APL\360 an interactive approach

APL\360

an interactive approach

LEONARD GILMAN

ALLEN J. ROSE

JOHN WILEY & SONS, INC.

New York · London · Sydney · Toronto

Library of Congress Catalogue Card Number: 71–147788

ISBN 0 471 30020 9

Printed in the United States of America

10 9 8 7 6

Preface

    As a result of increasing interest in APL, a formal educational program was begun in 1967 at the Thomas J. Watson Research Center in Yorktown Heights, New York. Within a year an APL "curriculum" had evolved which has been put on videotape. This text follows the same instructional sequence and uses essentially the same examples given on the videotapes.

    With but a few exceptions not necessary to the understanding of the topics following, the level of mathematical sophistication required does not exceed that associated with most current high school mathematics programs. In addition, no previous programming experience on the part of the reader is assumed. The authors believe, therefore, that the text is suitable for use by both secondary school and college-level classes, as well as by those in business and industry who are interested in the data processing capabilities of APL. Preliminary versions of the text have been used extensively in classroom situations and independent study by many individuals.

    At the end of each chapter except the first are problem sets with drill exercises and practice in the writing of APL expressions and programs (function definition). These have in general been chosen to emphasize and reinforce the concepts presented in the chapters which they follow. Past experience has indicated that students readily develop their own applications of APL once having learned the language.

    Finally, nearly all of the example functions that the student will encounter in the text have been placed in a block of storage (called a workspace in APL) which has the name $CLASS$. If not in your system, this workspace is obtainable from Scientific Time Sharing Corp. The work of the student will be facilitated if he has access to this workspace.

    We wish to acknowledge our debt to the many individuals who gave us their helpful comments and suggestions with regard to the layout and contents of the text. In particular we want to give credit to the following persons: Robert Hurley, for invaluable technical assistance in the early development of the course; Miss Colleen Conroy, for proofreading the text at several stages in its preparation; Eugene McDonnell, for suggesting solutions to a number of problems; Horst Feistel, for his ideas and exercises in the section on cryptography (chapter 21); Miss Linda Alvord, for her work in graphing (on which the latter part of chapter 30 is based);

Raymond Polivka, for his kind permission to use a number of problems which he had developed earlier in his own *APL* teaching. And last, but by no means least, in gratitude for a task that at times appeared endless, thanks are due to Mrs. Frances Verzeni and Mrs. Ann Tiller for preparing the copy for publication.

Yorktown Heights, New York   Leonard Gilman
June, 1970   Allen J. Rose

Foreword

APL is a language for describing procedures in the processing of information. It can be used to describe mathematical procedures having nothing to do with computers, or to describe (to a human being) how a computer works. Most commonly, however, at least at this time, it is used for programming in the ordinary sense of directing a computer how to process numeric or alphabetic data.

The language was invented by Kenneth E. Iverson while at Harvard, and was described in a 1962 Wiley book appropriately titled <u>A Programming</u> <u>Language</u>. In 1966 an experimental time-sharing system for the IBM System/360 became available within IBM, and is now an IBM program product. A number of universities and at least one public school system (Atlanta) are using *APL* on a wide scale for student instruction, and several universities and computer manufacturers are currently producing implementations for various computers. *APL* is clearly gaining acceptance at this time as a computer programming language.

This acceptance is not hard to understand. *APL* is one of the most concise, consistent, and powerful programming languages ever devised. Operations on single items (scalars) extend in a simple and natural way to arrays of any size and shape. Thus, for instance, a matrix addition that in other languages might require two loops and a half dozen statements, becomes simply $A+B$ in *APL*. Since computer programming typically involves a great deal of work with various kinds of data structures, the simplification offered by *APL*'s rich and powerful handling of arrays is central to its strength.

Again, since so many computer operations are describable by single *APL* operators, since data declarations are seldom required, and since procedure definitions are always independent of other definitions, *APL* is ideal for on-line interactive use of computers. Programs can readily be checked out in easy-to-manage segments.

From a pedagogical standpoint *APL* has a number of advantages. The material can be taught and used in small pieces. A student can be trying his hand on simple operations after five minutes of instruction. What he doesn't know won't hurt him (a statement that cannot be made about most other languages). If he tries something illegal, such as division by zero or adding a number and a letter, he gets an understandable error message and is free to try something else. Nothing the user can do will cause the system to crash.

As a new user becomes familiar with simple *APL* features, he moves on to more advanced concepts. Perhaps he tries operations on vectors, or samples the *APL* operator called reduction, which with two character strokes replaces complete loops in other languages. Some users will never have any occasion to become intimately familiar with all *APL* operators; their work will just not require them. Those who do need the advanced features will find the effort needed to master them rewarded with the availability of some extremely powerful operators, the equivalent of which are not to be found in other programming languages.

It is indubitably true that a "clever" programmer can use these advanced operators in such a way as to produce an "opaque" program, that is, one so compact and concise as to be nearly impossible for anyone else to understand. Whatever else may be said about such programs, which are questionable in many contexts anyway, they should not be used in demonstrations of *APL*. Experienced programmers who have seen *APL* demonstrated in terms of the fantastic cleverness angle sometimes criticize the language as being hard to understand, when their criticism more properly should have been directed at the demonstrator. Such misplaced cleverness is not to be found in this book. All operators are thoroughly covered, but there is no attempt to show off the ingenuity of the authors in writing ingeniously condensed programs.

APL is being taught successfully to high school students, in courses where the intent is more to teach mathematics than to teach programming. It is being used by engineers and statisticians to assist in their work, employing *APL* program packages designed to make such work more easy. And it is also used for various kinds of text processing, such as checking out compiling schemes and writing *APL* interpreters of other languages. Many other application areas could be cited. *APL* may not be all things to all men, but, to a greater degree than is true of most programming languages, it is many things to many.

This book concentrates on no special class of users. The features of the language are explained thoroughly, in a sequence chosen to facilitate learning. The authors have very extensive experience teaching *APL* to a wide variety of users. As the subtitle indicates (An Interactive Approach), the presentation is built around the assumption that the reader has access to an *APL* terminal. This, of course, is unquestionably the best way to learn *APL*, and such a reader will find the book well suited to his needs.

Nonetheless, the reader who wants to find out what *APL* is all about, not yet having access to a terminal, will discover that the presentation is easily readable. The text displays the terminal printouts just as they would appear to a user executing the commands under discussion. Being on a terminal oneself is surely the best way to learn an interactive language, but if that is not possible this may be the next best thing.

Ossining, New York
June, 1970

Daniel D. McCracken

Contents

CHAPTER 1

Getting started

Communication with the computer

Language is the means whereby we, as users, can tell the computer what to do, and it, in turn, can tell us what it has done with the information we have furnished it. It would be highly desirable to have a language that is as near as possible to what people ordinarily use. At the same time, the computer has to be able to interpret the given commands and execute them.

As a result of the recent development of time-sharing, in which regular telephone lines are used to connect remote inexpensive typewriters equipped for teleprocessing ("terminals") to a single central computer, a number of specialized languages have appeared with features adapted to this environment. Among them is _APL_ , the name being an acronym for A Programming Language, which is the title of a book by Dr. K. E. Iverson* (New York, John Wiley, 1962) defining the language in detail.

Since it is similar in many respects to algebraic notation and, in addition, contains many useful functions not expressible concisely with conventional symbols, it has proved to be very efficient for describing algorithms (problem-solving procedures). The text, therefore, will concentrate on the use of the _APL_ language for problem-solving on the terminal, following a brief introduction to the operation of the terminal and the establishing of the telephone connection. No consideration will be given to the characteristics and operation of any of the other components of the _APL_ system since the user of a time-sharing system is removed from the immediate vicinity of the computer, and need not be concerned with anything other than his terminal.

What the _APL_ system does

The following is a typical session in which a user interacts with the central computer via an _APL_ terminal. The student is cautioned that the display of terminal copy below was obtained from a terminal with access to programs in storage not necessarily available to him, such as _STATISTICS_ , which will result in a value error if execution is attempted.

*Presently Scientific Consultant for the IBM Scientific Center Complex, Data Processing Division.

```
      2+2
4
      3÷4
0.75
      3.1×5
15.5
```

As the illustration shows we can use the terminal as a desk calculator, with commands and data entered by the user via the keyboard (beginning six spaces to the right of the margin). Following the entry the return key is depressed to signal the computer that the user is finished. The response of the computer begins at the left margin.

Or we can assign a string of numbers to a variable called X , and ask the computer to execute the command shown, $+/X$, with the response 17.1:

```
      X←3  4  1.1  3  6
      +/X
17.1
```

This is the sum of all the numbers assigned to X.

The variable X can be further operated on, as, for example,

```
      2+X
5    6    3.1    5    8
```

And we have the ability to call upon programs previously stored in the system. Here is one that enables us to carry out statistical calculations on data:

```
      STATISTICS
ENTER DATA
☐:
      4  3  4.4  5  1  6.2
6 OBSERVATIONS ENTERED
AVERAGE IS 3.933333333
RANGE IS 5.2
STANDARD DEVIATION IS 1.787363048
TO TERMINATE TYPE  STOP
☐:
```

The program is expecting yet another set of data, which will now be entered:

```
      8  9  7.8  6.4
4 OBSERVATIONS ENTERED
AVERAGE IS 7.8
RANGE IS 2.6
STANDARD DEVIATION IS 1.070825227
TO TERMINATE TYPE  STOP
☐:
      STOP
```

As the instructions indicated, we terminated execution by typing $STOP$.

The hardware

Let's take a brief look at the physical equipment. It will be assumed in the remainder of the notes that the communications terminal you will be using is an IBM 2741* with an *APL* typeball, connected to a computer via a dataset telephone.

Note that on the left side of the stand on which the 2741 terminal is mounted there is a switch marked COM/LCL. When the switch is in the LCL position ("local"), the terminal can be used as an ordinary electric typewriter. The COM ("communicate") position is the correct one for *APL* .

Now look at the keyboard, reproduced below:

Although the alphabetic and numeric characters are in the standard positions, you will find most of the remaining symbols are not only probably not familiar to you but in addition the conventional symbols are not located where you might expect them to be.

The shift key is used in the usual manner for upper shift characters, and the return key on the right tells the system that you, the user, are finished with whatever you are entering, and are now ready for the terminal to respond.

To the right of the return key is the on-off switch, which is the main power control for the terminal. The space bar (not shown) is at the bottom of the keyboard.

Sign-on

At this point, turn the terminal on and set the switch on the left side to LCL. Practice entering the following with the terminal in the local mode:

)*USER NUMBER*:*PASSWORD* ⌊ if any ⌋

with

)1421:*JAY*

as an example.

---

* Several other terminals can be used with *APL*. Among these are the DATEL 20-31, DURA 1021 and 1051, TST 707, NOVAR 5-50, and IBM 2740 and 1050. In general, the control functions are similar, but the student should consult the vendor of the terminal or the *APL* time sharing service for specific information.

If you forget to hold down the shift key, you will get] instead of).
This will result in an incorrect entry and you will not be able to sign on.
Repeat the above exercise.

When you are finished practicing, put the left switch back on COM and
leave the power switch on.

Now examine the dataset. You will be concerned only with the two rightmost buttons: TALK and DATA. When the TALK button is depressed, the
dataset is a conventional telephone. Use it to dial the computer.

If you have made a proper connection, you will hear a high-pitched tone.
At this point, press the DATA button, replace the handset, and you are
ready to sign on as above.

Here is a summary of the sign-on procedure:

    1.   turn on-off switch on
    2.   put LCL-COM switch to COM
    3.   depress TALK button
    4.   dial telephone number
    5.   on tone, press DATA button
    6.   replace handset
    7.   enter)your user number:password [if any]
        press return key

The complete sign-on with the terminal response looks like this:

```
     )1500:DG
OPR:  196K WS APL SYS AVAILABLE EVES, SAT.
057)  9.44.03 03/13/70 LGILMAN

    A  P  L \ 3  6  0
```

057) tells on which port (tel. line) you are coming into the computer, and
is followed by the time in hours, minutes and seconds, the date and the
user's name. The next line identifies the system. At times there may also
be a message from the operator with APL news for all users.

Having signed on, we are at the place where we can do simple calculations:

```
     3+5
8
     2+2
4
```

Sign-off

At this point you are ready to work. It is foreordained, in the scheme of
things, that somebody is bound to come in and interrupt you. If the inter-
ruption is a lengthy one and you are unable to continue at the terminal for
some time, you will need to know how to sign off. Do not sign off at this
point unless you have to leave the terminal.

Here is the sign-off procedure:

    1.   enter)OFF
    2.   press return key

3. after terminal response, turn on-off switch off

The terminal's response will show how long you were connected and the actual time the central processing unit (CPU) of the computer was working for you both since sign-on and cumulatively since the last billing:

```
     )OFF
057   13.41.40 03/10/70 LGI
CONNECTED      0.00.22   TO DATE      4.19.26
CPU TIME       0.00.00   TO DATE      0.00.01
```

CHAPTER 2:

Some elementary operations

From this point on, the notes will make the assumption that you are seated at an active terminal. Many of the chapters will have instructions to get you into a special workspace, which is a block of internal storage (called "memory"), and in which there are a number of programs and exercises that you will use. More about this later.

In the early chapters, try to get as much finger practice as you can. Remember that the slowest link in the *APL* system is you, the user. You are limited by the speed with which you can enter information on the keyboard.

Elementary arithmetic operations

We'll begin with the simple arithmetic operations, + × - ÷, the symbols for which are in the upper right portion of the keyboard. The decimal point, which will be introduced here, is in the lower right part of the keyboard. All these symbols are used in the conventional manner.

     Addition:

```
      3+4
7
      .5+.6
1.1
      1.45+5.99
7.44
```

You've just barely started, but already there is one error that you are free to make. Suppose we type

```
      3+
```

You ask: 3+ what? Clearly this isn't a meaningful statement because you haven't indicated a second value for the plus symbol to operate on. The response of the computer is to type out the following error message:

SYNTAX ERROR
>   3+
>   ∧

The caret marks where the error was detected.

>   Multiplication:

>   5.1×7.9
40.29
>   3×6
18

>   Subtraction:

>   5-2
3
>   2-5
⁻3

Notice the high bar in the last response. This symbol means "negative."
In a way it is a description (like the decimal point) attached to the number
that follows it. It is not an indication of an operation to be performed.
For this, the subtraction sign is used.

Let's try some additional examples using the negative sign:

>   3+⁻2
1
>   ⁻2+3
1
>   -2+3
⁻5

If you think that there's something peculiar about the last example, where
a subtraction sign was used in place of the negative, relax—the explanation
will come in a later chapter.

>   Division:

>   3÷5
0.6
>   5÷3
1.666666667

By now you have probably noticed in your own practice with the arithmetic
operations that at most ten significant figures will be printed in the
response. APL carries out all calculations to approximately sixteen places
and rounds off to ten places in the output. Zeros on the right are not
printed. In chapter 34 a command will be introduced that will allow the
number of places printed to vary from 2 to 16.

So far so good. Now how about

>   5÷0
DOMAIN ERROR
>   5÷0
>   ∧

Here we see a second type of error occurring. The explanation is that the operation ÷ is a valid one, but we tried to divide by 0 , which is not in the "domain" of possible divisors in our number system. This seems reasonable enough, until you try

```
        0÷0
1
```

The current version of *APL* here follows the rule that any real number divided by itself is 1. If you want 0÷0 to result in a domain error, try 0×1÷0.

Corrections

Now suppose we have to enter one or more numbers that are a little harder to type than what we have been using thus far, and (heaven forbid!) we've made a mistake. Specifically, we typed 2×3.14169 and really meant 2×3.14159 , but haven't yet hit the return key.

There is a simple correcting mechanism on the 2741 terminal. We strike the backspace key gently (it may be typamatic on some terminals) to move the typeball over to where the error begins. If we then hit the ATTN (attention) button, an inverted caret will appear under the character at that point. This signifies that everything above and to the right of the caret is wiped out from the memory of the system and the corrections may be typed.

Here are some illustrations:

```
        2×3.14169
                v
                59
6.28318
        2×1.1058
                v

2.21
```

In the following example we want 23×506 but actually type 3×506 . All we need do is to backspace just before the 3 and type 2 as shown, provided, of course, that the return key hasn't yet been pressed:

```
        23×506
11638
        3×506
1518
        3×506
        2
11638
```

The fact that the 2 is on another line is immaterial, since the system doesn't know that we have manually moved the roller and paper.

You have undoubtedly guessed, by this time, that the way to get rid of a whole line is to backspace all the way to the beginning and make the correction:

```
      1234567×12345678
 v
```

The correction mechanism may also be used to enter comments:

```
      THIS IS A COMMENT
 v
```

Otherwise the system doesn't recognize the entry and an error message is recorded.

And while we're on the subject, the combination upper shift *C* and the small circle (upper shift *J*) overstruck is interpreted as indicating that a comment follows. It may contain any *APL* symbols and calls for no response from the system.

```
      ⍝THIS IS A COMMENT
```

This doesn't mean that all combinations of overstruck characters are possible in *APL*. Here the times and divide signs have been overstruck, with a resulting character error. Those combinations which are legal will be taken up in succeeding chapters.

```
      34⍟73
CHARACTER ERROR
      34
         ∧
```

An introduction to vectors

Imagine a store which, following a disastrous fire, is left with just three items for sale, A, B, C. Here is the sales record of the number of items sold over a two-week period:

```
              A   B   C
      week 1│ 9   7   8
      week 2│ 3   4   5
```

Before they go out of business, what are the total sales for each item?

The obvious answer is to add the weekly totals for each item separately as

```
      9+3
12
      7+4
11
      8+5
13
```

But there ought to be a more compact way and, in *APL*, there is:

```
      9  7  8+3  4  5
12   11    13
```

This leads us into a unique and time-saving feature of *APL*—its ability to process arrays of numbers. In the previous example the array was one-dimensional, with the elements all arranged in a single chain, called a vector. We shall see later that *APL\360* can handle multi-dimensional arrays as well.

Let's now change the problem:

	A	B	C
week 1	9	7	8
week 2	5	5	5

Treating this as a problem involving vectors, we enter

```
      9 7 8+5 5 5
14    12   13
```

To save still more typing time, where all the elements of one of the vectors are identical, it suffices to type just one of the numbers in that vector, leaving it to the system to extend it automatically to match the other vector in length:

```
      9 7 8+5
14    12   13
```

Now for some do's and don'ts. First, suppose we run all the numbers together:

```
      978+555
1533
```

Apparently the lack of space between the digits causes the system to interpret the series as a single number. Does this mean that the numbers (or the operation symbol, for that matter) must be separated by any fixed number of blanks? The following example makes clear that one blank is sufficient as a separator, but extra blanks don't hurt.

```
      9      7   8+      5
14    12   13
```

What if the two vectors don't have the same number of elements?

```
      9 7 8+5 3
LENGTH ERROR
      9 7 8 + 5 3
            ^
```

Here we get an obvious error message because the computer doesn't know which number goes with which. The only exception to this is where all the elements are identical (as in the previous example) and only one element needs to be typed.

You might argue that if we had

          9 7 8+5 3 0
14   10   8

we ought to be able to leave off the 0 since it doesn't contribute anything to the sum. But 0 is not the same as a blank. The former means
that the element in that position where it occurs has the value 0 , while
the latter occurs in place of some unknown element, possibly, but not
necessarily, 0 , and impossible for the computer to determine.

This parallel processing of vectors, to give it a name, works equally well
with other arithmetic operations:

          1.2 3 4×2
2   4   6   8

If, for example, a cookie recipe required 6, 4 and 1 cups respectively of
three ingredients, and we wished to make only a third of a batch, then the
required amounts are

          6 4 1÷3
2   1.333333333   0.3333333333

Again, suppose that the above three ingredients cost respectively 1, 5 and
7 cents per cup. What is the total cost for each ingredient?

          6 4 1×.01 .05 .07
0.06   0.2   0.07

As we shall see in subsequent chapters, not only are there a large number of
standard operations that can be used with vectors, but we will also
be able to invent functions that behave in many ways just like our ordinary
arithmetic operations in that, among other things, they too can be used with
vectors.

PROBLEMS

1. Drill. (Some of the drill problems may result in error messages.)

    6 8 2 4+3 9 1 1   5 4 3×6   1 2 8÷1 2 0

    1 0 9 8-4 2 2 3   10÷10 5 2 1   ¯2 0 .81+15 6 ¯5

    3-¯1 ¯56.7 0 ¯.19   3 4×1 2 3   2¯¯3

2. Additional finger exercises (use the ATTN key to delete each statement
    in turn):

    NOW IS THE TIME FOR ALL GOOD MEN TO COME TO THE AID OF

    IF AT FIRST YOU DON'T SUCCEED, TRY AGAIN

    HOW NOW BROWN COW

PRACTICE MAKES PERFECT

THE SLOWEST PART OF THE APL SYSTEM IS GENERALLY THE USER

3. At a basketball game a ticket seller sold 155 adult tickets at $1.25 each, 89 student tickets at $.50 each, and accepted 45 courtesy passes at $.25 each. Write an *APL* expression which gives the income from each class of tickets.

4. A taxi fleet owner recorded mileages of 1263, 2016, 1997 and 3028 for each of his four cars. Operating expenses for each car during the same period were $59.50, $72.50, $79.50 and $83.00, respectively. What was his cost per mile for each car?

CHAPTER 3:

Scalar dyadic functions

In the previous chapter we dealt with individual numbers, which we will call scalars, and chains of numbers, for which the term vectors was used. Left unanswered, at that time, was the question of what combinations of these are allowed in *APL* , as well as what the shape of the result might be. Let's now address ourselves to the question by formulating a few simple rules and appropriate names for the concepts to be considered.

Standard scalar dyadic functions

There are four mathematical rules that govern the ways in which vectors and scalars can be combined. In what follows, the symbol ∘ stands for any of the arithmetic operations that we have already introduced. Later in this section we will further classify and categorize these operations to make more evident their connection with other operations yet to be defined.

1. scalar ← scalar ∘ scalar
2. vector ← scalar ∘ vector
3. vector ← vector ∘ scalar
4. vector ← vector ∘ vector

The term on the left of the arrow tells us the shape of the result when various operations are performed on quantities having the shapes on the right.

This is as good a place as any to introduce a little additional terminology. Why? You ask. Naming something doesn't tell us any more about it and, in fact, can mislead us by enabling us to talk more glibly of things we may not know much about. But mathematicians, being the perverse creatures that they are, insist on more formal names for the tools and concepts they work with. And having a name for something does have the advantage of letting the namer identify without ambiguity (we hope!) what is under discussion.

First, if ∘ stands for an operation to be performed, the things it is to operate on will be called arguments. Thus, in 5x6, 5 is the left argument and 6 is the right argument. The arguments can both be scalars (rule 1)

```
      3+5
8
```

or vectors, either on the right or left (rules 2, 3)

```
      2+3 5 7
5   7   9
      5 6 8×3
15   18   24
```

or both arguments can be vectors (rule 4)

```
      3 6 8÷2 1 4
1.5   6   2
```

the only stipulation being, as previously mentioned, that both arguments have the same length. As an obvious corollary, the lengths of the result-ing vectors in the two examples at the top of the page are the same as those of the vector arguments.

The operators that we have been working with are more properly called functions, because once the arguments and operation are specified, a single result is obtained. In a crude sense, this is what the mathematician also thinks of when he uses the term more formally.

Furthermore, the label dyadic is attached to these functions, since they require, at least as we have been using them thus far, two arguments. Also they are called in *APL* standard or primitive because they are immediately available on the *APL* keyboard. And, finally (at long last!), they are referred to as scalar because functions of this type are defined first for scalars and then extended component by component to vectors.

Summarizing, the operations + - × ÷ are called in *APL* standard scalar dyadic functions.

Operation tables for the arithmetic functions

For each of the functions thus far introduced, we can construct an operation table, with the left arguments down the vertical column on the left and the right arguments across the top. To save space, only the integers 1-4 are used as arguments:

+	1	2	3	4
1	2	3	4	5
2	3	4	5	6
3	4	5	6	7
4	5	6	7	8

-	1	2	3	4
1	0	¯1	¯2	¯3
2	1	0	¯1	¯2
3	2	1	0	¯1
4	3	2	1	0

×	1	2	3	4
1	1	2	3	4
2	2	4	6	8
3	3	6	9	12
4	4	8	12	16

÷	1	2	3	4
1	1	.5	.33...	.25
2	2	1	.66...	.5
3	3	1.5	1	.75
4	4	2	1.33...	1

Here is one in which no function is specified. Can you guess what it is?

	1	2	3	4
1	1	1	1	1
2	2	4	8	16
3	3	9	27	81
4	4	16	64	256

Power function

You should be able to see that the above table represents the power function, with the left arguments being raised to the powers indicated by the right arguments. Clearly, this power function exhibits the characteristics we would expect from a standard scalar dyadic function.

All we need is a symbol for it. This brings up an interesting aspect (or failing if you prefer) of conventional mathematical notation, and one which will become even more apparent as we go along.

Notice how we write the four arithmetic functions:

$$2 + 3$$
$$2 - 3$$
$$2 \times 3$$
$$2 \div 3$$

And then we come along and write for the power function

$$2^3$$

The operation to be performed is specified not by a symbol but by position, which is not only inconsistent but downright dangerous, since it is very easy sometimes to miss the elevated position of the power in writing.

In *APL*, the symbol * (uppershift *P*) is chosen, yielding

        2 * 3
8

* , being a standard scalar dyadic function, extends to vectors as well:

        2 4 3 * 2
4   16   9

In mathematics courses, roots are shown to be equivalent to fractional powers, e.g., the square root is the 1/2 power. So, instead of writing

$\sqrt{2}$ to mean the square root of 2 , in *APL* this is

        2*.5
1.414213562

and

        9 64*.5
3   8

Negative powers, which are the equivalent of the reciprocal of the number raised to the corresponding positive power, are also available to the *APL* user, as in the following example:

        2*$^-$2
0.25

Our power function can be used to generate quite large numbers:

        100*8
1*E*16

Exponential notation

In the last example you saw a new notation, which some of you may recognize as being similar to what is used in other higher level programming languages, and evidently intended to avoid writing a monster like

                10,000,000,000,000,000

The *E* may be interpreted as "times 10 to the ...power."

This notation is equally convenient for very small numbers:

        .01*9
1*E*$^-$18

and can be employed in many different ways to express the same number, say, 530:

53*E*1	which is	53×10^1
5.3*E*2		5.3×10^2
.0053*E*5		$.0053 \times 10^5$
530*E*0		530×10^0
5300*E*$^-$1		5300×10^{-1}

APL not only produces results in the *E*-notation, but it is possible to enter data this way:

```
      0+33
33
      0+3.3E1
33
      0+.33E2
33
      0+330E¯1
33
```

The choice is up to the user.

Logarithmic function

There is another function which is closely related to the power function,
the logarithmic function (the logarithm of a number N to the base B is
that power to which B must be raised to equal N). In APL, this is written
$B \circledast N$, the symbol being that for exponentiation overstruck with the large
circle (upper shift 0).

Thus, since

```
      10*3
1000
```

the base — 10 log (to use the usual abbreviation) of 1000 is

```
      10⊛1000
3
```

and

```
      10⊛100 1000 10
2   3   1
```

Similarly, since

```
      2*3
8
```

then the log of 8 to the base 2 is 3:

```
      2⊛8
3
```

Notice that the base is the left argument and the number whose log is to
be found the right argument.

Maximum and minimum functions

Finally, try the following exercise, exploring the working of the symbol $\lceil$
(upper shift S):

```
        3⌈5
5
        5⌈3
5
        5⌈5
5
```

Lest you be tempted into saying "aha! ⌈ always generates a 5", look at

```
        3⌈3
3
```

If you play around with this function for a while, you will see that it selects the larger of the left and right argument, and is appropriately named the <u>maximum</u> function. Its operation table looks like this:

⌈	1	2	3	4
1	1	2	3	4
2	2	2	3	4
3	3	3	3	4
4	4	4	4	4

Where there's a maximum, there ought analogously to be a minimum function. This is found on the upper shift ⌐ , and selects the lesser of the two arguments:

```
        3⌊5
3
        ⁻5⌊1
⁻5
```

It has the operation table

⌊	1	2	3	4
1	1	1	1	1
2	1	2	2	2
3	1	2	3	3
4	1	2	3	4

"Lesser" and "greater" are relative terms, and indeed the mathematician defines them according to position on the real number line:

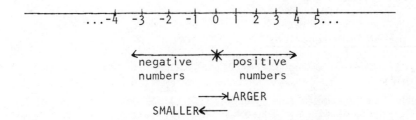

Thus, the lesser of two numbers is that one which is farther to the left, and the greater one, farther to the right.

Let's consider a couple of simple problems. There are three students who got grades of 90, 80 and 55 in a certain exam, and on a retest received 70, 80 and 75, respectively. The instructor wishes to record for each student only the larger of the two grades received. How can he do it in *APL*?

What we want to do is to select out 90 for the first student, 80 for the second, and 75 for the third, i.e.,

```
      90 80 55⌈70 80 75
90   80    75
```

A second problem: We have purchased an odd lot consisting of 4 boards of lengths 5, 8.1, 10, and 7.9 ft. Unfortunately, our truck can carry boards no longer than 8 ft. without running afoul of the law. Can we identify which boards have to be trimmed? This is

```
      8⌊5 8.1 10 7.9
5   8   8   7.9
```

and, from the position of the 8's in the result, we see which boards have to be cut down. These are two trivial examples, but as our store of new functions increases, we will be able to solve much more complex problems later.

It should be noted before concluding this chapter that all the new functions introduced, $*$ ⍟ ⌈ ⌊ , are standard scalar dyadic functions, but that the maximum and minimum functions mathematically are different from all others in one significant respect: no knowledge of an operation table is needed to use them, only the ability to distinguish greater and less.

PROBLEMS

1. Drill

3⌈3 7 ¯10.8 2 0	10⍟1 2 3 4 5	¯8$*$.3333333333333
1 9 ¯5 ¯2⌊0 6 4 3	2 3 4 5 6⍟2	10⍟0
5 ¯1 52⌈6	2⌊0 5 ¯8	1$*$0 1 10 100 1000
1⍟1	¯2⍟25	¯7.11E4÷9.45E¯3
2$*$.5 .333 .25 .2	¯2$*$.5	21.268E1+4.56E¯2
3$*$4 2 1 0 ¯5	1⍟55	8.2E0×7.9E¯3+56

2. Key in 1E0,1E1,...1E11 Do likewise with 1E¯1,...1E¯6. Note where the break point is in *APL* for the display on large and small numbers in *E*-notation.

3. Store A sells 5 vegetable items for 15, 20, 18, 32, and 29 cents a pound. At store B the prices are 18, 20, 15, 10 and 49 cents a pound, respectively. The policy of a third store C is to meet the competition's prices. Write

an *APL* expression to determine store C's selling prices for the 5 items.

4. The pH of a solution is a measure of its acidity or basicity, and is defined as the logarithm (base 10) of the reciprocal of the hydrogen ion concentration in moles/liter of solution. Use *APL* to express the pH of a solution whose concentration is C.

CHAPTER 4:

Two more scalar dyadic functions

Combinations

A relatively simple combinatorial problem in mathematics is to find the number of ways one can take 2 things out of a population of 4. Let's solve the problem by brute force, with 4 objects, A, B, C, D. Listing the possible combinations, we have

AB AC AD BC BD CD

We'll assume the order is not significant, so that CA and AC, for example, will be considered to be the same. Thus, there are 6 ways of taking 2 things out of a population of 4.

In combinatorial theory it is shown that the formula

$$\frac{m!}{n!\,(m-n)!}$$

gives the number of ways of taking m objects n at a time. For the case above, this would be

$$\frac{4!}{2!\,(4-2)!}$$

or 6. As a reminder to those of you whose math is rusty, m! means $(m)(m-1)(m-2)\ldots(1)$, so that 4! is the same as 4x3x2x1.

As you might suspect, the process is somewhat easier in APL. It is done with the same symbol !. On the keyboard it is formed by striking the period, backspacing, and hitting the quote symbol (upper shift K) so that the two characters line up. The correct format is n ! m and, for our example above,

        2!4
6

This is the place to emphasize that ! like ⍟ is <u>not</u> a keyboard character, but is formed by overstriking as described above. The symbols ' and . must be lined up. Otherwise no answer appears and the typeball doesn't space over. If we try to do anything else, like a simple addition, the terminal fails to respond:

```
      2.'4
(no response from the terminal)

2+2

(still no response)
```

When this happens, the cure is to type a single ' only. Then hit the return key and live with whatever error results.

```
'
```

SYNTAX ERROR

```
      '
      ^
```

and we are back in desk calculator mode once more.

! is a standard scalar dyadic function and can take vector arguments:

```
      0 1 2 3 4!4
1   4   6   4   1
      2!2 3 4
1   3   6
```

Its operation table looks like this:

!	0	1	2	3	4
0	1	1	1	1	1
1	0	1	2	3	4
2	0	0	1	3	6
3	0	0	0	1	4
4	0	0	0	0	1

What we generated above corresponds to the last column and the boxed in part of the third row. That portion of the table consisting of nonzero integers can be removed to form what in mathematics is called Pascal's triangle:

```
1  1  1  1  1
   1  2  3  4
      1  3  6
         1  4
            1
```

which is a device for calculating and displaying the coefficients generated in the expansion of an expression of the form $(a-b)^n$ by the Binomial Theorem.

Finally, to complete the picture, our arguments don't have to be integers:

```
      2.1!5.6
13.48487115
```

which, for the benefit of the more mathematically sophisticated, is related to the complete β-function of probability theory. (Don't panic. It won't be mentioned again!)

Residue

The next standard scalar dyadic function we will consider is one called residue. We can illustrate it with a simple example.

Assume that we have 7 peanuts and 3 children who are to share the wealth evenly. We aren't able to cut up a single peanut. How many do we have left?

Clearly the simple-minded way to do this would be to start with 7 and take away 3, leaving 4. Then take 3 more away, with 1 remaining. In formal language, the 3 residue of 7 is 1. This isn't the only way to do the problem. We could also divide 7 by 3, see that it goes in twice, and get a remainder of 1.

The symbol for residue is |, which is the upper shift M. In APL, the 3 residue of 7 is

```
        3|7
1
```

Our peanut problem can be enlarged by considering the distribution of varying amounts of peanuts to the 3 children:

```
        3|0 1 2 3 4 5 6 7
0   1   2   0   1   2   0   1
```

Here is another problem in which 5 peanuts are distributed among 1, 2, and 3 children:

```
        1 2 3|5
0   1   2
```

The residue function is a handy one for generating all kinds of useful information. For instance, try

```
        1|2.5
0.5
        1|31.23
0.23
```

Asking for the 1 residue of a number is a convenient way to get the nonintegral part of the number.

Now, what about the residue of negative numbers, say 3|¯4 ? Previously we saw that a recurring pattern was generated by

```
        3|0 1 2 3 4 5 6 7
0   1   2   0   1   2   0   1
```

so when we try

```
        3|¯4 ¯3 ¯2 ¯1 0 1 2 3 4 5 6 7
2   0   1   2   0   1   2   0   1   2   0   1
```

we expect and get a continuation of the recurring pattern. If you think about it a bit, you will see another way to obtain the residue of a negative number. For our example above, add 3 to ¯4 to get ¯1. Then add 3 again to get 2. In general, the rule is to keep adding until the result is 0 or positive.

Suppose the left argument is negative. Then its absolute value (i.e., magnitude without regard to the negative sign) is taken:

```
      3| ¯4
2
     ¯3| ¯4
2
```

There is one residue class of particular interest in the computing industry: the 2 residues of the integers:

```
      2|0 1 2 3 4 5
0   1   0   1   0   1
```

Here we have a continuing pattern of 0 and 1 as the only integers. If we so choose, we can let 0 represent the state of a circuit with a switch open (no current) and 1 with the switch closed. We'll have more to say about this in a later chapter.

PROBLEMS

1. Drill

```
      1 9 8|3 4 6            1|3.4 ¯2.2 .019

      ¯3 ¯2 ¯1|3             0 1 2 3 4!3 4 5 6 7

      0|1 2 3                4!3 4 5 6 7

      3|¯3 ¯2 0 1 2 3        ¯2 4 ¯5|8    13    3.78
```

2. Given that A and B are integers modulo 5 (i.e., A and B belong to the set S of integers generated by taking $5|N$ for any integer $N \geq 4$), show that $5|A+B$, $5|A \times B$, and $5|A*B$ are in S.

3. How can the residue function be used to tell whether one number A is divisible by another number B?

4. Write an APL expression to tell what clock time it is, given the number of elapsed hours H since 12:00.

5. Find the number of possible solutions in positive integers of the equation
$$X+Y+Z+W=50$$
    (Hint: think of 50 units partitioned into 4 blocks by separators)

6. How many quadrilaterals can be formed by joining groups of 4 points in a collection of 30 points in a plane, no 3 of which lie on a straight line?

7. If $1|N$ produces the fractional part of N, how can the residue function be used to get the integral part of the number?

8. Write an expression to get the fractional part of a negative number.

CHAPTER 5:

Relational and logical functions

In this chapter we will introduce ten new functions falling into two classes—the relationals and logicals. If you think that this is far too many for a single presentation and will leave you hopelessly confused, you may breathe easier. All of these functions have one thing in common—they call for an answer of 0 or 1 only, which at this stage shouldn't be too taxing.

Relational functions

There are, in *APL*, six relational functions, $< \leq = \geq > \neq$, which are the upper shift 3 through 8. They have the usual mathematical meanings, less than, less than or equal, equal, greater than or equal, greater than, and not equal, respectively. The reason they are called relational is that they inquire about the truth or falsity of the relationship between two quantities, say A<B.

This statement is really a question asked of the computer: Is A less than B? It calls for a response, yes or no, because either A is less than B or it is not. Let's try this on the terminal:

```
      3 < 5
1
      5 < 3
0
```

Clearly, a 1 response means the statement is true, and 0 false.

Vectors work well with this function too:

```
      3 < 1  2  3  4  5
0  0   0   1   1
```

and we can now use this function to help us in a selection problem.

Suppose, as a store owner, we have a number of accounts, with \$3, \$$^-$2, \$0, \$2, and \$$^-$3 as balances, and we want to flag or mark those accounts which are overdrawn (represented by negative values). The "less than" function will solve our problem, although it is by no means the only way to do it:

```
        3 ¯2 0 2 ¯3<0
0   1   0   0   1
```

Does < have all the qualities of a standard scalar dyadic function? Here is its operation table:

<	1	2	3	4
1	0	1	1	1
2	0	0	1	1
3	0	0	0	1
4	0	0	0	0

By this time you ought to be able to convince yourself that "less than" meets our criteria for a standard scalar dyadic function, as indeed do the rest of the relationals. We won't go through them all, but let's explore just one more, =. Typing

```
        3 ¯2 5 0 2 ¯3=0
0   0   0   1   0   0
```

generates a listing of those accounts from the previous example whose balance is 0, to complement the list of those overdrawn. You should be able to see many other possibilities. For instance, to get vectors of all 1's or all 0's

```
        0 1 2 3=0 1 2 3
1   1   1   1
        0 1 2 3=3 2 1 0
0   0   0   0
```

Logical functions

Not all the juice has been squeezed out of the subset 1,0 of the real numbers that we previously looked at in connection with the relationals. Here is a function ∧ (upper shift 0) called and, whose operation table is

∧	0	1
0	0	0
1	0	1

The result is 1 if and only if both arguments are 1. In fact, we can generate all the entries in the table by

```
        0 0 1 1∧0 1 0 1
0   0   0   1
```

You have probably noticed that only 0 and 1 were used as arguments in the table. Notice what happens when we try

```
      2∧0
DOMAIN ERROR
      2∧0
       ∧
```

The last time we got a domain error was when we typed

```
      5÷0
DOMAIN ERROR
      5÷0
       ∧
```

It seems clear, then, that the arguments are restricted to 0 and 1.

For those who have some background in mathematical logic, the analogy between 0 and 1 and the true-false entries in the truth tables for and will be apparent. In any event, this function provides yet another means of generating 0's and 1's, and will be useful in writing programs later on.

Another logical function is ∨, called or:

```
      ∨ | 0   1
     ───┼───────
      0 | 0   1
      1 | 1   1
```

The result is 1 if either or both arguments are 1. As before, we can generate all the entries in the table with

```
      0 0 1 1∨0 1 0 1
0    1    1    1
```

There are yet two more functions in this class, ⍲, nand, and ⍱, nor. You may have guessed already that nand stands for "not and," and nor for "not or." The overstruck ~ (upper shift T) is used for negation. Below are their operation tables,

```
      ⍲ | 0   1              ⍱ | 0   1
     ───┼───────            ───┼───────
      0 | 1   1              0 | 1   0
      1 | 1   0              1 | 0   0
```

Here is an example:

```
      1⍱0
0
```

You can see that everywhere 0 appears in the table for ∧, a 1 appears for ⍲, and vice versa. The same holds for ∨ and ⍱.

Although it was suggested earlier that the logical functions had a use in programming, for generating 0's or 1's at the appropriate point, there is another, physical situation which could be represented by them, namely piping networks:

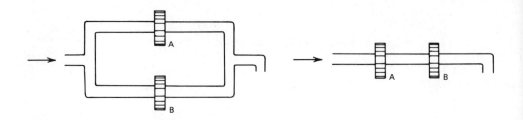

In Figure 1, fluid flows if either valve A or valve B is open, while in the second figure flow occurs only if both A and B are open.   Read "0" for closed and "1" for open, and the figure correspond to the or and and tables, respectively.   Keep in mind that it is a short step to go from pipes to electrical circuits.   Hence their value in computer design.

Actually, there are 16 possible logical connectives, of which we have taken up only 4.   To illustrate how the others can be generated, let's assume we want a function that gives us an exclusive or, with operation table

	0	1
0	0	1
1	1	0

the result being 0 if and only if, both arguments are 0 or both are 1.   Can we get this in *APL*?

The answer is yes.   It is that part of the operation table for ≠ where both arguments are 0 or 1:

≠	0	1	2	3
0	0	1	1	1
1	1	0	1	1
2	1	1	0	1
3	1	1	1	0

A similar approach yields the others.

Summary

Thus far, we have introduced and illustrated a large number of standard scalar dyadic functions.   Here is a brief recapitulation up to this point:

A+B	sum of A and B
A−B	B subtracted from A
A×B	product of A and B
A÷B	A divided by B
A*B	A raised to the power B

A⊛B	base-A logarithm of B
A⌈B	larger of A and B
A⌊B	smaller of A and B
A∣B	A residue of B
A!B	combinations of B items taken A at a time

A<B	
A≤B	
A=B	relations yield
A≥B	1 if true
A>B	0 if false
A≠B	

A∨B	logical or of A and B
A∧B	logical and of A and B
A⍱B	logical nor of A and B
A⍲B	logical nand of A and B

Keep in mind that every one of these functions can be used to replace the symbol ∘ in the rules (p. 13) for combining scalars and vectors.

PROBLEMS

1. Drill

    0 0 1 1∨0 1 0 1   2 3 0<5 ‾1 4

    1 0 1 0∧1 0 0 1   3 1 2≠1 2 3

    2 4 7 ‾2>6 ‾1 0 4   ~0 1

    0 1 2 3=0 1 3 2   0 0 1 1⍱0 1 0 1

    4 ‾5 ‾1 ‾6.8≥4 1 ‾1 2   1 0 1 0⍲1 0 0 1

    8 7 6 5 4 3 2 1≤1 2 3 4 5 6 7 8

2. How can the functions = and ∣ be used in *APL* to identify the factors of an integer N?

3. *A* is a vector of accounts, with the negative values representing those overdrawn. Use one or more of the relational functions to flag those accounts not overdrawn.

4. Write an *APL* expression to return a 1 if either condition A is true or condition B is false.

5. Execute 1 0 1 0=0 1 1 0. Compare this with the operation table on page 28. What name would be appropriate to assign to this logical connective?

6. Explain the results of executing 0 0 1 1∧~0 0 1 1 and 0 0 1 1∨~0 0 1 1.

CHAPTER 6:

Assignment and algorithms

Up to this point, all of our work has been done in desk calculator mode. This has the disadvantage that once we type in the arguments and the function and then press the return key, execution proceeds, we get an answer (unless we tried to do something illegal), but the work is lost. No longer is it available to us for any future calculation.

In this chapter we shall see how APL handles these situations and, in addition, we shall solve a well-known problem in geometry by a stepwise procedure.

Assignment

Any good desk calculator has the ability to store constant factors so that they can be used over and over again without having to be reentered each time. For instance, suppose we are given a series of problems all involving the constant 0.75 :

```
      2×.75
1.5
      4+.75
4.75
      .75*2
0.5625
```

As it stands, .75 has to be typed each time. What we'd like is some way to save this number and have it available for reuse. It may seem trivial at this point because our repeated factor, .75, doesn't take many typestrokes, but what if the expression you had to repeat had a large number of characters in it?

In APL the terms specification or assignment are used to describe the placing of an expression in storage. It works this way:

```
      A←.75
```

Incidentally, the expression above is frequently read as "A is assigned the value .75." The name A is given by means of the arrow ← to the quantity .75 and, from this point on, unless the contents of our workspace are destroyed or A reassigned to another quantity, typing A will be the same as typing .75. Since A is a name to which we are free to assign any value we want, even though we have chosen a specific one here, it and other names used in a similar manner are often called <u>variables</u>.

Here are a couple of calculations we can do with A:

```
        2×A
1.5
        4+A
4.75
        A*2
0.5625
        A
0.75
```

Flushed with success, you ought to be ready to try your hand at another:

```
        B←1  2  3  4  5
        2×B
2  ´4   6   8   10
```

Then, since we still have A (like death and taxes) with us,

```
        A+B
1.75    2.75    3.75    4.75    5.75
        B*2
1   4   9   16   25
```

If we keep this up, sooner or later we are going to run out of letters of the alphabet. What then? The next logical step is to use multiple letter names:

```
        PI←3.14159
        PI*2
9.869587728
```

A is still in storage. Here it is again:

```
        A
0.75
```

You should have noticed by now that when an assignment is made, no explicit result is returned by the terminal on the paper. This is reasonable enough, since all we are asking when we make an assignment is for something to be placed in storage.

What happens if we mistakenly (or otherwise) use the same letter for a second assignment? For instance, we let

```
        A←2+B
```

If we call for A now, we get

```
      A
3   4   5   6   7
      2+B
3   4   5   6   7
```

The new values of A supersede the old, which are lost. Moral of the story:
If you want to save the values stored under a variable name, don't override
the assignment. Use a different name.

There are several ways to extend the number of possibilities for variable
names. Underlining (upper shift F) is one way.

```
      A̲←3.2
      A̲+5
8.2
      A
3   4   5   6   7
```

$A̲$ is clearly different from A, which still has its last assigned value.
In effect, this gives us 52 letters to choose from, alone or in multiple
character names like

```
      DATA←5  2  7  8
```

APL recognizes up to 77 characters in a variable name, but it doesn't pay
to make it too long. Remember, you are the one who will have to type it.
Numbers can also be included in any position except initially, as shown by

```
      X3Y2←20
      3XY2←20
SYNTAX ERROR
      3 XY2←20
        ∧
```

but spaces, punctuation marks, and special symbols for operations may not.
Something new has been added here: a syntax error message. In plain
English, this means that a statement has been improperly formulated in APL,
i.e., is "ungrammatical."

It is possible in APL to make multiple specifications on the same line.
In certain cases this turns out to be a handy timesaver. Here is an
example:

```
      A←2+B←3  1  5
      B
3   1   5
      A
5   3   7
```

Now, let's try asking the computer for

```
      A+W
VALUE ERROR
      A+W
        ∧
```

It should be obvious what's wrong. The computer didn't recognize the
variable name W because there isn't any value currently stored under that
name. Hence the error message. A is still a valid variable, but not W.

```
        A
5    3  7
        W
VALUE ERROR
        W
        ∧
```

This raises another question: How can you find out what variable names you
have already in storage? The command $)VARS$ (abbreviation for "variables")
produces an alphabetical listing of the variables already in storage.

```
      )VARS
A        B        DATA    PI      XY2      X3Y2      A̲
```

Note that the underlined $A̲$ comes after the nonunderlined letters of the
alphabet.

Expressions which begin with a right parenthesis followed by a word or
abbreviation are known as system commands. You already know two of them,
sign-on and sign-off, and more will be introduced in succeeding chapters
as the need arises.

If we give W a value and then call for $A+W$, we no longer get an error
message:

```
      W←0.1
      A+W
5.1    3.1   7.1
```

and not only is execution completed, but W is added to the list of variables
in storage:

```
      )VARS
A        B        DATA    PI      W        XY2      X3Y2      A̲
```

Now W behaves just like the other variables and can be respecified:

```
      W←2×W
      W
0.2
```

Algorithms

We can use the notion of assignment as motivation for this next section,
which is concerned with the concept of an algorithm. An algorithm is
nothing but a series of steps that together comprise a prescription for
defining a function or solving a problem.

Here is an example taken from plane geometry. The problem is to calculate
the hypotenuse of a right triangle, given the sides:

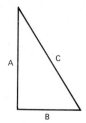

A convenient and time-honored rule for finding C is the Pythagorean Theorem. It states that to get C we have to square A and add it to the square of B, then find the square root of the sum.

This sequence of steps can be executed in APL by the following scheme:

```
      A←3
      B←4
      A2←A*2
      A2
9
      B2←B*2
      S←A2+B2
      S
25
      C←S*.5
      C
5
```

There is one point worth commenting on. We had to specify A and B initially in this sequence; otherwise, when we called for the values of $A2$, $B2$, and S along the way as checks on our work, we would have gotten value errors.

We'll see later, when we learn how to write and store programs, that the specification of values for the variables need not be done beforehand.

Let's go through the same steps and, this time, solve for a family of triangles:

```
      A←1 3
      B←1 4
      A
1    3
      A2←A*2
      A2
1    9
      B2←B*2
      B2
1   16
      S←A2+B2
      C←S*.5
```

As before the result for C doesn't appear on the paper because our last step, which was an assignment of a value to C, merely put it in storage. So, in order to get the result, we have to type C:

$$C$$
1.414213562   5

if we didn't want to save the result by storing it under C, we could eliminate the assignment and merely call for

$$S*.5$$
1.414213562   5

and the results now are printed.

Finally, we can check on the variables we have in storage in the usual
manner:

```
         )VARS
A          A2         B         B2       C       DATA     PI       S
W          XY2        X3Y2      A
```

and the new variables specified in our right triangle algorithm are now
included.

PROBLEMS

1. Given $A \leftarrow 1\ 0\ 1\ 0$
          $B \leftarrow 0\ 1\ 0\ 1$
          $C \leftarrow 0\ 0\ 0\ 0$
          $D \leftarrow 1\ 1\ 1\ 1$

    Evaluate each of the following:

    $\sim A \vee \sim B$ $\sim B \wedge \sim C$

    $\sim A \wedge B$ $\sim C \neq D$

    $\sim B \vee C$ $\sim D = B$

    Were the results what you expected? Can you explain the discrepancies?

2. Write an algorithm which will produce a logical vector C with 1's corre-
    sponding to the even numbers in a vector $A \leftarrow \bar{}6\ 7\ 2\ 4\ \bar{}21$

3. Given a cube each of whose edges have length E. Write in APL the steps
    needed to find its surface area. Execute for $E \leftarrow 3\ 7\ 15\ 2.7$

4. Show how in a series of steps you could obtain the cube of $X \leftarrow 5\ 6\ 7$
    without using $*$.

5. You happen to have in storage a vector S of four positive elements.
    Use S to generate in at least five different ways   A) A vector Z of four
    zeros, and   B) A vector W of four ones.

6. Assign the vector $3\ 4\ 5\ 6\ 7$ to the name A and twice it to the name B
    on one line.

CHAPTER 7:

Reduction

Previously you saw how the introduction of vectors enabled parallel processing of data to take place, with a resulting saving in time and number of
typestrokes required. In this lecture this concept will be extended to
show how meaningful operations can be effectively performed on the elements
of a single vector. Continuing the analogy with electrical circuits, we
may call such operations series processing.

Conventional notation

Let's begin with a problem in invoice extension. Assume that several different items, each with its own cost, have been purchased. We'll use Q and C
to represent the numbers and the costs, respectively.

        $Q \leftarrow 6\ \ 2\ \ 3\ \ 1\ \ 0$
        $C \leftarrow 2\ \ 4\ \ 3\ \ 5\ \ 10$

To get the vector of total costs, we execute

        $Q \times C$
12   8   9   5   0

But now, in order to obtain the grand total, we have to add up all the
elements of this vector.

In conventional notation, the mathematician indicates the sum of the components of a vector by writing

$$\sum_{i=1}^{n} x_i$$

Σ (sigma) means "sum," while "i" is a running variable from 1 to n, identify-
ing the individual components of the vector. n is the total number of components, 5 in the invoice extension problem we are working on.

If this seems potentially like a lot of work, don't be too concerned. In the
next section we will show how to carry out the summation in APL with minimal
effort.

Reduction

Our objective is to sum across the components of a vector. To do this, let

$$X \leftarrow Q \times C$$

so X contains

$$X$$
12 8 9 5 0

In APL the sum is achieved by $+/X$. This is read as "plus reducing X," or the "plus reduction of X," and the symbol / (lower right corner of the keyboard) is called "reduction," because it reduces the vector to a single component.

$$+/X$$
34

How this operation works is worth discussing in more detail. If

$$X \leftarrow 12\ 8\ 9\ 5\ 0$$

then

$$+/12\ 8\ 9\ 5\ 0$$
34

What the system does is to insert the function symbol which appears to the left of the slash between each pair of components of the vector and group them (internally) as follows:

$$12+(8+(9+(5+0)))$$

The reason for the grouping is that in the APL system each symbol operates on everything to the right of it. If you think about what this means, you will see that this is equivalent to operating on the rightmost pair of elements first, taking that answer together with the next element to the left, and so on, i.e., using the above illustration, step by step we obtain

$$12+(8+(9+5))$$
$$12+(8+14)$$
$$12+22$$
$$34$$

You may be inclined to argue that we are making a big todo about nothing, since with addition it doesn't really make any difference whether we work from right to left or left to right. We'll see later, however, that this commutative property is not general.

"Times" reduction

Now consider still another problem. A rectangular box has the dimensions

2''x3''x4.''   What is its volume? Clearly, to answer the question we want

        $2 \times 3 \times 4$
24

If we assign Z to the vector of dimensions, $\times/Z$ should give us our answer.

        $Z \leftarrow 2\ \ 3\ \ 4$
        $\times/Z$
24

In this case, $\times$ is planted between each neighboring pair of components, and the system stepwise does the following:

$$2 \times (3 \times 4)$$
$$2 \times 12$$
$$24$$

An algorithm for averaging

At this point we can profitably talk about an algorithm to get the average of the components of a vector X where

        $X \leftarrow 2\ \ 4\ \ 3\ \ 3\ \ 2.5\ \ 2$

In order to get an average we need two things: the sum T of all the components in the vector we are averaging and the number of components. The first is easy:

        $+/X$
16.5

We can get the average by dividing this sum by the number of components (obtained by manually counting them), but on the terminal there is a simpler, if somewhat sneaky, way to accomplish this. On your terminal type

        $X = X$

The response is

1   1   1   1   1   1

As you can see, this generates a vector consisting of as many 1's as there are components in X. The next step? You guessed it—plus reduction over $X=X$. Summarizing and storing the intermediate results:

        $M \leftarrow X = X$
        $N \leftarrow +/M$
        N
6

Let's look at the sum T:

```
        T
VALUE ERROR
        T
        ^
```

We forgot to set T, so naturally we got a value error.   Now

```
        T←+/X
        T÷N
2.75
```

2.75 is the average of the components of X:

```
        X
2   4   3   3   2.5   2
```

Maximum, minimum and logical reduction

If + and × were the only functions that could be used with reduction, the operation wouldn't be particularly useful.   But it turns out that all standard scalar dyadic functions can be employed in this manner.

Here is an illustration using the maximum function.   Remember Z, the vector of dimensions of the rectangular box we introduced earlier?

```
        Z
2   3   4
```

Suppose we wanted to get the longest dimension in Z, i.e., pick out the maximum value.   Then by analogy, just as we had

$$2+(3+4)\equiv2+7\equiv9$$
$$2\times(3\times4)\equiv2\times12\equiv24$$

("$\equiv$" denotes " is equivalent to", and is <u>not</u> a function)

for +/Z and ×/Z,

$$2\lceil(3\lceil4)\equiv2\lceil4\equiv4$$

represents $\lceil/Z$

On the terminal

```
        ⌈/Z
4
```

In the same fashion

$$2\lfloor(3\lfloor4)\equiv2\lfloor3\equiv2$$

is $\lfloor/Z$:

```
        ⌊/Z
2
```

Note that in every case the symbol before the reduction is placed between each pair of neighboring elements, and the groupings are identical.

Yet another simple application involves the logical functions in an accounts identification problem. Let X be a vector of accounts:

        $X \leftarrow 3 \quad 4 \quad 2 \quad {}^-2 \quad 1$

Our next job is to see if any have negative balances. The first step is to specify a vector of the same length as X, containing a 1 in each place where X is less than 0, i.e.:

        $LZ \leftarrow X < 0$
        LZ
0   0   0   1   0

Completing the algorithm:

        $\vee/LZ$
1

(Remember that the logical <u>or</u> returns a 1 if either or both arguments are 1.) Our answer can be interpreted as follows:

                if 1, then at least one account is negative
                if 0, then no accounts are negative

Let's reset X and repeat the problem to illustrate the second possibility:

        $X \leftarrow 3 \quad 6 \quad 1 \quad 0 \quad 3$
        $LZ \leftarrow X < 0$
        $\vee/LZ$
0

Can you tell what the significance of the answers might be if we had used $\wedge/LZ$ in the algorithm instead of $\vee/LZ$?

<u>Minus reduction</u>

We're not through with reduction yet. How about minus reducing a vector?

        $-/3 \quad 2 \quad 1 \quad 4$
${}^-2$

If you are puzzled by this result, the following step by step breakdown should help:

                        $3-(2-(1-4))$
                        $3-(2-{}^-3)$
                        $3-5$
                        ${}^-2$

Since $-{}^-$ in succession is equivalent to a +, you should be able to see that the above is the same as

3-2+1-4   (do by hand from left to right)

In other words, -/ is a way to get an alternating sum, to give such a sequence
its proper name.

Here is a somewhat messy example that gives a value for PI using -/

$$PI=4\times\left(\frac{1}{1} - \frac{1}{3} + \frac{1}{5} - \frac{1}{7} + \frac{1}{9} - \ldots + \ldots\right)$$

(This comes from integrating $1\div(1+X^2)$ termwise after dividing. The result
is a series for arctan X. If we let X=1, arctan 1 is PI÷4, and substitution
of 1 for X on the right hand side gives the expression in parentheses above.)

Let's construct an algorithm to obtain PI. Our first requirement is to get
the vector 1 3 5 7 9 11 13 15 17 19, stopping after 10 terms. Next, we take
their reciprocals, find the alternating sum, and multiply by 4, in that order.

Practically speaking, this isn't a very good way to get PI because the series
converges so slowly that a very large number of terms are needed to obtain
an accurate value.

However, since it is for illustrative purposes, we'll begin not by specifying
a vector 1 3 5 7 9.... Instead, it will be more instructive to see how this
vector, which we'll name N, can be generated in other ways. If

        $N\leftarrow 1$ 2 3 4 5 6 7 8 9 10

then

        $2\times N$
2   4   6   8   10   12   14   16   18   20

and

        $N\leftarrow 2\times N$
        $N\leftarrow N-1$
        N
1   3   5   7   9   11   13   15   17   19

gives us the series we want. The respecification of N as $2\times N$ and $N-1$ de-
stroys the previously assigned values of N, as discussed on page 32.

The reciprocals can be obtained by specifying

        $R\leftarrow 1\div N$
        R
1   0.3333333333   0.2   0.1428571429   0.1111111111
        0.09090909091   0.07692307692   0.06666666667
        0.05882352941   0.05263157895

and the alternating sum by

        $S\leftarrow -/R$

Our answer for PI (at last!) is

```
PI←4×S
PI
```
3.041839619

which is about .1 off for the reason described on the previous page.

Two final comments. If -/ is the alternating sum, then ÷/ is the alternating product, which you can verify for yourself on the terminal. Note
also that the result of reducing a vector is a scalar. Hence, generalizing
the operation, reduction is often thought of as a reduction of rank, where
a vector is said to be an array of rank 1, a scalar of rank 0. As we shall
see later, a matrix is an array of rank 2.

PROBLEMS

1. Drill

    +/3 7 ¯10 15 22   -/2 4 6 8 10   ×/2 4 6 8 10

    ÷/3 5 2   */3 2 1   ∧/1 0 1 1

    ∧/1 1 1   ∨/0 1 0 1   ∨/0 0 0

    =/3 2 2   >/1 ¯2 ¯4   ⌊/¯2 4 0 ¯8

    ⌈/1 ¯14.7 22 6

2. State in words what tests are represented by ∧/,∨/ and =/.

3. For $AV←3\ 6\ 8\ 2\ 4$, evaluate +/3×AV.

4. Write a one-line APL expression to specify Q as the vector 1 7 ¯2 ¯3
    and find the largest element in Q.

5. Set up an algorithm in APL to calculate the area of a triangle by
    Hero's formula, given below in conventional notation:

    $$\text{Area}=\sqrt{S(S-A)(S-B)(S-C)}$$

    A, B, and C are the sides of the triangle, while S is the semiperimeter.
    In your algorithm use L as the vector of sides of the triangle.

6. Write an APL expression to give the slope of the line passing through
    the points with coordinates P and Q. By definition, the slope of a
    straight line is the difference in the values of the vertical coordinates
    of two points on the line divided by the difference in the values of the
    corresponding horizontal coordinates.

CHAPTER 8:

Order of execution

Further applications

In the last chapter we stated that in reduction the effective order of execution was from right to left, since each function operated on everything to the right of it. It was as a result of the operation of this rule that -/ gave us the alternating sum.

Does this order of execution concept apply to all functions in *APL* ? You should make up a number of examples to convince yourself, at this point, that it does.

One good illustration is our previous problem (pages 41-42) to calculate a value for PI. There we used a large number of steps to get the result, but a much more elegant and neater way to write the algorithm is

        PI←4×-/1÷ ¯1+2×1 2 3 4 5 6 7 8 9 10
        PI
3.041839619

Here, working from right to left, the first thing the computer does is to multiply 2 by the numbers 1 2 3...10. Then ¯1 is added, which gives us the odd numbers 1 3 5.... These are divided into 1, yielding the reciprocals, and after -/ makes an alternating sum out of the reciprocals, the terms are multiplied by 4 to give PI.

The same approach can be taken with our old friend the invoice extension problem (page 36). In this case the total cost of the products Q with individual costs C can be written as +/X, where X is the vector $Q×C$. Numerically,

        +/6 2 3 1 0×2 4 3 5 10
34

Changing the order of execution

Don't be tempted by these examples into thinking that all problems can be solved this neatly. A case in point is our previous calculation of the hypotenuse of a right triangle. Without putting it on the terminal, try to figure out what would happen if we were so foolish as to write

$$C \leftarrow A * 2 + B * 2 * . 5$$

Going from right to left, 2 is raised to the .5 power, B is then raised to the power representing that result, and—we might as well stop here because it is obvious we goofed.

Really, what is needed is

$$C \leftarrow ((A * 2) + (B * 2)) * . 5$$

This is a good place to make three observations: (1) pairs of parentheses are used in APL in exactly the same way as in conventional mathematical notation, i.e., the normal order of execution is interrupted and expressions within parentheses are evaluated first; (2) aside from the above use of parentheses, there is no preferred order of execution in APL; and (3) a single right parenthesis is used in APL for system commands as contrasted to grouping, where a pair is required.

Getting back to the hypotenuse example, A and B are squared, added, and then the sum is raised to the .5 power. Let's execute this for specific values of A and B:

```
      A←3
      B←4
      C←((A*2)+(B*2)).5
SYNTAX ERROR
      C←((A*2)+(B*2)) 0.5
                    ∧
```

The error message is clearly due to the fact that an * was omitted before the .5, so that the line isn't a valid APL expression. Contrast this with the omission of × between expressions in ( ) in conventional notation, where multiplication is implied by the absence of the ×.

Redoing C, we can now call for its execution:

```
      C←((A*2)+(B*2))*.5
      C
5
```

The parentheses around $B*2$ aren't necessary. Why?

```
      ((A*2)+B*2)*.5
5
```

Now, one more rehash of an old problem—the calculation of averages. We saw that it was necessary to get the sum of the components of the vector X and divide this by the number of components in X. In one line

```
      X←1 2 3
      (+/X)÷+/X=X
2
```

From right to left, $X=X$ generates a vector of three 1's which are then added (+/) and divided into each of the three components of X before summing again.

Parentheses aren't needed around the expression +/X on the extreme left, but for a reason different from what you might expect. This can be shown by looking at +/1 2 3÷3, which is arithmetically equivalent to 1/3+2/3+3/3, or 2. This is exactly the same as (1+2+3)/3, the slashes in the last two expressions being used in the conventional way to indicate division. It doesn't make one bit of difference if we divide the elements of the vector by 3 before summing or after, as long, of course, as the divisor (here 3) is the same for all the elements.

Every nice simple-looking procedure has its fly-in-the-ointment. The following is a case where omission of the parentheses is significant.

        3×2+4
18

In *APL* 2 is added to the 4 to give 6, which is multiplied by 3. But in conventional notation, because of the accepted hierachy of order in which × precedes +, 3x2 is 6, which, adding 4, gives 10. So we should write

        (3×2)+4
10

or better still

        4+3×2
10

which requires fewer keystrokes.

The conventional rules in arithmetic aren't too bad to work with when only a relatively few functions are involved. Things tend to get a bit sticky, however, when you deal with the multitude of functions, standard and defined, that you have already been introduced to, or will soon encounter. It is here that the simplicity of the *APL* rule, that execution is from right to left subject only to the occurrence of parentheses, proves its worth.

At this stage of the game, as you start to build up expressions with many functions, don't hesitate to overparenthesize. When you are more at home in your understanding of the *APL* language, you will find yourself beginning to leave out the nonessential parentheses.

A polynomial illustration

An elegant demonstration of the order of execution rule and the power and versatility of *APL* can be seen in the following example showing how a polynomial can be written and evaluated.

Consider a typical algebraic polynomial expression

$$3-2X+9X^2+4X^3$$

which we want to evaluate for X, say, 10. How can this be represented in *APL*?

The most obvious and simplest to understand is a direct transliteration from the conventional notation:

$X \leftarrow 10$
$3+(^-2 \times X)+(9 \times X \star 2)+4 \times X \star 3$
4883

A little better version, which eliminates the parentheses, is

$3+X \times ^-2+X \times 9+X \times 4$
4883

Working from right to left, to 4X we add 9, giving

$$9+4X \text{ (conventional notation)}$$

This is then multiplied by X (remember that without parentheses the X multiplies <u>everything</u> to the right of it)

$$9X+4X^2$$

−2 is added

$$-2+9X+4X^2$$

X is again used as a multiplier

$$-2X+9X^2+4X^3$$

and, finally, 3 is added

$$3-2X+9X^2+4X^3$$

But you can't appreciate the economy of the *APL* notation until you have taken advantage of its ability to handle arrays. Here is the <u>pièce de résistance</u> of our problem:

$+/3 \ ^-2 \ 9 \ 4 \times X \star 0 \ 1 \ 2 \ 3$
4883

In this version, X is raised to the powers 0 1 2 3 to give

$$1 \ X \ X^2 \ X^3 \text{ (conventional notation)}$$

These, in turn, are multiplied by 3 −2 9 4, yielding

$$3 \ -2X \ 9X^2 \ 4X^3$$

and then +/ results in

$$3-2X+9X^2+4X^3$$

PROBLEMS

1. Drill

    4*3⌈3*4   1÷2+X←¯5 6 0 4 8 ¯6

    (4*3)⌈3*4   76÷+/2+3×1 2 3 4

    5*3×5   6÷2-4*3

2. Of the following five expressions which have the same value?

    (B*2)-4×A×C

    ((B*2)-4×(A×C))

    B*2-4×A×C

    (B×B)-(4×A)×C

    B×B-(4×A)×C

3. Construct *APL* expressions for each of the following:

    A) Three-fourths plus five-sixths minus seven-eighths
    B) The quotient of two differences nine-sevenths and
       eight-tenths, and one-third and two-fifths.

4. The geometric mean of a set of N positive numbers X is the nth root
    of their product. Write an *APL* expression to calculate this for
    X←1 7 4 2.5 51 19

5. For A←0 1 0 1, B←1 0 0 1, and C←1 1 0 0, evaluate

    (~A)v~B

    AvC∧B

    (A∧~B)∧AvC

    (~B)vAv~C

6. What is wrong with the expression A+B=B+A to show that the operation of
    addition is commutative, i.e., the order of the arguments is immaterial?

7. The Gregorian calendar provides that all years from 1582 to about 20,000
    that are divisible by 4 are leap years, with the provisos that of the
    centesimal years (1600, 1700, etc.) only those divisible by 400 are
    leap years, and of the millenial years those divisible by 4000 are not.
    Write a one-line *APL* expression to determine whether a given year Y
    is a leap year.

8. Why isn't the following a valid *APL* expression for $X^2-2XY+Y^2$ (conven-
    tional notation)? Correct it.

    (X*2)-(2×X×Y)+Y*2

9. The intensity level β of a sound wave is measured in decibels, and is defined as (conventional notation) β=10×log I/I_o where I_o is some arbitrary reference level of intensity. Write an *APL* expression for this formula.

10. Rewrite the following polynomial expression without parentheses. Do not use reduction:

$$({}^-3 \times X * 4) + (2 \times X * 2) - 8$$

11. Write an *APL* expression to compute the root-mean square of the components of a vector. (This is the square root of the average of the squares).

12. What is a possible interpretation of the following?

PROPOSE←RING∧WEATHER∧(JILL<JACK)∧JACK<AGELIMIT

13. Write an *APL* expression to calculate the interest on P dollars at R percent compounded annually for T years. How would you change your answer to provide for compounding quarterly?

CHAPTER 9:

Scalar monadic functions

Standard scalar monadic functions

Just as on page 14 we introduced the term <u>dyadic</u> to describe functions which require two arguments, so we will use <u>monadic</u> where only a single argument is needed.

Take a look at how some of the monadic functions are represented in conventional mathematical notation:

$$
\begin{array}{ll}
-X & \text{arithmetic negation} \\
X! & \text{factorial} \\
|X| & \text{absolute value} \\
\left.\begin{array}{l} 1/X \\ X^{-1} \end{array}\right\} & \text{reciprocal} \\
e^X & \text{exponential} \\
\ln X & \text{Natural logarithm} \\
\sqrt{X} & \text{square root} \\
\overline{X} & \text{logical negation}
\end{array}
$$

Whatever other merits this mishmash has, consistency certainly isn't one of them, for the symbol which is the functional indicator may appear on the left, the right, both sides, on top, or be in a special position, or be represented by an alphabetical label.

These same functions are effectively treated in *APL* as follows:

$$
\begin{array}{ll}
-X & \text{arithmetic negation} \\
!X & \text{factorial} \\
|X & \text{absolute value} \\
\div X & \text{reciprocal} \\
\ast X & \text{exponential} \\
\circledast X & \text{natural logarithm} \\
X\ast.5 & \text{square root (dyadic)} \\
\sim X & \text{logical negation}
\end{array}
$$

Notice that, for all the monadics in this list, the symbol precedes the argument. Most of them look like symbols for certain dyadic functions, but the interpretations may not always be closely related.

Let's run through some of them on the terminal and, as you do, note that both scalars and vectors can be used as arguments:

Arithmetic negation:

This function simply negates the argument that follows it:

```
      -3 4 ‾1 0 ‾8
‾3  ‾4  1  0  8
```

Factorial:

An expression like !X (X is an integer) is to be interpreted as the product (X)(X-1)(X-2)...(1) (see page 21). For example, if X is 4,

```
      !4
24
      1×2×3×4
24
```

and

```
      !1 2 3 4
1  2  6  24
```

To make sure your terminal is operating properly type

```
      2+2
4
```

If you got the result, ignore the next comment. If not, you didn't line up ' and . as in the precautions stated in our discussion of the dyadic ! on page 21. The way to get out of this hangup is to type a single ', followed by the return key.

This factorial function works also with nonintegers and zero:

```
      !2.5
3.32335097
      !0
1
```

(For those with a considerable background in mathematics, the factorial can be defined by use of the gamma function, given by the following integral:

$$\Gamma(n+1) = \int_0^\infty x^n e^{-X} dx$$

which can be shown to be equivalent to !n with n not restricted to integer values. If n is 0, incidentally, the definite integral has the value 1, which justifies the terminal result for !0.

For those with minimal math background—forget it.)

Absolute value:

The absolute value function is defined as follows:

$$|X \equiv \begin{cases} X & \text{if } X \geq 0 \\ -X & \text{if } X < 0 \end{cases}$$

In plain English this means: take the magnitude of the number and ignore any negative sign that may be present.

```
      |3 5 ¯2 7 ¯3
3   5   2   7   3
```

Reciprocal:

In *APL* the monadic ÷X is equivalent to the dyadic 1÷X. Thus,

```
      ÷1 2 3 4 5
1   0.5   0.3333333333   0.25   0.2
      1÷1 2 3 4 5
1   0.5   0.3333333333   0.25   0.2
```

Exponential:

*X is equivalent to raising e, the base of the system of natural logarithms, which has the value 2.71828..., to the X power. This means that *X is the same as 2.71828...*X.

```
      *2.5
12.18249396
```

and

```
      *1
2.718281828
```

which gives the value of e itself.

Natural logarithm:

⍟X yields the same result as the dyadic log, 2.71828...⍟X, i.e., e⍟X. See page 17 for a discussion of the dyadic log.

Since the base e is very common, the practice is to use "ln" to stand for "$\log_e$." Base 2 would be represented as "$\log_2$," base 10 as "$\log_{10}$" or simply "log," etc. Logarithms were originally invented as an aid in doing calculations involving products, quotients, powers, and roots. With the advent of modern calculators and computers they are rarely used nowadays for this purpose. More important, they do occur frequently in the solutions to equations representing a variety of physical problems, especially where the changes involved in the phenomenon to be analyzed are exponential in nature. Here is an illustration:

```
      ⍟10
2.302585093
```

In fact, from the definition of the logarithm, finding the logarithm and exponentiating are inverse processes, that is, each undoes the effect of the other, as the example below shows:

```
      ⍟*1 2 3
1   2   3
```

Square root:

This dyadic function was discussed earlier on page 16 and will not be taken up further, except to cite an example:

```
      25*.5
5
```

Logical negation:

Like the other logical functions, ∧ ∨ ⍲ ⍱, logical negation can have only 0 or 1 as an argument. As you have undoubtedly guessed

```
      ~1
0
      ~0
1
      ~1 0 1 1
0   1   0   0
```

and

```
      ~~1 0 1
1   0   1
```

i.e., logical negation is its own inverse. When we try to obtain

```
      ~3
DOMAIN ERROR
      ~3
      ∧
```

an error message is received since 3 is not an allowable argument for this function.

There are still additional monadic functions in *APL* that, for the most part, have no corresponding symbol in conventional notation. These are printed below and are taken up in sequence:

```
                    ⌈X   ceiling
                    ⌊X   floor
                    ?X   roll (random number generator)
                    +X   additive identity
                    ×X   signum
```

Ceiling:

This is the monadic ⌈, and is defined as the smallest integer not smaller

than the argument. Practically speaking, taking the ceiling of a number
"rounds up" the number.

```
      ⌈3.14
4
      ⌈4
4
      ⌈4.1
5
```

   Floor:

Analogous to the ceiling function, this results in the smallest integer
not larger than the argument ("rounding down").

```
      ⌊3.14
3
      ⌊3
3
      ⌊2.999
2
```

What about the ceiling and floor of a negative number? Let's try a few
examples:

```
      ⌈⁻4.1
⁻4
      ⌊⁻4.1
⁻5
```

If this puzzles you, it can be cleared up by reference to the number line
(page 18). Rounding up with ⌈⁻4.1 gives the next largest integer, ⁻4,
while rounding down gives ⁻5.

Finally, before going on to an illustrative problem, if we specify X as

```
      X←1.1 4.2 ⁻3.9 3
```

then

```
      ⌊X
1   4   ⁻4   3
      -⌈-X
1   4   ⁻4   3
```

and

```
      ⌈X
2   5   ⁻3   3
      -⌊-X
2   5   ⁻3   3
```

and our APL system is richer by two identities, no simple equivalent of
which exists in conventional notation. Additional identities will be
introduced from time to time in the text.

Here is a practical problem which involves the floor and ceiling functions. It considers rounding off bills with fractional pennies (so-called half cent adjust). After studying the solution you should be able to come up with a number of other related applications.

For purposes of illustration, let's specify a vector X:

        X←3 3.1 3.49 3.5 3.9 4

To make the half cent adjust work properly, we round up if the fractional part is 0.5 or more, and round down if it is less than 0.5. So for the above figures we want the following:

                    3 3 3 4 4 4

Looking at the floor of X:

        LX
3   3   3   3   3   4

This isn't what we want. What about the ceiling?

        ⌈X
3   4   4   4   4   4

which isn't right either.

Suppose we add 0.5 to each component of X and then try the floor again:

        X+.5
3.5   3.6   3.99   4   4.4   4.5
        LX+.5
3   3   3   4   4   4

Success! And the result suggests that a half cent adjust that rounds down (i.e., makes 3.5 come out 3 instead of 4) might be obtained by

        ⌈X-.5
3   3   3   3   4   4

We can summarize these results in the following table:

		X	3	3.1	3.49	3.5	3.9	4
		⌈X	3	4	4	4	4	4
		LX	3	3	3	3	3	4
		X+.5	3.5	3.6	3.99	4	4.4	4.5
		LX+.5	3	3	3	4	4	4
		⌈X-.5	3	3	3	3	4	4
Desired Results			3	3	3	4	4	4

Roll:

Just to be different, let's call for the execution of the monadic roll
several times:

          ?6 6
1   5
          ?6 6
3   4
          ?6 6
2   1

What kind of oddball function can this be that doesn't return the same
result each time? We seem to be getting numbers at random from it. In
fact, if you play around with it some more, you will see that $?X$ returns
a random integer from 1 to X inclusive.

This means that ?6 6 simulates the roll of a pair of dice, while ?2

          ?2
2

could be a simulation of a coin toss, with 1 standing for heads, say, and 2
for tails.

When we try to execute the roll function (also called "random" or "query")
with a noninteger, we get

          ?4.5
$DOMAIN\ ERROR$
          ?4.5
          ^

and in fact, its domain consists of positive integers only.

In APL each time you sign on the terminal you will get the same sequence
of random numbers if the same upper limit is specified. There is a
practical reason for this. In checking out algorithms (debugging), it is
often necessary for testing purposes to use the same set of numbers so
that valid comparisons can be made each time through in the checking process.

Finally, the reason why the starting point is 1 and the way in which it can
be altered will be covered in chapter 34.

          Additive identity:

This function is included for completeness. $+X$ is equivalent to $0+X$:

          +2 4 6
2   4   6

and is not to be confused with $+/X$:

          +/2 4 6
12

Signum:

$\times X$ results in 0, 1 or $^-$1, depending on whether the argument is 0, positive or negative:

```
        ×1 ‾3 0
1   ‾1   0
```

As before, it shouldn't be mixed up with $\times/X$:

```
        ×/2 4 6
48
```

Calculation of the cosine

To show a useful application of some of these monadic functions, let's calculate the cosine of some angle X (in radians) in APL.

The cosine is a trigonometric function which can be defined in a number of ways, including the following:

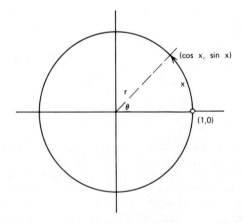

In a circle of unit radius, if we measure counterclockwise from the point (1,0) a distance X along the curve, the coordinates of the end point are defined to be cosine X (cos X) for the horizontal coordinate and sine x (sin x) for the vertical coordinate.

A radian is a unit of angular measure such that the angle theta (θ) shown in the figure, measured in radians, is the length of the curve intercepted, as indicated by the arrow, divided by the radius. Since the length of the whole circumference is 2xPIxr and r is 1 in this circle, there are 2xPI radians in a unit circle. Arguments involving geometric similarity lead us to the same conclusions for all circles. Thus, PI radians are equivalent to 180°.

It can be shown in calculus, by application of a Maclaurin's series to the cosine function, that (in conventional notation)

$$\cos X = \frac{X^0}{0!} - \frac{X^2}{2!} + \frac{X^4}{4!} - \frac{X^6}{6!} + \frac{X^8}{8!} - \ldots + \ldots$$

where X is in radians.

Notice the regularity of the terms, the numerators and denominators being all even and increasing regularly. This will help us in developing a compact *APL* expression for them.

Our first step is to set a value for X. Let's choose PI÷4 (45°):

        $X \leftarrow 3.1415 \div 4$

Working with the numerators, we have

        $TOP \leftarrow X \star 0 \ 2 \ 4 \ 6 \ 8 \ 10 \ 12$
        TOP
1   0.616849233   0.3805029763   0.2347129691   0.1447825149
        0.0893089833   0.05509017785

Similarly, the denominators can be assigned to a vector called *BOT*:

        $BOT \leftarrow !0 \ 2 \ 4 \ 6 \ 8 \ 10 \ 12$
        BOT
1   2   24   720   40320   3628800   479001600

Our last two steps are to divide *TOP* by *BOT* and take the alternating sum:

        $-/TOP \div BOT$

yielding

0.7071072503

as the cosine of PI÷4.

This can be done all on one line, and gives us a good excuse to introduce another new idea in *APL* at the same time. Here it is:

        $-/(X \star V) \div !V \leftarrow 0 \ 2 \ 4 \ 6 \ 8 \ 10 \ 12$
0.7071072503

We have combined an assignment and several functions in a single line. Reading from right to left, we defined a vector of even numbers and stored it under the variable name V (since it is needed for both numerators and denominators). Next we got the factorials of V which were then divided into the vector $X \star V$. Lastly, -/ gave us the alternating sum.

As a corollary to this problem, the Maclaurin's series for sin x is

$$\sin X = \frac{X^1}{1!} - \frac{X^3}{3!} + \frac{X^5}{5!} - \ldots + \ldots$$

so that to calculate sin X all we have to do in our algorithm is to change V to 1+0 2 4 6....

A drill exercise in *APL*

In the *APL* system (located in common library 1 of the system on which this
text is based) there is a drill exercise in the various functions that have
been described so far. This is a stored program, much like *STAT* was in
the first chapter. The details of how such programs are written and stored
will be covered in later chapters.

Follow this sequence carefully on your terminal. You should also check
with your own system librarian to see what exercises (if any) may have
been developed locally or duplicated for storage in the system you have
access to. The more practice you get at this early stage, the better you
will understand how they can be used in programming.

First execute the following command:

```
    )LOAD 1 APLCOURSE
SAVED   11.07.53 09/01/69
```

A message comes back stating when the workspace (block of storage) we have
asked for was last saved. This command, about which more will be said
later, in effect puts an exact image of the workspace *APLCOURSE* into our
own active workspace so that we can access it.

You will now go through an exercise in which you and the *APL* system will
exchange roles. It will ask you to do problems and you will be required to
type the answers in. To start off type *EASYDRILL* and put *Y*'s under all
the functions printed, as shown in the copy below. Be sure to type *Y* for
the exercises in vectors because vectors are so easily handled in *APL* .
Ditto for reduction. None of the problems require answers which are not
integers, and the problems are relatively easy computationally.

```
    EASYDRILL
TYPE Y UNDER EACH FUNCTION FOR WHICH YOU WANT EXERCISE
SCALAR DYADIC FUNCTIONS
+-×÷*⌈⌊<≤=≥>≠!|∧∨⊕⍲⍱
YYYYYYYYYYYYYYYYYYYYYY
SCALAR MONADIC FUNCTIONS
+-×÷⌈⌊!|~
YYYYYYYYY
TYPE Y IF EXERCISE IN VECTORS IS DESIRED, N OTHERWISE
Y
TYPE Y IF EXERCISE IN REDUCTION IS DESIRED, N OTHERWISE
Y
```

Here are some sample problems generated by the program. These will be
different each time you ask for the program, as well as different for each
person who asks:

```
              ¯1   9   ¯9   5 >   ¯8   ¯10   4   8
□:
     1  1  0  0
                      -  8   ¯6   ¯4   ¯3   0
□:
     ¯8  6  4  3  0
```

If the problem is correctly answered, you get another. Let's do this one wrong:

```
                          ⊛/ 2   2
□:
      0 1
TRY AGAIN
□:
      1
```

You get three tries altogether, after which you are furnished with the answer and, to add insult to injury, you get another problem of the same kind.

```
                          ∨/ 0   0   1   1
□:
      1
                          ⌊ ‾2.333333333   ‾2   1.666666667   ‾2.666666667    ‾3
□:
      3 4 5 6
TRY AGAIN
□:
      4 2 10 4
TRY AGAIN
□:
      3 1 9 7
ANSWER IS  ‾3  ‾2   1   ‾3   ‾3
                          ⌊ ‾1
□:
     ‾1
                          + ‾7   ‾4
```

Typing PLEASE gives you the answer and another problem of the same kind. The only way out of a particular type of problem is to type the correct answer. However, since any valid APL expression equivalent to the answer is acceptable, the problem itself can be entered as its own answer—not particularly instructive from a pedagogical point of view, but it works. To get out of the drill, type STOP, after which you receive a record of your performance (only part of which is shown here). Typing STOPSHORT exits you from the program, but doesn't print your record.

```
□:
     ‾7 ‾4
                          ⌊ 1.333333333   ‾0.6666666667
□:
     PLEASE
ANSWER IS 1  ‾1
                          ⌊ 0.5  1.75
□:
     STOP
YOUR RECORD IS
FUNCTION     FIRST TRY   SECOND TRY    THIRD TRY     FAILED
    +
    ‒
    ×
    ÷
    *
```

PROBLEMS

1. Drill

    ⌊ ¯2.7|¯15   ⌈8.1|32.68 |3.1 0 ¯5.6 ¯8

    ?10 10 10 10   *3 4.7 ¯1.5   !3 5 7 4

    ⍟14.1 86 .108   ⌈ ¯1.8 0 ¯21 5.6   ⌊5.5 6.8 ¯9.1 ¯.12

    × ¯5.6 0 42   ?3 4 5   - ¯1.2 ¯6.7 .52 19.5

    +8.7 ¯19.1 23   ÷3.5 ¯67 ¯.287   14×⌈5.8×¯31.046

2. Using the residue function, write one-line definitions in *APL* of ⌊*X*
    and ⌈*X*.

3. If *A*←3, and *B*←3 2 3 1 ¯6, evaluate

    $$*2+A1←(¯1+A*3)÷2$$

    $$~(2≤A)∧∨/3=B$$

    $$C≠⌊C←((A*2)+(A+1)*2)*.5$$

4. Write an algorithm to test an integer N for the following if the final
    digit is deleted, the original number is divisible by the new one.

5. January 1 falls on Thursday (the fifth day of the week) in 1970.
    Determine the day of the week on which January 1 falls in any given
    year Y. For simplicity assume any year divisible by 4 is a leap year.

6. Given a vector *V* which is made up of one- and two-digit integers.
    A) Write an expression that will yield a logical vector whose 1's
    correspond in position to the one-digit members of *V*.   B) Do the
    same for the two-digit members of *V*.

7. After executing each of the following, write an expression to round a
    positive number N to D places to the right of the decimal point:

    $$(10*¯1)×⌊.5+6.18×10*1$$

    $$(10*¯2)×⌊.5+4.75×10*2$$

8. Modify the answer to the previous problem to handle negative numbers
    only. What further changes are needed, if any to make your expression
    work for either positive or negative numbers.

9. Let *M*←84.6129999993 Display *M*. Compare 1*E*5×*M* with ⌊1*E*5×*M*. (See
    under "fuzz" in chapter 34 for an explanation).

10. Construct an *APL* expression that will determine whether or not the first
    N significant figures of two whole numbers X and Y are identical.

11. A) You are given D dollars with which to make purchases of books at
    B dollars each. How many books can be purchased?

    B) How many books can be bought if it is required that the D dollars
    be used up and supplemented, if necessary?

12. Carry out the following instructions and explain the answers:

> ```
> A←15.8
> B←(A←4)×A
> B
> ```
16
> ```
> A←15.8
> B←(A←4)×⌈A
> B
> ```
64

13. Write an *APL* expression that rounds numbers down if the decimal part
is less than .5, and up if greater than .5. For numbers ending in .5,
your expression should round to the nearest <u>even</u> integer.

CHAPTER 10:

Function definition

Earlier we introduced the idea of an algorithm in calculating the hypotenuse
of a right triangle. If you recall, at that time we stated the problem and
went through a sequence of simple operations to solve it. Then we refined
our treatment and reduced the number of steps needed by taking advantage
of the simple order of execution rule in APL.

In a very real sense the operation of getting the hypotenuse exhibits the
characteristics of a standard scalar dyadic function. And it should be
clear that what we did was by no means unique. Literally an infinite
number of algorithms exist for solving all kinds of problems and behaving
like our hypotenuse function, if indeed we may call it that.

This suggests that we need a way to label and record these algorithms so
that they can be used over and over again by using the appropriate name
and arguments, just like the standard APL functions studied so far.

More specifically, let's review what was done in the hypotenuse problem
with our ultimate objective being to define it for repeated use:

        (1) A was specified
        (2) B was specified
        (3) C was specified as the sum of A squared and B
              squared, all raised to the one-half power (see page 34)

This was our last revision, with the algorithm reduced to one line.

The defined function HYP

What is most desirable is to be able to give to the terminal values for
A and B and a simple message to get the hypotenuse, much like asking for
2+2 and getting 4 back. Here + is the simple message which tells the computer what to do.

By analogy A HYP B, HYP being the message in this case, sounds like just
the thing to do the dirty work of calculating the hypotenuse for us. Such
a function has already been provided for you in the APL system. Don't
worry at this point how it got there. (The student's attention is called

to the note in the preface about the common library, which will be heavily used from this point on.)

Now enter on your keyboard

>   )LOAD 1 CLASS

after which you should get a message back about when this workspace was saved last.

SAVED   15.02.39 07/29/69

The workspace CLASS, incidentally, contains a large number of functions and illustrations which will be of considerable value to us in subsequent chapters.

Typing

>   3 HYP 4

elicits the response

5

It works with vector arguments too, as the next example shows:

>   1 3 HYP 1 4
> 1.414213562   5

Here we are solving a family of triangles, with sides 1 1 and 3 4 at the same time. In short, the function HYP acts just like + in the problem

>   1 3+1 4
> 2   7

and apparently behaves and is used like a standard scalar dyadic function.

Thus far we've looked at the external behavior of the function HYP. In order for us to go on and design our own functions in the future we will have to be able to understand how HYP is constructed.

Function definition

There is a command which will display any defined function like HYP stored in the active workspace. It is the following, which you should enter on your keyboard at this point. DON'T press the return key until your entry looks exactly like the one below. If you make a mistake, correct it before, not after:

>   ∇HYP[□]∇

The symbol ∇ (pronounced "del") is the upper shift G and the box □ (called "quad") is the upper shift L. No attempt will be made at this point to explain the rationale behind the particular combination of symbols, but you will see shortly how this command is related to a number of others that will be needed to define, display and edit functions.

Here is the system's response:

```
      ∇  C←A  HYP  B
[1]      C←((A*2)+B*2)*0.5
      ∇
```

The first line, beginning with ∇, is called the "header" of the function. *HYP* is the name of the function, and it has two arguments, *A* and *B*, with a resultant (i.e., the answer) which is stored under the variable name *C*. Notice that the arguments are separated by spaces from the function name. Can you imagine what would happen if the spaces were omitted?

Line 1 gives the rule for calculating *C* and is the same as before. If you are wondering what purpose the ∇'s serve, it should not be too difficult to see that, since they open the function on the header line and close it after the one and only line needed (in this particular case) to complete the function, they must be a signal to the system that function definition is about to begin or is ending.

As we pointed out before, *HYP* can be used just like a standard scalar dyadic function:

```
      1+3
4
      1  HYP  3
3.16227766
```

Let's get some practice in entering this function ourselves in our own workspace. First type

```
      )CLEAR
```

which is another system command, to be discussed in more detail later, but which has the effect of clearing out your active workspace and replacing it with a fresh blank workspace, just like the one you received when you signed on. The response is

CLEAR WS

Suppose we try to execute *HYP* now:

```
      3  HYP  4
SYNTAX ERROR
      3  HYP  4
          ∧
```

Are you surprised that we got an error message? You shouldn't be. After all, our new workspace isn't supposed to have anything in it, and this leaves the way open for us to insert the function *HYP* ourselves. Start by typing

```
      ∇C←A  HYP  B
```

which tells the system you want to enter a function. To give it its proper name, after you type the opening ∇, you are said to be in "function definition mode," as opposed to desk calculator mode.

Having pressed the return key you should get the response

[1]

i.e., the system in effect tells you it is ready to accept the first line of your function. Enter the line as follows, then press the return key:

[1] $C \leftarrow ((A*2)+B*2)*.5$

The response this time is

[2]

since the system doesn't know how many lines your function will ultimately have. There being nothing more to enter, type a second ∇ to signal the system that you are finished:

[2]   ∇

Now the function, having been duly entered, is executable:

        3 *HYP* 4
5

If at this point you don't get 5, type)*CLEAR* and enter the function over again.

We haven't squeezed all the juice out of *HYP* yet. Just as we can type

        $2 \times 3+4$
14

so we can ask the system for

        2×3 *HYP* 4
10

What makes this possible is the fact that the calculation involved in *HYP* produced a resultant which was stored away temporarily under the name *C* and hence was available for further calculations. Such a function is said to return an explicit result. More about this in the next chapter, where we will see examples which can't be used as *HYP* above.

A defined monadic function

For an example of a standard scalar monadic function we'll develop a square root function and complicate it a bit for purposes of illustration. If we had one called, say *SQRT*, then in *HYP* we could write

        [1] $C \leftarrow SQRT(A*2)+B*2$

for line 1 instead of what we actually have.

Let's go ahead and define such a function with the header

        $\nabla R \leftarrow SQRT \ X$

Again as a reminder, don't forget the space between $SQRT$ and X. Clearly, only the one argument X is needed here, namely the number we are calculating the square root of, and it is placed on the <u>right</u> of the function name. The system responds, as before, with

[1]

Incidentally, this suggests that a good way to tell whether you are in function definition or desk calculator mode is to see if you get a number in brackets when the return key is pressed. Just remember that if you do get it, anything you type from that point on until the closing ∇ becomes part of the function definition.

If you were to press the return key again, you would get

[1]

and the system returns yet another indication to you that it is still waiting for line 1.

Now for the rule and the closing out of the function:

```
[1]    R←X*.5
[2]    ∇
```

A few examples show that $SQRT$ seems to work acceptably:

```
      SQRT 4
2
      SQRT 1 2 4
1   1.414213562   2
```

Since earlier we had indicated that $SQRT$ could be used to simplify the function HYP, and we have now defined $SQRT$, let's write another HYP function in which $SQRT$ can be imbedded. Starting off as before, type the function header and wait for the response:

```
      ∇R←A HYP B
DEFN ERROR
      ∇R←A HYP B
                ∧
```

But, this time, it appears that something is wrong. Apparently reentering the function with the same name and in the same workspace doesn't wipe out the old function. In this there exists no analogy between the behavior of a function header and an assignment of values to a variable, the old values of which are wiped out when a new assignment is made.

You may argue that this replacement feature could be a very handy thing to have around for function headers, but if you think about it you will see that it can have some grave consequences too. Suppose, for example, you had a big complex function that was really valuable in your work, and you inadvertently used the same function name for something else. All your hard work, unless you kept a record of it somewhere else, would then be gone. So the *APL* system deliberately makes it hard for you to destroy work accidentally.

This leaves you with two alternatives for redefining *HYP*: You can get rid of *HYP* by an appropriate system command (to be taken up later) or, better yet, use another name for your new function, say, *HY*.

Here is the function *HY*:

```
        ∇R←A HY B
[1]     R←SQRT (A*2)+B*2
[2]     ∇
```

and it appears to work just as well as *HYP* does:

```
        3 HY 4
5
        1 3 HY 1 4
1.414213562   5
```

The cosine function

For another by no means new example in this lecture, let's define a monadic function which incorporates the cosine algorithm. In this problem, just to be different, *T* is used for the resultant in the header and body of the function:

```
        ∇T←COS X
[1]     T←-/(X*V)÷!V←0 2 4 6 8 10 12
[2]     ∇
```

RESEND

Unexpectedly we get a *RESEND* message, which is indicative of a transmission error. Pressing the return key gives us a second *RESEND*. (Seated at your own terminal, you probably won't get these messages.)

RESEND

After the return key is pressed once more, the system returns a [2]:

[2]

Since, at this stage, we can't be sure whether our function exists in storage, we retype line 1 of the function, followed by the return key:

```
[2]     T←-/(X*V)÷!V←0 2 4 6 8 10 12
```

We get back an error message and [2]:

CHARACTER ERROR

^

[2]

Apparently line 1 of the function was accepted previously, so we close the function out with ∇:

[2]   ∇

Now we are out of function definition mode and can do

      2+2
4

A word of caution, however. If we had tried the calculation before closing out the function, we would have been in hot water. Can you explain why?

As a value for the argument, we'll use $PI\div4$ and execute the function:

      PI←3.14159
      COS PI÷4
0.7071072503

We get a meaningful result, so it seems to be working OK so far.

Some additional system commands

Our workspace, which was originally blank, now has four functions. As users, we may at times want to find out what is in our workspace at the moment. This can be done quite easily by the system command

)FNS

which works in exactly the same way as)VARS did earlier, that is, it provides us with an alphabetical listing of the functions available in the active workspace. Here is the response:

COS   HY   HYP   SQRT

One additional point about the system commands)FNS and)VARS. If the listing is long and we are interested only in whether a particular name, say, HYP is included we can ask for

)FNS H
HY   HYP   SQRT

and we get that part of the listing from the letter H on. Printing of the list can be interrupted at any time by pressing the ATTN key. For variable names, the same syntax prevails. Since we have only PI in storage at this point, let's define a number of additional variables, and then call for a partial listing:

      A←B←C←D←F←G←J←T←10
)VARS F
F   G   J   PI   T

We can observe the behavior of the system as we add and delete functions. For example, add the following simple monadic function designed to give the square of a number:

```
        ∇R←SQ U
[1]     R←U×U∇
```

Two observations should be made at this point. In the first place, the rule could have been stated in either of two ways: $U×U$ or $U*2$. Second, waiting until the next line number is returned by the system is really unnecessary. Since the function is finished at the end of line 1, it is perfectly proper to close it out there, as was done in this case.

SQ seems to be all right:

```
        SQ 4
16
```

and, in fact, SQ and $SQRT$ are inverse functions:

```
        SQRT SQ 4
4
```

Displaying the list of functions now available, we see SQ has been added to the list:

```
        )FNS
COS      HY      HYP      SQ      SQRT
```

We haven't said yet how to delete a function from the workspace. This is done by the system command

```
        )ERASE HYP
```

and a new display of the functions shows that HYP is gone:

```
        )FNS
COS      HY      SQ      SQRT
```

As a side note here, the $ERASE$ command can be used to delete more than one function at a time, as well as variables, so that the proper syntax for its use is $)ERASE\ FN1\ FN2...VAR1...$, depending on what is to be deleted. Of course, to get rid of all the functions at once, type

```
        )CLEAR
CLEAR WS
```

and then the command $)FNS$ elicits an "empty" response from the system, the typeball merely moving over six spaces.

PROBLEMS

1. Define a function EQ which evaluates the expression $(X-2)×X-3$ for various integer values of X and identifies the solutions to the equation $0=(X-2)×X-3$.

2. Define a function BB which generates the batting averages of players by dividing the number of hits obtained by the number of times at bat for each player.

3. Define a function *HERO* to calculate the area of a triangle by Hero's formula. (See problem 5, chapter 7.)

4. The ABC Manufacturing Company reimburses its employees 100% of the first $200 spent per semester for college work in an approved program, and 50% of the next $300. No reimbursement is made for expenses above $500 per semester. Write a function called *REFUND* that will calculate the refund due each employee in the program.

5. A well-known formula in electrical work gives the combined resistance RT of several resistances R1, R2, etc., wired in parallel as follows (conventional notation):

$$\frac{1}{RT} = \frac{1}{R_1} + \frac{1}{R_2} + \ \cdots$$

Define a function *PR* that will calculate *RT* for a vector *M* of resistances in parallel.

6. To find the standard deviation of a set of numbers, the following steps are necessary: (1) Compute the mean; (2) Find the difference of each number from the mean; (3) Square these differences; (4) Take the square root of the average of step 3. Write a function *SD* to compute the standard deviation of some data *X*. Assume you already have a monadic function *AVG* (which computes averages) in storage.

7. In relativity theory the mass of a body depends on its velocity V relative to the observer. Specifically, (in conventional notation)

$$m = m_o \div \sqrt{1 - v^2/c^2}$$

Where m_o is the mass of the object at rest and c is the velocity of light ($\bar{3}E8$ meters/sec). Write a defined function *REL* to yield the "mass" of a body moving at speed *V* and with a rest mass *MR*.

8. Define functions called *PLUS*, *MINUS*, *TIMES*, *DIVIDEDBY* to give mathematical meaning to these words, e.g., 3 *PLUS* 4 returns 7, etc.

CHAPTER 11:

The syntax of functions

The last chapter discussed some of the ways in which functions can be designed and used. It should be apparent that they differ from the standard
functions accessible on the keyboard in a number of ways, but the differences
are of form and appearance rather than intent. As a matter of fact, if our
keyboard had a hundred more keys on it, many of the more useful defined
functions could then appear as symbols. If the function $SQRT$ happened to
be one of these so favored, all that would be necessary to get a square
root then is to key in the appropriate symbol and argument. Practical con-
siderations prevent the keyboard from being larger than it is, so only the
most useful functions are incorporated.

The richness of the APL language is such that many other function types
than have been introduced so far are possible. Already you have worked
with two kinds, the dyadics HYP and HY and the monadics $SQRT$ and SQ.

A number of illustrations that will be helpful to us are stored in the
workspace called 1 $CLASS$, which has been accessed before in the last
chapter. Let's reload this workspace and find out what is in it by executing the following sequence of commands. The system responses are
included after each command:

```
        )LOAD 1 CLASS
SAVED   15.02.39 07/29/69
        )FNS
ADD       AGAIN    AVG      AVG1      AVG2      AVG3      AVG4     AVG5
BASE      C        CMP      CMPX      CMPY      COLCAT1   COLCAT2
COLCAT3   COS      COSINE   CP        CPUTIME   CP1       DEC
DELAY     DESCRIBE          DFT       DICE      E         FACT
FACTLOOP           GEO2     GEO3      HEXA      HY        HYP
INSERT    INV      MEAN     PI        RECT      REP       REVERSE
ROWCAT    RUN      S        SD        SETVARIABLES        SIGN     SORT
SPELL     SQRT     STAT     STATISTICS          SUB       SUMSCAN  TIME
TIMEFACT           TRA      TRACETIME
```

Your listing may not be identical with this one, since changes are made from
time to time in the common library workspaces. Be that as it may, most of
the functions will be explained and used as we go through the remaining
chapters. The ones we will be interested in at this time are HYP, $SIGN$,
$DICE$, $RECT$, $STAT$, and $TIME$

71

Remember that to display the contents of a function we type

        ∇ name [ ] ∇

after which the system prints out the function header followed by all the
steps which comprise the function, and includes even the opening and
closing dels. Our old friend *HYP* is an example:

        ∇*HYP*[ ]∇
      ∇ *C←A HYP B*
[1]   *C←((A*2)+B*2)*0.5*
      ∇

Function headers

In *APL* there are six ways of writing function headers, and each has its
own particular uses, as will be seen from the illustrative examples to be
displayed. These six forms are summarized in the table below.

	DYADIC	MONADIC	NILADIC
returns explicit result	∇*C←A HYP B*	∇*R←SIGN X*	∇*R←DICE*
no explicit result	∇*L RECT H*	∇*STAT X*	∇*TIME*

Don't worry, for the moment, about what all this means; everything in good
time.

To start off, display the function *SIGN*:

        ∇*SIGN*[ ]∇
      ∇ *R←SIGN X*
[1]   *R←(X>0)-X<0*
      ∇

It takes a single argument which, if negative, returns ⁻1, if positive, 1
and if zero, it returns 0. In fact, it duplicates the monadic signum
function introduced earlier. Executing this for various arguments; we get

        SIGN ⁻5.2
  ⁻1
        SIGN 0
  0
        SIGN 569
  1
        SIGN 3 ⁻2 0
  1 ⁻1 0

If you look at the rule for '*SIGN*, you should be able to see how it works
by tracing it through. If *X* is negative, *X*<0 would be 1 and *X*>0 would be 0.
so 0-1 gives ⁻1. Similarly, for *X* positive, *X*<0 is 0, *X*>0 is 1, with 1-0
resulting in 1. And for *X*=0, *X*<0 is 0 and *X*>0, so that 0-0 gives 0.

Now, type *DICE* several times and display it:

```
      DICE
6
      DICE
7
      DICE
3
      ∇DICE[☐]∇
   ∇ R←DICE
[1]   R←+/? 6 6
   ∇
```

This is simply the sum of random roll of two dice. Notice in the header
that *DICE* has no arguments. It is a "niladic" function, to use a coined
word. The reason for the lack of arguments is that the function really
doesn't need any. It is designed to select the numbers for the roll itself.

So far, we have seen three types of function headers, requiring 0, 1, or 2
arguments. They all return explicit results, i.e., a result that can be
used for subsequent computation. Now let's look at one that doesn't give
explicit results, but merely prints them on the paper.

Display the function *RECT*:

```
      ∇RECT[☐]∇
   ∇ L RECT H
[1]   2×L+H
[2]   L HYP H
[3]   L×H
   ∇
```

The first thing that should hit your eye is that there is no ← in the header.
Line 1 gives the perimeter of a rectangle of length *L* and height *H*; line 2
is the length of the diagonal, using the previously defined *HYP*; line 3 is
the area of the rectangle.

Notice also that there is no specification arrow on any line. This means
that the results of that line aren't stored anywhere and will, as mentioned
above, be printed out on the paper.

For example:

```
      3 RECT 4
14
5
12
```

The purpose of this function, as defined, is to give information, not for
further work:

```
      5+3 RECT 4
14
5
12
VALUE ERROR
      5+3 RECT 4
      ∧
```

Here the results of the function's three lines again print out because that
is done in the body of the function, but we can't add 5 to these results
because the numbers weren't stored anywhere, as in

          5+3 *HYP* 4
10

The two headers differ in that a specification is made in *HYP* and not in
RECT, and in the body of *RECT* again there were no assignments of results
to any variables. We will have more to say about the significance of the
variables used in the header assignment and in the function itself in
chapter 13.

Now consider the monadic *STAT* :

          ∇*STAT*[☐]∇
      ∇ *STAT X*
[1]   *N*←+/*X*=*X*
[2]   (+/*X*)÷*N*
[3]   ⌈/*X*
[4]   ⌊/*X*
      ∇

Again there is no explicit result implied in the header form, so the result
will be three lines. The first two give us the average of the components
of *X*, and could actually be combined into one line. *N* is just a convenient
handle for transferring the results of line 1 (which is the number of components) to line 2. Lines 3 and 4 print out the largest and smallest components of *X*. Executing *STAT*, we get

          STAT 3 2 1 3 2 1
2
3
1

Since no explicit results are returned, it doesn't make any sense to work
further with them. If we try it, we get an error message as before.

          2×*STAT X*
3.333333333   2.333333333   2.666666667
6   3   4
0   2   1
VALUE ERROR
          2×*STAT X*
             ∧

To complete the table, execute (but don't display) the function *TIME* :

          TIME
11:11:07 *AM EASTERN*

Obviously it doesn't need any arguments to give the time of day, and is
designed so that you can't do anything with it.

Another function of this type that you have already encountered is
EASYDRILL in the workspace 1 *APLCOURSE*. This too required no arguments

and returned no explicit results.   It typed out the answers and accepted inputs, but you couldn't do any computations with them.   Functions of this type are commonly called <u>main programs</u>.

PROBLEMS

For problems 1 to 6 define functions as follows, having the stated characteristics:

1. Dyadic, explicit result: to calculate the FICA (social security tax) at the rate of P percent on gross yearly income IN up to a maximum of $7800.

2. Dyadic, no explicit result; to store under the name T the square of the difference of two arguments.

3. Monadic, explicit result: to generate prime numbers, using Fermat's formula, $2^{2^N} + 1$ (conventional notation).

4. Monadic, no explicit result: to calculate the ceiling of X, using the residue function.

5. Niladic, explicit result: to produce four random numbers from 1 to 100.

6. Niladic, no explicit result: to see if either one of two previously defined variables divides the other evenly.

7. Enter the function HYP (see page 72) and use it to evaluate each of the following:

$$(3 \ HYP \ 4) \ HYP \ 3 \ HYP \ 1$$
$$4 + 3 \ HYP \ 4 - 3$$
$$(4 + 3) \ HYP \ 4 - 3$$

8. After executing the command $)LOAD$ 1 $CLASS$, derive a dyadic function called D which returns an explicit result and gives the larger of the two arguments.   Explain the system's response.

9. Assume that you have a monadic function AVG that returns an explicit result (there is one in 1 $CLASS$).   Write a one-line APL expression which uses AVG to obtain the average of a vector of numbers X, stores the result under the name A, and calculates and stores in F the 10 log of A.

CHAPTER 12:

Function editing

Up to now we have been examining the different ways to enter functions on the *APL* system, but have yet to consider how we might change a function which has already been put in. Since we can't do much without the capability for such change, this chapter will be concerned with ways of editing functions after they have been written and entered.

To speed things up, we'll use a prepared function in the workspace 1 *CLASS*. Type)*LOAD* 1 *CLASS*:

```
      )LOAD 1 CLASS
SAVED  15.02.39 07/29/69
```

By way of review, let's look at what's in this workspace:

```
      )FNS
ADD       AGAIN   AVG     AVG1    AVG2     AVG3    AVG4     AVG5
BASE      C       CMP     CMPX    CMPY     COLCAT1 COLCAT2
COLCAT3   COS     COSINE  CP      CPUTIME  CP1     DEC
DELAY   DESCRIBE          DFT     DICE     E       FACT
FACTLOOP          GEO2    GEO3    HEXA     HY      HYP
INSERT    INV     MEAN    PI      RECT     REP     REVERSE
ROWCAT    RUN     S       SD      SETVARIABLES     SIGN     SORT
SPELL    SQRT    STAT    STATISTICS        SUB     SUMSCAN  TIME
TIMEFACT         TRA     TRACETIME
```

The function we will be demonstrating on is *STAT*. Remember how to display it?

```
      ∇STAT[▯]∇
    ∇ STAT X
[1]    N←+/X=X
[2]    (+/X)÷N
[3]    ⌈/X
[4]    ⌊/X
    ∇
```

It isn't possible to enter it or redefine it because we already have a copy of it in our active workspace. Suppose we didn't know that it was already in and tried to reenter it:

```
      ∇STAT X
DEFN ERROR
      ∇STAT X
            ∧
```

An error message is obtained, showing, as was discussed earlier on page 66, that the system has built-in protection against accidental replacement of a function.

But we can make changes in the function as already defined. This *APL* feature is a necessity, for otherwise finding errors and debugging and modifying programs would be considerably more difficult.

Adding a line

The four lines of the function, as presently written, give information on the average and largest and smallest components of a vector X. Let's suppose we've decided to add a fifth line which will give the range (difference between the largest and smallest components).

How is this done? The first step is to open up the function by typing a single ∇ and the function name, followed by the return key as usual:

```
      ∇STAT
[5]
```

Notice that the system responds with [5]. In general the next available line number will be returned. It's as though we had just entered the first four lines and are ready to continue our writing on the fifth line. This is one way, if somewhat sneaky, to find out, incidentally, how many lines are in the function. Now type in

```
[5]    (⌈/X)-⌊/X
[6]    ∇
```

and the system has responded with a [6], waiting for the next line of input. Since we don't want to add anything further, a closing ∇ has been typed in as a signal that we want to get out of function definition mode and back into desk calculator mode.

Execution with a vector 2 9 1 gives us four lines of output, the fourth line being the range as we had intended:

```
      STAT 2 9 1
4
9
1
8
```

If we now ask for the function to be displayed, we see that line 5 has indeed been added:

```
        ∇STAT[□]∇
     ∇ STAT X
[1]    N←+/X=X
[2]    (+/X)÷N
[3]    ⌈/X
[4]    ⌊/X
[5]    (⌈/X)-⌊/X
     ∇
```

Replacing a line with another line

Also in the workspace 1 *CLASS* is a function called *AVG* which computes
the average of the components of an argument *X*. Let's change line 2 of
STAT to *AVG X*. First we'll check out *AVG* to see if it works:

```
     AVG 1 2 3
2
```

In order to replace line 2, we need to open up the function as before by
typing

```
     ∇STAT
```

The system's response is [6], which we can override by typing in a [2]:

```
[6]    [2]
```

After pressing the return key, the system replies with a [2] and we can now
enter *AVG X*:

```
[2]    AVG X
```

Since we don't plan at this point to make any further changes on line 3, a
del is used to close out the function:

```
[3]    ∇
```

It should be emphasized that in making this change lines 3, 4, and 5 are <u>not</u>
affected.

Here is an execution of *STAT* followed by a display of the revised function:

```
     STAT 2 9 1
4
9
1
8
        ∇STAT[□]∇
     ∇ STAT X
[1]    N←+/X=X
[2]    AVG X
[3]    ⌈/X
[4]    ⌊/X
[5]    (⌈/X)-⌊/X
     ∇
```

The change has gone through, leaving the rest of the function unaltered.

Inserting a line between two other lines

Suppose we want to insert between lines 1 and 2 a statement whose purpose
is to return, i.e., print out, the original values of X. This can be
accomplished in the following way.   First open up the function and type
in some number in brackets, say [1.1], after the response [6]:

```
        ∇STAT
[6]     [1.1]
```

(Any number will do as long as it is between the numbers of the two lines
where the insertion is to be made.)

The system returns [1.1] and we can enter the single symbol X, which when
encountered during execution will cause a printout of X

```
[1.1] X
```

Now a 1 is added by the system to the last place of the number chosen for
the inserted line to provide for still other entries between lines 1 and 2,
but since we don't want to close out the function just yet, let's ask
first for a display of what we have so far while we're still in function
definition mode, and then close it out:

```
[1.2] [□]∇
      ∇ STAT X
[1]       N←+/X=X
[1.1]   X
[2]       AVG X
[3]       ⌈/X
[4]       L/X
[5]       (⌈/X)-L/X
      ∇
```

Your typeball should have moved over six spaces after this. If it does,
you are in desk calculator mode. If, however, a number in [ ] was returned,
type ∇, followed by the return key.

Of course, a line numbered 1.1 is somewhat awkward, to say the least.
Fortunately, after the function is closed out, the steps are automatically
renumbered, as seen in the following display:

```
      ∇STAT[□]
      ∇ STAT X
[1]       N←+/X=X
[2]       X
[3]       AVG X
[4]       ⌈/X
[5]       L/X
[6]       (⌈/X)-L/X
      ∇
[7]
```

and the renumbering has actually taken place. But since [7] was returned, we are still in function definition mode. Striking the return key gives [7] again, and since there is to be no added entry at this time, we close out the function:

[7]   ∇

Now we are back in desk calculator mode.

Doing several things at once

In *APL* it is possible to put several of the editing instructions on a single line. For our example we'll take line 3, *AVG X* , change it back to what it was originally, and then return to desk calculator mode. To do this, type the following:

$$\nabla STAT[3](+/X)\div N\nabla$$

Typing [3] gets control to line 3, what follows it is the new line 3, and the second ∇ closes it out after the change. We can check this with a display of the function in the usual manner:

```
      ∇STAT[□]∇
   ∇  STAT  X
[1]    N←+/X=X
[2]    X
[3]    (+/X)÷N
[4]    ⌈/X
[5]    ⌊/X
[6]    (⌈/X)-⌊/X
   ∇
```

Getting rid of a line

How do we remove a line completely? For example, suppose we want to get rid of line 4. As usual, we first open up the function and direct control to line 4:

$$\nabla STAT[4]$$

The computer responds with a [4] and in effect asks us what we intend to do with line 4. Pressing the ATTN button, followed by the return key, is the only combination that will delete a line. Again, as you have already seen, *APL* makes it difficult to destroy things once entered.

[4]
        ∇

Next [5] is returned, and now we ask for a display of the function, but without closing it out:

```
[5]    [□]
    ∇ STAT X
[1]    N←+/X=X
[2]    X
[3]    (+/X)÷N
[5]    L/X
[6]    (⌈/X)-L/X
    ∇
```

Notice that line 4 has been deleted. The response continues with a [7], but since we have nothing more to add, let's close it out:

```
[7]    ∇
```

The lines are now renumbered, as can be seen if the function is once more displayed:

```
    ∇STAT[□]∇
    ∇ STAT X
[1]    N←+/X=X
[2]    X
[3]    (+/X)÷N
[4]    L/X
[5]    (⌈/X)-L/X
    ∇
```

Just remember that if the number of dels <u>you</u> (not the system) have typed is even, you are in desk calculator mode; if odd, you are in function definition mode.

Displaying only part of a function

Thus far, we have asked for the entire function to be displayed. What if the function is a long one and we are interested only in a single line, say 4? The display command for this is very similar:

```
    ∇STAT[4□]∇
[4]    L/X
```

If there had been no second del, line 4 would have been displayed and then the system would ask us what, if anything, we wanted to do with it by return-ing a [4] again:

```
    ∇STAT[4□]
[4]    L/X
[4]
```

and now we can close out the function:

```
[4]    ∇
```

By now you should be getting the idea that the quad □ is used to display things. Fancifully speaking, you might think of it as a window to see what's going on inside the function. Just remember

                    [⎕]   displays everything
                    [4⎕] displays a particular line, here 4

Here is another useful variation which will display all lines from the
number specified on:

         ∇STAT[⎕3]
[3]   ⌈/X
[4]   ⌊/X
[4]   ∇

But what if the function has fifty lines and you want lines 5, 6, and 7
only? The way to display only these lines is to ask, as above, for lines 5
on to be displayed and let the terminal run on until you want it to stop.
Pressing the ATTN button (on most terminals) activates an interrupt feature
that will stop the display. If your terminal doesn't have this feature,
you may either let the display run on until the end or use the following
procedure:

                 (1) Lift up receiver of Dataset
                 (2) Depress TALK button for a few seconds
                 (3) Depress DATA button and replace receiver

However, note that unless the original display command was closed with a
del, you will still be in function definition mode after interrupting.
Plan your next step accordingly.

Detailed editing of part of a line

Getting into more specific and limited changes, let's start over again
from the beginning. Load a fresh copy of 1 CLASS:

)LOAD 1 CLASS
SAVED   15.02.39 07/29/69

As has been discussed previously, this wipes out what was in our active
workspace and replaces it with an exact image of the workspace loaded.

Now display STAT, but without closing out the function:

         ∇STAT[⎕]
     ∇ STAT X
[1]   N←+/X=X
[2]   (+/X)÷N
[3]   ⌈/X
[4]   ⌊/X
     ∇
[5]

It is again in its original form, and the system is waiting for us to add
something on line 5.

Up to now we have made changes involving entire lines. But suppose a line
is very long and complicated, and our change is to involve only a few
characters without having to type the rest of the line over and quite possibly make a mistake. For example, say we'd like to change the letter N to

$COUNT$ in lines 1 and 2 of $STAT$.

In this case, obviously, we could type both lines over since they are quite short. However, it will be more instructive to use the detailed editing capabilities of APL to make the changes.

We're still in function definition mode, since when we press the return key we get

[5]

To direct the typeball to specific characters that need revising, what we type in has the following format:

[line number ☐ estimate of what print position
the first change occurs]

In this case we'll deliberately make the typeball space over twenty positions (from the margin) and then backspace manually to the N to show that our estimate doesn't have to be accurate:

[5]   [1☐20]

The system will respond by displaying line 1 and then position the typeball twenty spaces over on the next line:

[1] $N \leftarrow + / X = X$
                          @

(typeball comes to rest in the position indicated by @)

We wish to strike out the letter N. For this, the slash (same symbol as reduction) is used. $COUNT$ has five characters for which space needs to be provided. To be sure that we get enough space we type 8 after the slash as shown, once we have manually backspaced the typeball under the N. This inserts eight spaces just prior to the character (here ←) above the number typed:

[1] $N \leftarrow + / X = X$
       /8

After striking the return key the system responds as follows:

[1] $\leftarrow + / X = X$

and we can type $COUNT$ in the space provided:

[1] $COUNT$ $\leftarrow + / X = X$

Having made this change we are asked if we want to do anything with line 2. Before doing anything else, display line 1:

[2]   [1☐]
[1] $COUNT \leftarrow + / X = X$
[1]

N is gone and $COUNT$ has been inserted.

Now directing control to the eighth position on line 2, we can go through the same procedure to insert *COUNT* at the end of the line. Eight spaces happen to be too few in this case, so we'll have to use the spacebar to move the typeball over some more after it comes to rest in the eighth position:

```
[1]    [2□8]
[2]    (+/X)÷N
               /
[2]    (+/X)÷COUNT
[3]    ∇
```

Displaying the entire revised function, we see that the changes have been made:

```
       ∇STAT[□]∇
    ∇ STAT X
[1]    COUNT←+/X=X
[2]    (+/X)÷COUNT
[3]    ⌈/X
[4]    ⌊/X
    ∇
```

Finally, for the sake of completeness, we include again the system command which deletes an entire function from the active workspace:

```
    )ERASE STAT
```

The response to a successful "erasure" is the typeball moving over 6 spaces. If we now try to display it, we get an error message:

```
       ∇STAT[□]∇
DEFN ERROR
       ∇STAT
            ∧
```

Can you think of a way to get *STAT* back in without typing it?

Review

Here is a summary of the editing capabilities of *APL*:

```
∇FN              open fn, control directed to first available line
∇FN[3]           open fn, control directed to line 3
∇FN[3□]          open fn, display line 3, control directed to line 3
∇FN[□]           open fn, display all lines, control directed to first avail.
                 line
∇FN[□3]          open fn, display line 3 and all following, control directed
                 to first available line
∇FN[3□10]        open fn, detailed editing at print position 10 of line 3
∇FN[3] ATTN RETURN    delete line 3
∇FN[3]X←2+A∇     open fn, rewrite line 3 as shown, close fn
∇FN[□]∇          display fn only
)ERASE FN        delete fn from active workspace
```

One last point. In our discussion of the function editing capabilities of
APL we have neglected the header. It is possible to change the header itself in exactly the same way as any line by using [0] as the line number:

```
      ∇STAT[0□]]
[0]   STAT X
[0]   STATE X
[1]   ∇
      ∇STAT[□]∇
DEFN ERROR
      ∇STAT
             ∧
```

and since *STAT* has been renamed *STATE*, we get an error message when we
call for *STAT* , which no longer exists. Just remember that any changes in
the header must be consistent with what is in the body of the function itself, unless, of course, the corresponding changes are made in the rest of
the function too.

PROBLEMS

Execute)*LOAD* 1 *CLASS* and enter the following program to calculate the
standard deviation of a set of numbers (see problem 6, chapter 10):

```
      ∇ STD N
[1]   R←AVG N
[2]   R←R-N
[3]   R←AVG R*2
[4]   ANS←R*0.5
      ∇
```

1. Display the function and direct control to line 5.

2. Use detailed editing to change *ANS* on line 4 to *R*.

3. Edit the header to return an explicit result *R*.

4. Eliminate line 2.

5. Display the function and remain in function definition mode.

6. Change line 3 to *R←AVG (R-N)*2* .

7. Display lines 3 and 4.

8. Close out the function

9. Use a single expression to open up the function again and reinsert the
    former contents of line 2.

10. Change line 3 back to its original form with detailed editing.

11. Insert just prior to line 1 a command that will print out the number
    of elements in *N*.

12. Delete the function from the active workspace.

CHAPTER 13:

Types of variables

Up to now all the variables that we have encountered have been considered by us to be alike in their behavior. In this chapter we will see that this isn't quite true, and that *APL*. has two very useful built-in features. One of these provides protection for variables against their being accidentally respecified as a result of a function execution, while the other enables the same variable names to be used repeatedly in different functions without the possibility of their being confused.

In the workspace 1 *CLASS*, which you should now load,

)*LOAD* 1 *CLASS*
SAVED   15.02.39 07/29/69

there are five functions, *AVG*1-*AVG*5 , which are quite similar and which are all used to calculate averages. It is the small but significant differences between them that we are going to explore now.

Dummy variables

First display *AVG*1 :

        ∇*AVG*1[□]∇
     ∇ *R*←*AVG*1 *X*
[1]   *N*←+/*X*=*X*
[2]   *R*←(+/*X*)÷*N*
     ∇

From the appearance of the header it is a monadic function that returns an explicit result. The first line calculates the number of components in X and stores that value in N, while the second divides the sum of the components by N and stores it in R for printing out as the average when the function is executed.

Let's give X and N values:

        X←⁻21.7
        N←3.1415

and now calculate

        AVG1 2 1 2 1 2 1
1.5

On checking what's in X and N, we get

        X
⁻21.7
        N
6

Something seems to be wrong here. We put in 3.1415 for N and got back 6,
while X was set at ⁻21.7. The function *AVG1* calculated the average
not of that X (which would have been ⁻21.7 since there is only one component) but of another X, 2 1 2 1 2 1, in the argument of the header.
According to what was presented in an earlier chapter, the latest value of
X is supposed to supersede a previous value. So why didn't we get
2 1 2 1 2 1 when we called for X?

To make a start on some answers to these questions, look at the function
header. There is an X in it as the argument. Apparently this isn't the
same variable as the X we set before (⁻21.7), even though the symbols are
the same. When we executed this function for 2 1 2 1 2 1, for the time
being X inside the function must have had the value 2 1 2 1 2 1. The
X outside (⁻21.7) was not affected, since we were able to retrieve it
afterwards unaltered.

Still confused? It isn't as bad as it looks, because part of the trouble
was due to our use of the same letter to represent two distinctly different
types of variables, as we shall see shortly. In the meantime, let's try to
come up with a set of rules governing the behavior of variables in this and
similar situations.

First, the variables used in the argument and resultant of the header are
in a very real sense "dummy" variables. This means that they have values
assigned to them only inside the function itself, and we can find out what
these values are only when we ourselves are inside the function, i.e., when
execution is suspended part way through because we interrupted it or because
of an error.

To illustrate the point further, imagine we have a function

        ∇*Z←A FN G*
[1]   *Z←A+G*
[2]   ∇

And we call for 3 *FN* 4 to be executed:

        3 *FN* 4
7

After execution, if we ask for A and G, we still get value errors:

        A
VALUE ERROR
        A
        ∧

```
      G
VALUE ERROR
      G
      ^
```

A and *G* no longer exist! However, now let's set *A* as, say, 1 and *G* as 2, and then call for *A* and *G* after execution:

```
      A←1
      G←2
      3 FN 4
7
      A
1
      G
2
```

We still don't get the 3 and 4 which were the arguments.

These values 3 and 4 were set as soon as we typed 3 *FN* 4 and are available until execution is finished, at which time they are relegated to limbo. Thus, calling for *A* and *G* after execution gives us as always the last set values of the variables, namely, 1 and 2, that the system has a record of.

Of course, if we were to execute 1 *FN* 2 and then call for *A* and *G*, we would indeed get 1 and 2. But this would be purely coincidental because our dummy variables in the function header happened to have the same set of values as *A* and *G* before execution was called for. So just as with our two *X*'s in *AVG*1, the two *A*'s and *G*'s aren't really the same, in spite of the fact that the same characters are used for both.

It should be dawning on you by this time that it ought not to make any difference what variables we put in for the arguments of *FN*. They serve only to indicate that two arguments are called for, and in this sense they act very much like the 0's in a number of the form .00032. All the 0's do is fill up space, but you need them to read the number correctly. This is why the arguments associated with the function name are called dummy variables.

One point by way of clarification here. Suppose we set

```
      X←1 2 3
```

and execute

```
      AVG1 X
2
```

How come? In executing the function, the system encountered the argument *X* (which is still a dummy variable in the header), searched its memory for a value for *X*, found the most recent assignment, 1 2 3, and then executed *AVG*1. This shows that we have a choice as to whether we wish to give values to the arguments at the time of execution or before. In either case, it is the most recently set value that is used.

Calling for the preset *X* after execution shows that it hasn't been affected, nor is it changed when we reexecute *AVG*1 for another set of values:

```
        X
1   2   3
        AVG1 3 4 5
4
        X
1   2   3
```

In a similar manner the resultant Z has no value before execution (unless we deliberately set it). It acquires a unique value during execution as soon as we get to that part of the function which determines what Z will be:

```
        Z
VALUE ERROR
        Z
        ∧
```

There should, of course, be such a place if we've written the function meaningfully. As in the case of the arguments, once execution is finished, the value is lost.

Global variables

Now (at last!) getting back to our original function AVG1 . We have answered the question of why calling for X returned the preset value ‾21.7 , but what about N?

Notice that N, contrasted with X, doesn't appear in the header, but only in the body of the function. Lacking any instructions from us to the contrary, it ought to behave the same way all of our variables had been behaving up to the point where we started to get involved in function definition. That is to say, whenever the system encounters an instruction respecifying a variable whose value has been previously set, it changes that value accordingly. In our case, N was originally set at 3.1415, but as execution proceeded it was reset at 6 as a result of the instructions contained in line 1.

Such variables as N and the X which was preset at ‾21.7, since they retain their original values in APL for all time in the workspace in which they appear, until, of course, they are respecified or deleted, are appropriately called "global" variables.

Local variables

Let's look at another way in which variables can be used in function definition. For this display AVG2 :

```
        ∇AVG2[□]∇
    ∇  R←AVG2 X;N
[1]     N←+/X=X
[2]     R←(+/X)÷N
    ∇
```

This time something new has been added—a variable N in the header preceded by a semicolon. When a variable is used in the header in this fashion, it is said to be a "local" variable, whose values are to be set and used only within the function itself, and behaving much like the dummy variables we discussed before.   In order to restore the values of the variables to what they were before we first executed $AVG1$ for comparison purposes, we'll have to reset X and N:

        $X \leftarrow {}^-21.7$
        $N \leftarrow 3.1415$

Using the same argument as before, let's execute $AVG2$ and then call for X and N:

        $AVG2$ 2 1 2 1 2 1
1.5
        X
$^-21.7$
        N
3.1415

As you might have expected, X hasn't changed, but this time N also returns the original value set when we made it a global variable.   The instructions for N on line 1 now refer to a different N, the local variable at the right of the header, it being only an accident of choice that we used the same symbol for both a local and a global variable.

It should now be clear that the APL system has the ability to keep straight its records of variables used in these different ways.   This is fortunate for us because we may have used the same variable name previously for something entirely different and want to preserve it.   To prevent accidental respecifying of the variable, it would seem wise to make it local by putting it in the header preceded by a semicolon.   If more than one variable is to be so localized, they can be strung out, separated from each other and the rest of the header by semicolons.

$AVG3$, displayed below, has a local variable P and is a niladic function returning an explicit result:

        $\nabla AVG3[\square] \nabla$
    ∇ $R \leftarrow AVG3 ; P$
[1] $P \leftarrow +/X = X$
[2] $R \leftarrow (+/X) \div P$
    ∇

Executing $AVG3$, we get

        $AVG3$
$^-21.7$
        X
$^-21.7$

By this time you ought to be able to figure out for yourself why the result $^-21.7$ was returned.   (HINT: is X a local, global or dummy variable?) Resetting X and executing $AVG3$ again:

```
      X←2 1 2 1 2 1
      AVG3
1.5
```

Clearly the X being averaged is from the most recent assignment.

Global variables as counters

AVG4 adds a new twist:

```
      ∇AVG4[☐]∇
    ∇ R←AVG4 X
[1]    R←(+/X)÷+/X=X
[2]    COUNT←COUNT+1
    ∇
```

This function is intended to illustrate a practical use for a global variable, and is designed so that each time it is used a counter (called COUNT) goes up by one. Thus, a record can be kept of the total number of times the function is executed.

Here is an execution of AVG4:

```
      AVG4 2 1 2 1 2 1
VALUE ERROR
AVG4[2] COUNT←COUNT+1
        ∧
```

Why do we get an error message? If you think about it, you will see that we goofed and failed to specify the initial value of COUNT. So naturally the system didn't know where to start counting and was unable to execute line 2. This is confirmed by asking for the value of COUNT:

```
      COUNT
VALUE ERROR
      COUNT
      ∧
```

Setting COUNT to 0 and reexecuting AVG4 twice, we get

```
      COUNT←0
      AVG4 2 1 2 1 2 1
1.5
      COUNT
1
      AVG4 5 4 3 2 1
3
      COUNT
2
```

COUNT now behaves as we had intended. It is a global variable because it doesn't appear in the header.

We are still plagued with our two X's. One is a global variable with the last set value (see page 90).

```
      X
2   1   2   1   2   1
```

while the other is a dummy variable in the header, which unfortunately happened to be set to the same value. Moral of the story? As an *APL* user with an enormous number of possible variable names at your disposal, there isn't any real necessity to be in a rut and use the same few over and over again.

Now display *AVG*5:

```
      ∇AVG5[☐]∇
    ∇ R←AVG5 X;COUNT
[1]   R←(+/X)÷+/X=X
[2]   COUNT←COUNT+1
    ∇
```

COUNT is a local variable in this monadic function. Executing *AVG*5:

```
      AVG5 2 3 2 3
VALUE ERROR
AVG5[2] COUNT←COUNT+1
             ∧
```

What's wrong? *COUNT* was set earlier to 0, so why the error message? True, *COUNT* was set, but as a global variable, and the set value can't be used in *AVG*5 because we said in the header that *COUNT* was local. This function just won't work.

We could consider putting in a line before line 1, setting *COUNT* to 0. But each time we execute it, the local variable *COUNT* will be reset to 0. It will never get beyond 1, and furthermore, since it's local, all trace of it is lost once we exit the function.

This means that if we have a global variable (name not in the header), we can reset it from within the function and obtain its last value, as in *AVG*4. If we make it local by preceding it with a semicolon in the header, there is no chance for confusion or destruction of values set previously. However, it is not possible to use a subfunction by the same name as a local variable. For example, if *COUNT* were also a function, we couldn't ask for it to be executed in *AVG*5 and still retain *COUNT* as a local variable.

Here is a good place to remind you how to keep track of all the global variables in your active workspace,)*VARS* , which will give you a listing of all the current variables which have been set.

Suspended functions

One last point. We had a couple of runs that resulted in functions being suspended at some point in their execution. We can find out what functions are suspended and where by the system commands

```
        )SI
AVG5[2] *
AVG4[2] *
        )SIV
AVG5[2] *        R       X        COUNT
AVG4[2] *        R       X
```

SI stands for "state indicator" and the commands tell which functions are suspended (*) and on what step. The most recent suspension is listed first. If the * is missing, it means that the function is held up because of a suspension elsewhere, as would be the case if we were to invent a function *AVG6* which used *AVG5* in one of its instructions. Calling then for *AVG6* would cause *AVG6* to execute only to the point where *AVG5*, which is in suspension, is needed. *AVG6* would then appear on the list under)*SI*, but without the star, indicating that *AVG6* is held up in execution pending clearing up of the suspension of the function *AVG5*. The command)*SIV* gives the same information as)*SI* but adds the variables appearing in the header as local or dummy.

It isn't good practice to leave many functions suspended, since this clutters up the available space. They should be removed as soon as possible from the suspended state. To show how the list grows, let's execute *AVG5* again:

```
        AVG5 7 4 2 4
VALUE ERROR
AVG5[2] COUNT←COUNT+1
               ^
        )SI
AVG5[2] *
AVG5[2] *
AVG4[2] *
```

Each time a function is suspended, you should find out what's wrong. For the time being without further explanation, the instructions →0 or simply →

```
        →0
4.25
```

will exit you from the most recently suspended function. The result shown, incidentally, is the average from the last computation. Looking at our list again,

```
        )SI
AVG5[2] *
AVG4[2] *
```

we exit from the next suspended function and continue this until the command)*SI* yields a list with no functions in it:

```
        →0
2.5
        )SI
AVG4[2] *
```

```
        →
        (no result prints out with this command)
        )SI
        (typeball moves over six spaces)
```

Of course any future executions of *AVG*5 will build up our list again:

```
        AVG5 4 2 1
VALUE ERROR
AVG5[2] COUNT←COUNT+1
              ∧
        )SI
AVG5[2] *
        →0
2.333333333
        )SI
        (typeball moves over six spaces)
```

PROBLEMS

1. Execute the command)*LOAD* 1 *CLASS*

    (A) Specify a global variable *C*←53 78 90
         Account for the result. /

    (B) Enter the following function *F*:

```
            ∇F
        [1]    Z←(A*2)+B*2
        [2]    Z←Z*.5∇
```

    After specifying values for *A* and *B*, execute *T*←*F*+7 and
    T←*Z*+7. Explain your results.

2. Below are several defined functions. Execute the command following each
    and give the values of the variables. Reset these variables to their
    initial values before each function is executed:

R	B	C	M	S
3	2	5	7	1

```
        ∇PERIM1              ∇R←B PERIM2 C              ∇R←PERIM3 C
    [1]    R←2×B+C∇      [1]    R←2×B+C∇          [1]    R←2×B+C∇

        PERIM1               S←M PERIM2 R               S←PERIM3 R
```

3. Redefine the second function of problem 2 to include a local variable
    P in the header. Make line 1 the sum of *B* and *C*, the result to be
    stored in *P*. The second line is to finish the algorithm for the
    perimeter.

CHAPTER 14:

Workspace movement

In the previous chapters all the work you placed in storage, both variables and defined functions, was lost when you signed off. The only recoverable work was in 1 *CLASS* and in 1 *APLCOURSE*. And the only reason we could still access it was that when we loaded one of these workspaces into our own active workspace, we were actually taking an exact copy of the original, not the original itself. Although we lost the copy in signing off, we could always obtain another in the same manner.

Clearly we need to know how to preserve what we've done for posterity. In this chapter, therefore, we will go through a series of exercises designed to show how workspaces can be manipulated by the *APL* user. In order to insure continuity, repeat the entire sequence of commands exactly as they are given.

Workspace contents

We will start off by typing

```
      )CLEAR
CLEAR WS
```

As we pointed out earlier (page 64), this is one of a family of so-called system commands, like the sign-on and sign-off. It has the effect of wiping out all the work done in the active workspace and replacing it with a clean workspace, such as is obtained at the sign-on. Remember that the active workspace is the one that you have currently available to you, in which all your work is now being done.

To show that this workspace is now empty as a result of the *CLEAR* command, we can use the commands

```
      )FNS
                    (in both cases the typeball moves over six spaces
      )VARS         after return, but prints nothing)
```

and we see there isn't anything in the active workspace.

Since we are going to save some work later, we'll need to put something tangible into it. For this, let's enter the function *HYP* :

95

```
        ∇R←A HYP B
[1]     R←((A*2)+B*2)*.5
[2]     ∇
```

Our listing of functions now shows

```
        )FNS
HYP
```

Let's add a couple of variables:

```
        PI←3.14159
        V←1 2 3 4 5
```

and the command

```
        )VARS
PI        V
```

now shows that *PI* and *V* are in storage.

For a second function, enter *TOSS*:

```
        ∇TOSS
[1]     ?2∇
```

and another listing of functions

```
        )FNS
HYP       TOSS
```

confirms that *TOSS* has been added.

Saving and recovering a workspace

We could continue entering material and checking on it for quite a while, but for purposes of illustration let's pretend that we are through with our work at this point and want to preserve these functions and variables.

The system command *SAVE* does this. However, since users are normally assigned more than one workspace, even though only one is being used at any one time, we have to assign a name to the workspace we are saving. This is so that we'll know what to ask for when we call for it again. *APL* recognizes only the first eleven characters of a workspace name.

For the work previously entered we'll use the name *FIRST*:

```
        )SAVE FIRST
15.52.19 03/20/70
```

We get a message back giving the time and date. This means that the *SAVE* was successful and a copy of the workspace is now in storage under the name *FIRST*. The workspace name, incidentally, may be followed by a colon and lock for greater protection if desired.

There is a command which lists all the saved workspaces so that we know

what we have in our own *APL* library ("library" in *APL* refers to a
collection of workspaces associated with a single identification number).
The command is

)*LIB*
FIRST

Only one workspace is listed because that's all we have saved so far.
)*FNS* shows that *HYP* and *TOSS* are still around:

)*FNS*
HYP   TOSS

Remember we saved a <u>copy</u> of the active workspace. Let's now get a fresh
workspace:

)*CLEAR*
CLEAR WS

Imagine that it is the following day and we are ready to do some work with
HYP and *TOSS* . They were lost from the active workspace when we cleared,
but there is an exact copy stored in our library under the name *FIRST*.. To
recover this copy, execute the command

)*LOAD FIRST*
SAVED   15.52.19 03/20/70

If a lock was originally associated with the name when it was saved, it
must be included here, separated from the name by a colon. The response
indicates that it was saved at a certain time and date, which, you will
note, is identical with what appears under the original *SAVE* command
on page 96.

Our functions and variables are available to us once again:

)*FNS*
HYP   TOSS
)*VARS*
PI   V

Here's a check on *V* to see whether it's still what it's supposed to be:

        V
1   2   3   4   5

Often it is the case that we have work to be saved in more than one workspace.
How do we go about this? To illustrate the procedure, type

)*CLEAR*
CLEAR WS

and enter the function *SQRT* :

        ∇*R←SQRT X*
[1]   *R←X∗.5*∇

This function, which is the only object in our active workspace at the moment, we'll save under the name *SECOND*:

```
     )SAVE SECOND
15.55.10    03/20/70
```

Before going on, let's be sure we understand what we have immediate access to at this point, namely a single workspace with only the function *SQRT* in it, a copy of which exists also in storage under the name *SECOND*:

```
     )FNS
SQRT
```

If we want to access *FIRST* now, we must execute

```
     )LOAD FIRST
SAVED   15.52.19 03/20/70
```

and we see that *HYP* and *TOSS* are back in the active workspace:

```
     )FNS
HYP      TOSS
```

Now we'll load *SECOND* (we don't need to clear between loadings because the act of loading replaces the contents of the active workspace with a copy of the material in the workspace being loaded):

```
     )LOAD SECOND
SAVED   15.55.10 03/20/70
     )FNS
SQRT
```

It should be obvious to you that we can access only one workspace at a time.

Let's save still another workspace under the name *THIRD*. This time, just to be different, we'll clear and load 1 *CLASS*:

```
     )CLEAR
CLEAR WS
     )LOAD 1 CLASS
SAVED   15.02.39 07/29/69
```

Here is a list of functions:

```
     )FNS
ADD      AGAIN    AVG      AVG1     AVG2     AVG3     AVG4      AVG5
BASE     C        CMP      CMPX     CMPY     COLCAT1  COLCAT2
COLCAT3 COS       COSINE   CP       CPUTIME  CP1      DEC
```

and we have cut off the printout by pressing the ATTN button because the list is too lengthy. The contents of 1 *CLASS* (or perhaps we should be more precise and say a <u>copy</u> of the contents) will now be saved under *THIRD*:

```
     )SAVE THIRD
15.58.27 03/20/70
```

Our listing of saved workspaces has grown:

```
      )LIB
FIRST
SECOND
THIRD
```

Let's clear again, define a couple of variables, and save them in *FOURTH* :

```
      )CLEAR
CLEAR WS
      X←4  6  8  10
      Y←2  5  8
      )SAVE FOURTH
NOT SAVED, WS QUOTA USED UP
```

The system tells us, in effect, that we have only three workspaces allotted to us and they are used up, so we're out of luck. Actually, it is possible to have more workspaces assigned, but this is a decision which depends on the configuration of the particular *APL* system being used and the amount of available storage.

Dropping a saved workspace

If *X* and *Y* were really some big functions or tables of data and we wanted desperately to save them, then our question is: Which of the three workspaces in our library can we afford to sacrifice? Again look at the list:

```
      )LIB
FIRST
SECOND
THIRD
```

Assuming we don't need *THIRD*, let's try to save *X* and *Y*, which are still in the active workspace, in *THIRD* :

```
      )SAVE THIRD
NOT SAVED, THIS WS IS CLEAR WS
```

We are prevented from saving it in *THIRD* because a stored workspace can't be named *CLEAR WS*, and again *APL* keeps you from destroying a workspace that was previously saved by replacing it with another workspace under the same name. As we'll soon see, there is a way to add *X* and *Y* to *THIRD* without destroying what is already there.

Suppose we really wanted to get rid of *THIRD* . The command

```
      )DROP THIRD
16.01.03 03/20/70
```

does this, the response giving the time and day when the workspace was dropped.   *THIRD* is now gone, as shown by

```
        )LIB
FIRST
SECOND
```

In the active workspace we have no functions but still the two variables
X and Y:

```
        )FNS
        (typeball moves over six spaces)
        )VARS
X         Y
```

which shouldn't surprise us, since we haven't done anything to the active
workspace yet. Now that an available slot exists, let's save these variables
in a workspace simply called XY for the sake of variety:

```
        )SAVE XY
  16.01.34 03/20/70
        )LIB
FIRST
SECOND
XY
```

and XY is added to our library.

Altering a saved workspace

What if we wanted to save X and Y into $FIRST$? See what happens when we
try this:

```
        )SAVE FIRST
NOT SAVED, THIS WS IS XY
```

What this means is that the contents of our active workspace have already
been saved under the name XY and therefore can't be saved also under the
name $FIRST$. In order to save the material in the active workspace into
$FIRST$ we would have to drop $FIRST$, and then save the active workspace
under the name $FIRST$ again. Later we'll see how the $COPY$ command can
be used to merge two workspaces.

Another way to change the status of a saved workspace is illustrated by
the following sequence:

```
        )LOAD FIRST
SAVED   15.52.19 03/20/70
```

It currently has

```
        )FNS
HYP       TOSS
```

Let's define the function $SIGN$:

```
        ∇R←SIGN X
[1]      R←(X>0)-X<0∇
```

Now our list includes the new function:

```
      )FNS
HYP      SIGN    TOSS
```

Here is what happens when we try to save this into *SECOND*:

```
      )SAVE SECOND
NOT SAVED, THIS WS IS FIRST
```

We are again prevented from doing so because the active workspace contains *FIRST*, and we already have a workspace named *SECOND* in storage, but not in the active workspace.

We can, however, save into *FIRST*, since a copy of *FIRST* exists in the active workspace:

```
      )SAVE FIRST
16.04.07 03/20/70
```

FIRST is now updated. This can be shown by clearing and reloading it:

```
      )CLEAR
CLEAR WS
      )FNS
      (typeball moves over six spaces)
      )LOAD FIRST
SAVED 16.04.07 03/20/70
      )FNS
HYP      SIGN    TOSS
```

Notice that the time and day given after the *LOAD* command is that associated with the most recent save.

Our library, once more, consists of

```
      )LIB
FIRST
SECOND
XY
```

but the contents of *FIRST* are not the same as when we last listed the workspace functions on page 100.

Summarizing, we can (1) preserve all storable material in the active workspace by saving it; (2) recall material from a saved workspace into the active workspace just as it was when it was last saved; and (3) delete a workspace with the *DROP* command.

PROBLEMS

Carry out the following instructions and *APL* system commands in the order given:

Define a number of arbitrary functions and variables.

```
)SAVE WORKONE
)CLEAR
```

Repeat these instructions several times until your workspace quota is used up. Use workspace names *WORKTWO*, *WORKTHREE*, etc.,

```
)LIB
```

How many workspaces can you save in your *APL* system?

```
)DROP WORKONE
)LIB
)LOAD WORKTHREE
)FNS
)VARS
```

Define additional functions and variables.

```
)SAVE WORKTWO
```

Why wasn't the material saved?

```
)SAVE WORKTHREE
)CLEAR
)LOAD WORKTHREE
)FNS
)VARS
```

Has *WORKTHREE* been updated?

Delete several functions and variables from *WORKTHREE*.

```
)ERASE FN1 FN2 V1 V2 ...
)SAVE
)LIB
)FNS
)VARS
```

CHAPTER 15:

Library management

In the last chapter you learned how to save, drop, and load material in the active workspace. The command *LIB* was introduced as a means of getting a listing of the saved workspaces in your personal *APL* library.

Let's see if the material from before is still there:

```
      )LIB
FIRST
SECOND
XY
```

We won't be needing the contents of these workspaces any more, but actually the command is a very useful one. Someone else may have saved workspaces in his library with the same names as yours, but there is no confusion whatever, since each person's workspaces are associated with his own user identification number. This leads us to an important feature of *APL* , the common or public libraries, to be discussed in the next section.

Public libraries

What about this 1 *CLASS* we've been loading all along? Library 1 on the system on which this text is based is a public library, available to all users. To find out what saved workspaces are in this library, type

```
      )LIB 1
CATALOG
MINIMA
WSFNS
TYPEDRILL
PLOTFORMAT
NEWS
CLASS
APLCOURSE
ADVANCEDEX
```

Your list may differ somewhat from this because the library contents aren't static and change from time to time. Notice that *CLASS* is in there. Ordinarily, individual *APL* users cannot save material into a public library or drop something from it. If you were to try to save 1 *CLASS* you won't be permitted to because yours wasn't the user number that saved it the first time:

>   )*SAVE* 1 *CLASS*
> *IMPROPER LIBRARY REFERENCE*

The rules for so doing depend on the *APL* system you are using, and changes in the contents would most likely be made through the system librarian, if there is one.

Library 1 is a general interest library which is entirely public—a true system library while library 10 is a special or limited interest library, intended for developmental purposes. Later, in this chapter, we'll be using some of the material from library 10.

Let's look at the contents of library 10.

>   )*LIB* 10
> *POLAR*
> *FUNCTIONS*
> *MATRIXALG*
> *ALGFORM*
> *PLOT*
> *INVESTMENTS*
> *THINKGAMES*
> *SWIVEL*
> *WHOSIT*
> *GAMBLE*
> *DOCONTROL*
> *SHAPE*
> *COGO*
> *FORLORN*
> *EDIT*
> *SNOBOL*
> *TEXT*
> *TICTACTOE*
> *LPAPL*

These lists may seem meaningless to you, but there is a practical way to find out what is in a strange workspace. As an example, type

>   )*LOAD* 1 *NEWS*
> *SAVED* 15.10.12 03/12/70

You have probably noticed that the load commands are slightly different for one's own workspaces as compared to those in the public libraries. As a matter of fact, for any other library than the user's, it is necessary to include the library number. Except for public libraries these would generally be the same as the number of the user with whom they are associated. The complete command has the form

>   )*LOAD LIB NO. WSNAME:LOCK* [if required]

The library number can be omitted for one's own library.

Having loaded the workspace *NEWS* , the best thing to do next is to get a
list of functions:

```
        )FNS
APLNOW   CLEAR    CLEARSKED       CREATE   EDIT    FILE    FLE
FMTDT    INDEX    NJ       POS    POSITION         POSTSKED
PRINT    REWORK   RWK      SCHEDULE        SETDATE SKEDNOTE
START    TDATE    TRYTEXT  TXF
```

By convention, if there is a function that contains the word *HOW* or
DESCRIBE or something similar, then executing it will give information
on what is in the workspace. At this time there doesn't appear to be any
such function in *NEWS*, which means that the only way we can find out about
the syntax and use of a particular function in *NEWS* is to display it and
try to figure it out. Of course it may be obvious from the name what it is,
as in *SCHEDULE* , which gives *APL* system information. This happens to be
niladic, so we just type

```
        SCHEDULE
```

```
ANTICIPATED CHANGES FROM THE NORMAL SCHEDULE, AS OF 03/12:
  04/05   900 - 1700
  04/12   900 - 1700
  04/19   900 - 1700
```

```
THE NORMAL SCHEDULE IS
```

```
MON-FRI          SAT OPER  SYSTEM      PHONES

9:00AM- 8:10PM       2291  RES. APL    5001,5011,5051,5201,5211
                                       5221,5231
8:30PM- 5:00AM 9-5 2291  RES. APL      5121,5128,5118,5119
6:45PM-10:00PM 9-5 1810  BIG WS APL    5105,5131
```

```
NOTE: DURING THE DAY CALL 1402 FOR RECORDING TELLING STATUS OF
      APL.
```

Another niladic function whose purpose is evident from the name is *TDATE* :

```
        TDATE
04/10/70
```

The syntax can't often be determined from just looking at the function name,
but in this case a niladic header is the most reasonable one because no arguments are needed. All we want is information.

Another workspace in library 1 is *PLOTFORMAT*. Let's take a look at it:

```
        )LOAD 1 PLOTFORMAT
SAVED    9.41.16 12/10/69
```

In it are

```
        )FNS
AND      DESCRIBE        DFT     EFT     PLOT    VS
```

There are a number of aids to plotting in this workspace. Since *DESCRIBE* is in here, we'll execute it and display part of the contents:

      DESCRIBE

THE WORKING FUNCTIONS IN THIS WORKSPACE ARE:

   AND   DFT   EFT   PLOT   VS

THE NAMES AND COMPOSITION OF THE GROUPS IN THIS WORKSPACE ARE:

   DFTGP: *AND   DFT*
   EFTGP: *AND   EFT*
   PLOTGP: *AND   PLOT   VS*
   DESGP: *DESCRIBE   HOWFORMAT   HOWPLOT*

DESGP   CAN BE USED TO CONVENIENTLY ERASE THE DESCRIPTIVE MATTER TO MAKE MORE ROOM IN THE WORKSPACE.   THE OTHER GROUPS CAN BE USED TO SELECTIVELY COPY THE INDICATED FUNCTIONS.

SYNTAX   *DESCRIPTION*
------   -----------

Z←A AND B   *ESSENTIALLY A COLUMN-CATENATOR, WITH SOME EXTRA EFFECTS WHEN THE ARGUMENTS ARE NOT MATRICES. THIS FUNCTION IS DESIGNED TO BE USED EITHER INDEPENDENTLY, OR IN CONJUNCTION WITH VS. TOGETHER, THEY PROVIDE A CONVENIENT WAY OF FORM ING INPUT TO THE PLOT FUNCTION.*

Z←A DFT B   *FORMS FIXED-POINT OUTPUT. MORE DETAILED DIREC TIONS CAN BE FOUND IN THE VARIABLE HOWFORMAT.*

The *COPY* command

We already know how to define the cosine and sine functions (see pages 56 and 57), but suppose we'd like to have the cosine function available in our workspace called *SECOND*. There is one in *CLASS*, but we don't need the whole workspace for this. Can we select just what we want and transfer it from *CLASS* to *SECOND*? The diagram on the next page shows the situation.

Each saved workspace may have many functions and variables. The active workspace may get its contents by your having loaded a saved workspace (your own or from another library) as well, of course, as from what you may be putting into storage yourself at the keyboard. In the diagram the arrows show the paths by which material can be transferred to your active workspace by the *LOAD* and *COPY* commands, the latter to be discussed shortly.

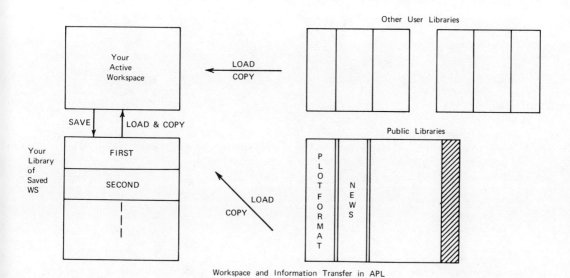

Workspace and Information Transfer in APL

Now our problem is to take *SECOND*, which isn't exactly bursting at the seams at the moment:

```
      )LOAD SECOND
SAVED   15.55.10 03/20/70
      )FNS
SQRT
```

and place the function *COS* and an accurate value of *PI* (also in *CLASS*) in it.

The sequence of steps is not too complicated. We first need to move *SECOND* into the active workspace by loading it. We've done it already, but there's no harm in doing it again:

```
      )LOAD SECOND
SAVED   15.55.10 03/20/70
```

To add *COS* and *PI*, the *COPY* command is used. The proper form is

```
            )COPY  LIB NO. WSNAME FNNAME
```

The response to a successful copy is the time and date that the workspace from which the copy was taken was last saved. Specifically, for our problem:

```
      )COPY 1 CLASS COS
SAVED    15.02.39 07/29/69
```

and now

```
     )FNS
COS      SQRT
```

COS has been added to the list of functions in *SECOND*. Repeating this
for *PI*:

```
     )COPY 1 CLASS PI
SAVED    15.02.39 07/29/69
     )FNS
COS      PI        SQRT
```

You might be tempted to think of *PI* as a variable with a specific value,
but the fact that it appears in the list above shows clearly that it is
a function. Why make it a function? Suppose we happened to specify a
less accurate value:

```
     PI←3.1415
SYNTAX ERROR
     PI←3.1415
     ʌ
```

and a syntax error is returned. We can't store a value under a function
name. Thus making it a function (it is niladic, returning an explicit
result, as you can see if you display it) makes it difficult to destroy the
stored value of *PI*.

To save this new material into *SECOND*, type

```
     )SAVE
16.45.23 03/20/70 SECOND
```

The system response gives the name of the active workspace to the contents
when none is specified.

This time, let's try to copy something that doesn't exist:

```
     )COPY 1 CLASS SIN
OBJECT NOT FOUND
```

No copy is found.

If we were to try to copy something that already existed in our active
workspace, as, for instance, *COS*, we get the response shown:

```
     )COPY 1 CLASS COS
SAVED    15.02.39 07/29/69
```

and the copy is successful. Having obtained *COS* from *CLASS*, the system
searches the active workspace to see if *COS* is in it. If it isn't, it is
entered. If it is, it is replaced by *COS* again. Clearly no protection is
needed in such a case, but if the *COS* function already in the active workspace happened to be different from the one in *CLASS*, it would be replaced
by the latter.

Let's now bring some more things into the active workspace, as, for instance

```
        )COPY 1 PLOTFORMAT AND
SAVED      9.41.16 12/10/69
```

Now we have

```
        )FNS
AND       COS      PI       SQRT
```

This could be saved into *SECOND* if we so desired. However, as we saw in
the last chapter, we are prohibited from saving into *FIRST* or *XY*, the other
two workspaces in our library:

```
        )LIB
FIRST
SECOND
XY
```

All copying takes place in the active workspace. We cannot copy from one
saved workspace into another saved workspace unless the latter happens
to be in the active workspace at the time of copying. We must load the
saved workspace first, copy into it, then resave to update or enlarge it.
Thus, *COPY* follows the same paths for transfer of material between
workspaces as *LOAD* (diagram, page 107). One final point. The *COPY* command is valid for all global objects. This means that global variables as
well as functions can be transferred in this manner.

The workspace *CONTINUE*

There is one more workspace in the user's personal library that needs
discussion. It is called *CONTINUE*. If you were to lose your telephone
connection with the *APL* system as a result of some local failure not
involving the central computer, everything in your active workspace will
automatically be available to you when you sign back on. This is because
the system plunks the contents of your active workspace into a workspace
named *CONTINUE*, available to all users, and reloads it at the next sign-
on, as indicated by the response *SAVED* right after "*APL\360*."

CONTINUE is really an extra workspace not part of the regular user
allotment, and can be used for emergencies if the other workspaces aren't
available. However, you have to be very careful with it. Each time there
is a line failure the contents of *CONTINUE* are replaced by whatever is
in the active workspace. So if you must, you can save work into *CONTINUE*,
since it is always available to you. But it isn't a wise move for long-term
storage because of the danger posed by the replacement of its contents
in the event of a line failure in the interim.

Summary of system commands

We have introduced and explained a number of system commands in the notes
thus far. For the convenience of the user these will be summarized and
classified. In addition, a few new commands will be included. These will
be explained briefly, but not illustrated. Their action should be evident
to the user from the discussion.

The first category consists of

SIGN-ON AND -OFF COMMANDS

)*USER NO.*	signs on; lock optional; clear ws activated unless previous connection broken, in which case *CONTINUE* is loaded
)*OFF*	signs off; deletes active ws; terminates phone connection
)*OFF HOLD*	same as)*OFF* but doesn't terminate phone connection for 60 seconds so that another user can sign on in that time
)*CONTINUE*	signs off; active ws saved in *CONTINUE* (same as what happens in case of a disconnect); terminates phone connection
)*CONTINUE HOLD*	same as)*CONTINUE* but phone connection held for 60 seconds

In all sign-offs when the command is followed by a colon and a lock, the lock will have to be included in subsequent sign-ons unless changed again.

A second category includes

COMMANDS CHANGING THE STATUS OF THE ACTIVE WS OR LIBRARY

)*CLEAR*	deletes everything in active ws
)*LOAD LIB NO. WSNAME*	moves image of ws to active ws; lib. no. not needed for user's own ws; lock optional after wsname
)*COPY LIB NO. WSNAME OBJ*	moves image of global object to active ws; lib. no. not needed for user's own ws; if no object name is given, all global objects in the ws are copied; lock optional after wsname
)*PCOPY LIB NO. WSNAME OBJ*	same as)*COPY* but protects the active ws in case of name duplication
)*SAVE WSNAME*	moves image of active ws into user's library; lock optional after wsname; omitting wsname saves active ws under name of last ws loaded
)*DROP WSNAME*	deletes ws from user's library
)*ERASE OBJNAME(S)*	deletes global object(s) from active ws

The *COPY* command should <u>not</u> be used in lieu of loading, since the CPU time used to copy an entire workspace is much greater than that required for loading. *COPY* should ordinarily be reserved for individual global objects. It can be used for merging two workspaces by loading one of them and copying the other into it.

The last category consists of

INQUIRY COMMANDS

)*LIB NO.*	lists ws's in library; no. not needed for user's own library
)*FNS LETTER*	alphabetically lists functions in active ws beginning with letter entered (if any)

)*VARS LETTER*	alphabetically lists global variables in active ws beginning with letter entered (if any)
)*SI*	lists functions which are suspended or pending, most recent function first
)*SIV*	same as)*SI* but includes names of local variables
)*PORTS*	lists ports in use at time of inquiry, with code names of users signed on
)*PORT CODE*	lists all port numbers associated with the given user code
)*WSID*	identifies active ws
)*WSID NAME*	changes identity of active ws to *NAME*

As was pointed out on page 93, it isn't a good idea to hang on to suspended functions. Try to find out what is wrong and remove the suspensions. This is especially important because when a workspace is saved or loaded, any suspensions present are carried along.

There are some additional commands changing the status of the active workspace, as well as one more category consisting of message commands. These will be considered in chapter 34.

PROBLEMS

1. Follow the instructions given and carry out the indicated system commands:

)*LIB* 1
)*LOAD* 1 *WSFNS*
)*FNS*
)*VARS*

    If there is a function or variable named *DESCRIBE* or *HOW*, execute it.

)*WSID*

    Define a function *RECT* which gives only the area of a rectangle of length L and width W. Display it after executing.

)*COPY* 1 *CLASS RECT*

    Was your own defined function *RECT* unchanged?

)*ERASE RECT*

    Redefine *RECT* as above to give only the area of a rectangle.

)*PCOPY* 1 *CLASS RECT*

    Does this command behave the same as *COPY*?

)*SAVE JONES*

    If the workspace was not saved, drop one of those in your library and then save it.

)*PORTS*

Change the name of your active workspace to *SMITH*

)*WSID SMITH*
)*SAVE*
)*CLEAR*
)*LOAD 1 NEWS*
)*SAVE 1 NEWS*

Why couldn't *NEWS* be saved?

)*CONTINUE HOLD*

Sign on again under your user number

)*LIB*
)*FNS*
)*VARS*

What was the effect òf signing off with *CONTINUE HOLD* ?

2. You have saved your work in a workspace called *GOOD* and have just
    developed a function *OK* in your active workspace. Write out a sequence
    of commands which will get *OK* into *GOOD* without carrying with it any
    unwanted "trash" which may be in the active workspace.

CHAPTER 16:

Mixed functions

Thus far we have worked with standard scalar dyadic and monadic functions.
One of their characteristics is that the shape of the result is the same
as that of the argument. For example, if the arguments are vectors, so is
the result. Ditto for scalars. In this and subsequent chapters, additional
functions will be introduced in which the shape of the result is not related
in such a consistent way to that of the arguments. Appropriately, these
are called "mixed" functions.

Index generator

To start off, let's consider a familiar algorithm: the one associated
with our earlier investigation of the cosine function. Here is a review of
the steps involved, the last being a one-line APL expression which does
the calculation:

$$\frac{x^0}{0!} - \frac{x^2}{2!} + \frac{x^4}{4!} - \frac{x^6}{6!} + \cdots - \cdots$$

```
X←3.14159÷4
TOP←X*0 2 4 6 8 10 12
BOT←!0 2 4 6 8 10 12
-/TOP÷BOT
-/(X*V)÷!V←0 2 4 6 8 10 12
```

Wouldn't it be nice to have a way to generate these sequences so as to
eliminate the monotony of typing? What's more, the only way now that we
can change the length of the sequence is to type in more or fewer numbers.

In APL the mixed function ι, which is upper shift I on the keyboard,
solves all your problems—or at least some of them, if you don't like
exaggeration. When used monadically with positive integer arguments, it
is called the <u>index generator</u>. Let's see how it works. Enter

```
      ι5
1   2   3   4   5
```

and a vector of integers from 1 to 5 is produced. Here is another:

113

```
      ι6
1   2   3   4   5   6
```

Now we're ready to use this function to produce the sequence needed for calculating the cosine. We know that multiplying any number by 2 produces an even number. Since our desired sequence is 0 2 4 6 8..., this suggests that we need

```
      2×ι6
2   4   6   8   10   12
```

Almost, but not quite there, 0 being omitted. The correct expression should be

```
      ¯2+2×ι6
0   2   4   6   8   10
```

and we have it. We can get something else out of this for free. If adding ¯2 gives an even sequence, then adding ¯1 should result in a sequence of odd numbers:

```
      ¯1+2×ι6
1   3   5   7   9   11
```

Getting back to our cosine function, we can now incorporate ιN for a variable number of terms. First

```
      )CLEAR
CLEAR WS
```

and we are ready to define the function. Since N, the number of terms, is now a variable, we ought to make the cos function dyadic. We may want to use the result for other calculations, so the header should be set to return an explicit result:

```
      ∇R←N COS X
[1]   V←¯2+2×ιN
[2]   R←-/(X*V)÷!V∇
```

In 1 CLASS there is an accurate value of PI. As we saw previously, we can transfer this to our active workspace by typing

```
      )COPY 1 CLASS PI
SAVED    15.02.39 07/29/69
```

Here is cos PI÷3 evaluated for a varying number of terms:

```
      2 COS PI÷3
0.4516886444
      4 COS PI÷3
0.4999645653
      6 COS PI÷3
0.4999999964
      8 COS PI÷3
0.5
```

Even though the last result is shown as .5, it is still approximate, the .5 being the best value to ten places.

Our ι function is good for all kinds of sequences.   Suppose we want a multiple of the first five integers.   Try

```
      ι 5 × 2
1   2   3   4   5   6   7   8   9   10
```

We forgot parentheses.   It should be

```
      ( ι 5 ) × 2
2   4   6   8   10
```

Sequences like powers of 2 can be obtained:

```
      2 * ι 5
2   4   8   16   32
```

This can be easily modified to get 2 raised to the 0 power:

```
      2 * ¯1 + ι 5
1   2   4   8   16
```

Now look at the following sequences:

```
      ι 5
1   2   3   4   5
      ι 4
1   2   3   4
      ι 3
1   2   3
      ι 2
1   2
```

So far, they seem straightforward.   Obviously, ι*N* generates a vector of *N* components.   Well, if you're so sure, what is ι1?

```
      ι 1
1
```

Carrying the analogy along, ι1 is a vector of length 1 containing the single component 1.   Is it the same as this 1?

```
      1
1
```

They look the same, but looks aren't everything.   The 1 we typed is a scalar. The result of ι1 is a vector.   In mathematics there is a term which is associated with the difference—rank, about which we'll have more to say later.

One (?) down, one to go.   What about

```
      ι 0
```
(typeball moves over 6 spaces but prints nothing.)

This must be a vector of no components, and the system in its response is trying to print a vector of length 0, but there just aren't any components to put on the paper!

What good is a vector of length 0? A good question. You can't really appreciate its uses until you begin to define functions for yourself. But, in the meantime, think about this: if you needed to generate vectors of varying length and you were looking for a starting place for a counter to keep track of what you were doing, what better place to start than with a vector of no components, the empty vector ι0?

Dimension vector

There is another mixed monadic function which gives the length or dimension of a vector. It is represented by the symbol ρ, pronounced "rho" (upper shift R). Let's define a couple of vectors X and Y and look at how this function works:

```
      X←2 3 5 7
      ρX
4
      Y←ι6
      ρY
6
```

This is just the thing we were looking for some time back when we were writing the awkward expression +/X=X to get the number of components in a vector for use in AVG, which can now be redefined a little more compactly:

```
      ∇R←AVG X
[1]   R←(+/X)÷ρX∇
```

Trying it out, it seems to work OK:

```
      AVG 1 2 1 2 1 2
1.5
```

Actually, ρ isn't as limited in its applicability as would appear from the above. It gives information about multidimensional arrays of numbers as well. In 1 $CLASS$ are some sample arrays for illustrative purposes called $TAB0$, $TAB1$, $TAB2$ and $TAB3$. Enter them in your active workspace with the $COPY$ command:

```
         )COPY 1 CLASS TAB0
SAVED    15.02.39 07/29/69
         )COPY 1 CLASS TAB1
SAVED    15.02.39 07/29/69
         )COPY 1 CLASS TAB2
SAVED    15.02.39 07/29/69
         )COPY 1 CLASS TAB3
SAVED    15.02.39 07/29/69
```

Now apologies are in order for making you do all the typing at this time. In chapter 34 a new command will be introduced which will enable you to group these four variables and copy them with a single instruction.

Display *TAB*0 :

        *TAB*0
4.1

It's just the scalar number 4.1. Look at ρ*TAB*0:

        ρ*TAB*0
        @

From this point on @ will be used to indicate the point where the typeball comes to rest when the result is an empty vector.

*TAB*0, the scalar, has no dimensions. It doesn't "extend out" any distance in any direction, unlike a vector or a matrix. In this sense it's like an idealized geometric point, which is also considered to be dimensionless.

Let's investigate *TAB*1 :

        *TAB*1
1.414213562   1.732050808   2   2.236067977
        ρ*TAB*1
4

ρ*TAB*1 yields a single number, which tells us that it is one-dimensional (a vector), with four components along that dimension.

Now for *TAB*2:

        *TAB*2

    3   1   7
    7   10   4
    6   9   1
    1   6   7
        ρ*TAB*2
4   3

Here we have a two-dimensional array (matrix), with four components along one dimension (no. of rows) and three components along the other (no. of columns).

Finally, display *TAB*3 :

```
      TAB3

 111   112   113
 121   122   123
 131   132   133
 141   142   143

 211   212   213
 221   222   223
 231   232   233
 241   242   243
      ρTAB3
2   4   3
```

This may look peculiar, but remember that we are restricted to two-dimensional paper to depict a three-dimensional array. If you think of the lower half of the table as being a second page lying behind the first, you will see where the third dimension comes in. The result of ρ TAB3 indicates that we do indeed have a three-dimensional array, two components deep (no. of planes), four components down (no. of rows), and three components across (no. of columns).

Rank

Earlier in this chapter, rank was mentioned as a distinguishing description of the number of dimensions of an array. Let's see how this is handled in APL . First, consider

```
      ρρTAB0
0
```

An unexpected response? Not really, when you think about it. Let's see if we can construct a plausible explanation. First we'll line up the responses from ρ TAB0-3:

```
      ρTAB0
@
      ρTAB1
4
      ρTAB2
4   3
      ρTAB3
2   4   3
```

What do you see? The shape of ρ applied to an array of N dimensions is a vector of N components. So ρTAB0 must really be a vector of length 0, i.e., ι0. Now you should be able to understand why ρρTAB0 results in 0:

```
      ρι0
0
```

Clearly the number of components in a vector of length 0 is 0, i.e., there are no components.

Similarly, we get

$\qquad \rho\rho\,TAB1$
1
$\qquad \rho\rho\,TAB2$
2
$\qquad \rho\rho\,TAB3$
3

Thus, $\rho\rho$ of any array gives the number of dimensions of the array, to which the name <u>rank</u> is attached. A scalar is of rank 0, a vector rank 1, and a <u>matrix</u> rank 2, while the array of rank 3 is sometimes called a <u>tensor</u>.

At last we are ready to tell the difference between

$\qquad \iota\,1$
1

and

$\qquad 1$
1

They have different ranks:

$\qquad \rho\rho\,1$
0
$\qquad \rho\rho\,\iota\,1$
1

PROBLEMS

1. <u>Drill</u>. Specify $A\leftarrow 0\ 8\ ^-3\ 4\ 6\ 10$

ρA	$\iota\,10$	$+/\iota\,15$
$\rho\rho A$	$(\iota\,5)+3$	$\div\iota\,5$
$\rho\rho\rho A$	$^-7\times\iota\,1$	$\iota\,28\div3+1$
$A\lceil 0.8\times\iota\,6$	$\iota\lceil/A$	$\iota\,10000$

2. What is the difference in meaning of the two expressions $\rho A=6$ and $6=\rho A$?

3. Load 1 $CLASS$ and execute each of the following:

$\times/\rho TAB0$	$\times/\rho TAB2$
$\times/\rho TAB1$	$\times/\rho TAB3$

What information is gained from these instructions?

4. For the vector A (prob. 1) execute $\iota\rho A$ and $\rho\iota\rho A$. What meaning can be assigned to each of these expressions?

5. Write one-line monadic functions returning an explicit result to give

   A) the sum of the square roots of the first N positive integers
   B) the square root of the sum of the first N positive integers
   C) the geometric mean of the first N positive integers (the
       nth root of the product of the N numbers)

6. Construct each of the following sequences using ι:

$$1 \ 3 \ 5 \ 7 \ 9 \ 11 \ 13 \ 15$$

$$^-7 \ ^-2 \ 3 \ 8 \ 13$$

$$0 \ 0.3 \ 0.6 \ 0.9 \ 1.2 \ 1.5$$

$$^-250 \ ^-150 \ ^-50 \ 50 \ 150 \ 250$$

$$5 \ 4 \ 3 \ 2 \ 1$$

$$1 \ 0 \ 1 \ 0 \ 1 \ 0$$

7. Enter $\iota3\times\iota3$. Account for the error message.

8. Write an *APL* expression to generate a vector of fifty 1's.

9. Rewrite each of the following statements without parentheses:

$$^-1+(-/(\iota5))\times2$$

$$+/(\iota5)-1$$

$$+/((\iota5)+1)=5$$

$$+/0=(\iota5)=6$$

10. Write functions that would approximate each of the following series to
    N terms:

$$1 - \frac{1}{2} + \frac{1}{3} - \frac{1}{4} + \ldots - \ldots$$

$$\frac{1}{0!} + \frac{X}{1!} + \frac{X^2}{2!} + \ldots$$

11. Write an *APL* expression that yields 1 if the array A is a scalar, 0
    otherwise.

CHAPTER 17:

More mixed functions

In our work with vectors, up to this point, we haven't said anything about
how we might add components to increase the length of the vector, which
would certainly be desirable if the vector represented, say, the bills run
up by a single customer in a department store. Our only recourse, thus far,
has been to respecify the vector by retyping it with the additions, which,
you'll agree, isn't very satisfactory.

Catenate

APL does have such a chaining feature for vectors on the keyboard. To
illustrate how it can be done, let's build a simple adding machine with
only a few keys on it. Here is the simulation:

KEY	PURPOSE/ACTION
C	clears accumulator
E	allows entry of values and prints no. of
	values accumulated since last entry
S	prints sum accumulated

Such a simulation is provided in 1 *CLASS*, which should be loaded now.

```
     )LOAD 1 CLASS
SAVED   15.02.39 07/29/69
```

Type
```
        C
        @
```

Next, type *E* and enter the data as shown:

```
        E 5 3 1
3
```

The system responds with a 3, indicating that three values have been entered.
Again make an entry:

```
        E 5 6
5
```

Typing S gives the sum of the values accumulated:

```
        S
20
```

We can continue to enter values and get the sum:

```
        E 2
6
        S
22
```

Now clear:

```
        C
        @
        S
0
        E 1 2 3
3
        S
6
```

What do the functions look like that comprise this simple desk calculator? First, let's display C:

```
        ∇C[□]∇
      ∇ C
[1]     VECT←ı0
      ∇
```

It is niladic and doesn't return explicit results, which is reasonable enough since its function is only to set the accumulator $VECT$ to ı0 each time it is executed. $VECT$ is a global variable and in C is an empty vector, a good place to start.

Here is E:

```
        ∇E[□]∇
      ∇ E X
[1]     ρVECT←VECT,X
      ∇
```

It has one argument, X, and takes the components in X and tacks them on to the back of $VECT$. This result is stored in $VECT$ and the number of components resulting is printed out. In effect we update $VECT$ and print out information about its components at the same time.

A new dyadic function is introduced in E. It is called catenate, the symbol for which is the comma, and its job is to catenate or chain together its two arguments.

Next, we'll display S:

```
        ∇S[□]∇
   ∇ R←S
[1]    R←+/VECT
   ∇
```

All S does is print out the sum of the accumulated values in $VECT$.

The catenate function has a number of characteristics worth noting.   If, for example,

```
        J←ι3
        K←9  8  7  6
```

and we catenate J and K and put the result in Y,

```
        Y←J,K
```

then there are seven components in Y:

```
        ρ Y
7
        Y
1    2    3    9    8    7    6
```

Two vectors can be catenated.   What about a scalar?   Can it be catenated to a vector?   Consider

```
        J,6
1    2    3    6
```

For purposes of catenation, the 6 is regarded as a vector of length 1.   If this is so, we ought to be able to catenate two scalars to make a vector:

```
        X←3,5
        X
3    5
```

X is now a vector of length 2, containing a 3 and a 5.

Catenating ι0 to a vector gives the same vector, as we would expect:

```
        J,ι0
1    2    3
        (ι0),J
1    2    3
```

What about catenating a vector of length 0 to a scalar?

```
        R←6
        ρρR
0
        T←R,ι0
        T
6
        ρT
1
```

```
      ρρT
1
```

T is a vector of one component, as shown by the last two results.   Clearly the result of catenation is always a vector.

Ravel

If we're not careful, this vector-scalar distinction can cause difficulties. Sometimes it is advantageous to have a vector of length 1 instead of a scalar.   As an example, look at AVG in 1 $CLASS$, which you should still have in your active workspace:

```
      ∇AVG[□]∇
    ∇ R←AVG X
[1]     R←(+/X)÷+/X=X
    ∇
```

It appears to work with both vector and scalar arguments:

```
      AVG 2 3 4
3
      AVG 4
4
```

Now let's use detailed editing to change $+/X=X$ to ρX:

```
      ∇AVG[1□10]
[1]     R←(+/X)÷+/X=X
                ////1
[1]     R←(+/X)÷ρXV
```

AVG is still in working order:

```
      AVG 2 3 4
3
```

or is it?

```
      AVG 4
      @
```

Something must be wrong.   One check is to see what ρAVG 4 is:

```
      ρAVG 4
0
```

which means that AVG 4 must result in a vector of length 0.   Why should this be?   Again let's display the function:

```
      ∇AVG[□]∇
    ∇ R←AVG X
[1]     R←(+/X)÷ρX
    ∇
```

Working from right to left on line 1, if X is a scalar, then ρX is an empty vector. But the algorithm calls for dividing $+/X$ (a scalar) by ρX (in this case a vector of length 0). Dividing a scalar by a vector gives a result which has the same shape as the vector argument. Need we say more?

Interesting though all this may be, it doesn't solve our problem. Our function, to be consistent, should return a result of 4 in this case. Somehow we have to make the argument X a vector if it isn't one already.

The APL function which does this is the monadic <u>ravel</u>, which uses the same symbol, the comma, as the dyadic catenate. We'll now insert this between ρ and X in AVG :

```
        ∇AVG[1☐10]
[1]     R←(+/X)÷ρX
        1
[1]     R←(+/X)÷ρ,X∇
```

Now executing AVG 4, we get the anticipated result:

```
        AVG 4
4
```

The ravel function has some interesting uses. $TAB2$ is a good example.

```
        TAB2

3    1    7
7   10    4
6    9    1
1    6    7
        ρTAB2
4    3
        ,TAB2
3   1   7   7   10   4   6   9   1   1   6   7
```

Notice that the last coordinate is raveled first, and there are as many components in the ravel as in the original array:

```
        ×/ρTAB2
12
        ρ,TAB2
12
```

If we try to catenate two arrays of different rank, we run into difficulties:

```
        4  5  6  7  8,2 3ρι6
RANK ERROR
        4  5  6  7  8 , 2 3 ρι6
                    ∧
```

This can be remedied by raveling the right argument first:

```
        4  5  6  7  8,,2 3ρι6
4    5    6    7    8    1    2    3    4    5    6
```

Again, with *TAB*3

```
      TAB3

 111   112   113
 121   122   123
 131   132   133
 141   142   143

 211   212   213
 221   222   223
 231   232   233
 241   242   243
      ,TAB3
111   112   113   121   122   123   131   132   133   141
      142   143   211   212   213   221   222   223   231
      232   233   241   242   243
```

Thus, no matter what the rank of the array with which we start, the monadic ravel converts the array to a vector.

Restructure

If we can reduce matrices to vectors, as we did in the last section, we also ought to be able to reshape vectors into matrices or higher rank arrays. The dyadic ρ, called <u>restructure</u>, does this for us. We'll start by specifying

```
      U←4 3 5 7 8 9
```

Suppose we want to build a two-dimensional table with the first row 4 3 5 and the second row 7 8 9. The restructure function rearranges the elements in the right argument to have the shape of the left argument:

```
      2 3ρU

4   3   5
7   8   9
```

Here is an example where the left argument contains only a single component:

```
      3ρU
4   3   5
```

Not only does the number of components in the left argument give the rank of the resulting array but, in addition, when we run out of numbers in the right argument, we go back to the beginning of the argument and start over. This will be evident from the following illustrations:

```
      5ρ3
3   3   3   3   3
      5ρ0 1
0   1   0   1   0
```

and if there are more numbers in the right argument than are needed to build the array,

```
      3ρ9 8 7 6 5 4 3
9  8   7
```

only as many as are called for in the restructure will be taken (in order).

So far our right arguments have been vectors. What happens when we have a matrix on the right?

```
      A←2 3ρ2 3 4 5 6 7
      A
```

```
2  3  4
5  6  7
      2 3 4ρA
```

```
2  3  4  5
6  7  2  3
4  5  6  7
```

```
2  3  4  5
6  7  2  3
4  5  6  7
      A←2 3 4 5 6 7
      2 3 4ρA
```

```
2  3  4  5
6  7  2  3
4  5  6  7
```

```
2  3  4  5
6  7  2  3
4  5  6  7
```

from which we can conclude that whatever the shape of the right argument A, for restructuring purposes it is in effect ,A. This is perfectly reasonable, since raveling an array of rank 2 or more before reshaping is just what most people would do if they had to do it by hand.

Finally, what if the right argument contains no components, i.e., is an empty vector?

```
      3ρι0
DOMAIN ERROR
      3ρι0
      ∧
```

There are no components on the right to perform the desired restructure on, so the instruction can't be carried out. But now try

```
      0ρι0
      @
      (ι0)ρι0
LENGTH ERROR
      (ι0)ρι0
      ∧
```

Can you think of an explanation for these results?

PROBLEMS

1. <u>Drill</u>. Specify $M \leftarrow 2\ 4\rho\iota 8$ and $V \leftarrow 3\ 3\rho\iota 9$

    ρM $5\ 4\rho V$ $3\ 3\rho 1, 3\rho 0$

    $(^-2)\ 1\ 2$ V, M $5\ 4\rho 0$

    $^-2, 1\ 2$ $6\rho 12$ $5, 4\rho 0$

    $\rho\rho V$ $10\rho 100$ $\rho\rho 0\rho 9\ 10\ 11\ 12$

2. What is the difference between $\rho A, \rho B$ and $(\rho A), \rho B$ for two vectors A and B?

3. Write an APL instruction to cause three 2's to be printed out in a vertical column.

4. Select 100 random positive integers, none of which is greater than 10.

5. A) Construct a matrix whose dimensions are always random and not greater than 8, made up of elements which are random positive integers not greater than 150.
    B) Modify your result for A) to make the upper bound for the elements itself a random number less than 300.

6. Use the ravel, restructure and catenate functions to reshape a 5 4 matrix A and a 7 4 matrix B into a 12 4 result R such that the first five rows of R contain A and the last seven, B.

7. This chapter introduces the function E as part of a simulated adding machine. Suppose the function E were dyadic. How could you tell the difference between it and, say, $6E8$ in exponential notation?

8. Make the scalar S a vector without using the ravel function.

9. You are given the job of designing a loop function in which the final result is a vector to be built up by tacking on the back end what comes out of each pass through the function. Assume there is nothing in the result to start with, and each time the loop is traversed the result is some vector Q. Write a two-step algorithm that will do this.

10. Define a monadic APL function that will take a vector V with an arbitrary number of components ≤ 7 and insert as many 0's in the front to make the result a seven-component vector, i.e., 3 2 5 7 becomes 0 0 0 3 2 5 7.

CHAPTER 18:

Character data

Have you noticed that except for variable and function names the input and
output that we have been working with has been entirely numerical? You
have undoubtedly observed that when by mistake you enter alphabetical characters without a specification you get a value error. This hasn't been
a real problem up to now, but what if in our output we wanted to label the
results or associate some message with them? We need a way to have such
literal (character) output alone or mixed with numerical information.

Some examples

In 1 *CLASS*, which should now be loaded,

```
        )LOAD 1 CLASS
SAVED   15.02.39 07/29/69
```

the function *RECT* shows the need for some kind of identification for the
output:

```
        ∇RECT[□]∇
     ∇  L RECT H
[1]      2×L+H
[2]      L HYP H
[3]      L×H
     ∇
        3 RECT 4
14
5
12
```

The three lines of output are the perimeter, diagonal and area (in that
order) of the rectangle whose sides are 3 and 4. But we had to look back
at the function to see what each of the numbers represented.

Also in 1 *CLASS* is a similar function *GEO2* , which does contain identify-
ing information. Try

```
      3 GEO2 4
PERIMETER IS:
14
AREA IS:
12
DIAGONAL IS:
5
```

This is more like it, so let's open up the function and look at it:

```
      ∇GEO2[⎕]∇
    ∇ L GEO2 H;X
[1]    X←' IS: '
[2]    'PERIMETER',X
[3]    2×L+H
[4]    'AREA',X
[5]    L×H
[6]    'DIAGONAL',X
[7]    L HYP H·
    ∇
```

Line 1 looks like nothing we've done so far. It appears to introduce a new use for the quote sign, namely, to enclose literal characters. As a matter of fact, not only are there obvious alphabetic characters I and S but also a colon used as a punctuation mark, and even blank spaces at either end.

APL interprets each of these, including the blanks, as a character of literal information. But it does more than that. Since, in line 2, catenation is used between the set of characters on the left and those on the right (stored in X), this suggests that such characters are components of an array, in this case of rank 1. It's a fancy way of calling what is between the quotes a vector. However, since we could conceivably have a table of characters, the rank will depend, as with numerical information, on the shape. X here is a vector of length 5.

Continuing down the function, lines 4 and 6 catenate the words $PERIMETER$ and $DIAGONAL$, respectively, to X, which consists of the word IS and the colon. Since even the spaces are counted as components of the literal vector, you should be able to see why at least the one before IS was necessary.

Don't get the idea that you have to be in function definition mode in order to deal with literals. For instance:

```
      A←'HELLO '
```

Again, notice the space after the O. Counting the space, it's a vector of length 6:

```
      ρA
6
```

We can do some rather cute things with these literals. As an example, if

```
      B←'HOW ARE YOU'
      B
HOW ARE YOU
```

then catenation forms the message

```
      A,B
HELLO HOW ARE YOU
```

However, there comes a time when we have to be serious in our use of literals. Suppose we had a family of rectangles we wanted information about:

```
      1 3 GEO2 1 4
PERIMETER IS:
4    14
AREA IS:
1    12
DIAGONAL IS:
1.414213562    5
```

Our answers are OK, but the labels don't look right. What would be nice to have is identification to match the output. Specifically, the labels should be followed by ARE or IS depending on the number of components in the arguments.

Try now

```
      1 3 GEO3 1 4
PERIMETERS ARE:
4    14
AREAS ARE:
1    12
DIAGONALS ARE:
1.414213562    5
```

If we give only a single rectangle to this function, we obtain

```
      3 GEO3 4
PERIMETER IS:
14
AREA IS:
12
DIAGONAL IS:
5
```

GEO3 does exactly what we want it to, and changes the alphabetical information to fit the conditions of the problem. Let's display GEO3:.

```
      ∇GEO3[□]∇
    ∇ L GEO3 H;X;FLAG
[1]    FLAG←((ρ,L)>1)∨(ρ,H)>1
[2]    X←((4×~FLAG)ρ' IS:'),(6×FLAG)ρ'S ARE:'
[3]    'PERIMETER',X
[4]    2×L+H
[5]    'AREA',X
[6]    L×H
[7]    'DIAGONAL',X
[8]    L HYP H
    ∇
```

The first thing to note is the presence of the two local variables X and
$FLAG$. Looking at line 1, if the number of components in either L or H
is greater than 1, then the variable $FLAG$ is set to 1. Otherwise, it is 0.
If the result of line 1 is 1 (i.e., we ask for information on more than one
rectangle), $6×FLAG$ is 6, and the 6 restructure of 'S ARE:' is simply the
characters $S ARE$. At the same time $~FLAG$ would be 0 and 4x0 is 0, so
that the 0 restructure of ' $IS:$' results in no characters being printed.
When catenated, the effect is just $S ARE$. You should be able to figure
out for yourself what happens in this line if $FLAG$ is 0. Line 2 thus tells
the system to pick up $IS:$ or $S ARE:$, depending on the length of the arguments. The rest of the function is like $GEO2$. Finally, here is some food
for thought before leaving this function: why must the arguments L and H
in line 1 be raveled before ρ is applied to them?

Rules for literals

It is important that when literal information is entered, <u>both</u> quotes appear.
Otherwise you have an open quote, not unlike the problem we faced before on
page 21 when in forming the symbol for the combination function we failed to
line up the quote and period.

We mentioned before that even spaces in quotes are characters. This brings
up the interesting question of what effect pressing the return key before
typing the second quote has on the output. Could the return itself be a
character? Here is an example:

```
      D←'ENGINEERING'
      ρD
11
      G←'ENGINE
ERING'
```

G types out as

```
      G
ENGINE
ERING
```

and has one more character than D:

```
      ρG
12
```

Occasionally a word to be entered has an apostrophe in it. Since this is
the same character as the quote, how can it be handled?

$$W \leftarrow 'ISN'T'$$

@

The typeball doesn't move over the usual six spaces after the return key.
Why? There are three quotes on the paper. Since quotes are used in pairs,
except where they are a part of an overstruck character, the cure is to
type another quote:

'

$$SYNTAX\ ERROR$$
$$\qquad W \leftarrow 'ISN'\ T\ '$$
$$\qquad\qquad\qquad \wedge$$

Now the system is back in desk calculator mode.

To get the apostrophe in, APL uses a double quote:

$$W \leftarrow 'ISN''T'$$
$$W$$
$$ISN'T$$

What about all the functions we've studied so far? Do they work with
literals? Let's try some and see:

$$A \leftarrow 'X'$$
$$B \leftarrow 'Y'$$
$$A + B$$
$$DOMAIN\ ERROR$$
$$\qquad A + B$$
$$\qquad \wedge$$
$$\qquad A < B$$
$$DOMAIN\ ERROR$$
$$\qquad A < B$$
$$\qquad \wedge$$

These functions make no sense operating on literals because literals aren't
orderable. Indeed, most of the standard functions would behave similarly.
But consider

$$A = B$$
0

Here we are asking the system to compare each component of the vector A with
the corresponding component of B. There is only one component on each side,
and they don't match, so the response is 0. The function $\neq$ works similarly:

$$A \neq B$$
1

A more sophisticated way in which = can be used is shown in the following
example, which asks how many occurrences of the letter E there are in the
vector D:

```
      D
ENGINEERING
      +/'E'=D
3
      'E'=D
1  0  0  0  0  1  1  0  0  0  0
```

Another function which works with a literal argument is the dyadic ρ, which isn't surprising since all it does is reshape the argument:

```
      ALF←'ABCDEFGHIJKLMNOPQRSTUVWXYZ'
      4 6ρALF

ABCDEF
GHIJKL
MNOPQR
STUVWX
```

Up to this point we have used only alphabetic characters, punctuation marks, spaces and the return as literals. Actually any keyboard character, including overstruck ones, can be employed in this manner. This can lead to some strange looking situations with numbers:

```
      T←'10'
      T
10
```

But T doesn't have the value 10:

```
      5+5
10
      T=10
0  0
```

Neither component of T matches the 10 on the right! If this is puzzling to you, remember that T is a <u>vector</u> of two components, 1 and 0, which obviously aren't equal to 10.

One other point about character entry. Take

```
      ρ'ABC'
3
      ρ'AB'
2
      ρ'A'
@
```

This means that a single character is considered to be a scalar, and in order to make it a vector we would have to ravel it:

```
      ρ,'A'
1
```

And, finally:

```
      ρ''
0
```

`''` is an empty vector (equivalent to ι0).

PROBLEMS

1. <u>Drill</u>.   Specify X←$'MISSISSIPPI'$ and Y←$'RIVER'$

$'ABCDE'='BBXDO'$	$1\ 2<'MP'$	$\rho\rho AL$←$3\ 3\rho 'ABCDEFGHI'$
ρV←$'3172'$	$\rho X,Y$	$X='S'$
$(\rho V)\rho V$	$+/X='S'$	$+/'P'=X$
$3172=V$	$+/X\ne 'S'$	$+/(X,'\ ',Y)\ne 'S'$
X,Y	$X,'\ ',Y$	$\lor/X='R'$

2. Here is a record of executions with an unknown vector D:

   ```
            D
            @
            ρD
   15
            5×D
   DOMAIN ERROR
            5×D
            ∧
            ' '=D
   1  1  1  1  1  1  1  1  1  1  1  1  1  1
   ```

   What is D?

3. Define a function F which takes a single argument A and prints out its dimension, rank, and number of elements with appropriate descriptive messages.   Assume rank $A\ge 1$.

4. Write a program that will add a row R to a matrix M and print out a message reading $THIS\ IS\ AN\ EXAMPLE\ OF\ CATENATION\ IN\ APL$

5. Copy the functions HYP and $GEO3$ in 1 $CLASS$. Open up the function and direct control to line [0.5]. Use the comment symbol ⍝ on this line and the next to write a message describing what the function does.   Then close out the function, display it and execute it.   Do comments introduced in this manner affect execution?

CHAPTER 19:

Mixed functions for ordering and selecting

Ranking

One of the points stressed at the end of the last chapter was that literal characters are unorderable, that is, it makes no sense to say, for example, that X is less than Y (X, Y literal). Yet there are clearly times when ordering is desirable, primarily for sorting and selection purposes.

In order to see how this can be done in *APL*, let's first get a clean workspace:

)*CLEAR*
CLEAR WS

and set

        X←'ABCDEFGHIJK'

Remember to close the quote before going on.

Now try

        *X*ι*'CAFE'*
3   1   6   5

This dyadic use of the mixed function ι is an interesting and useful one. The response has four components, the same as the length of the right argument, and it isn't too hard to tell what they stand for. *C* is the third character in *X*, *A* the first, *F* the sixth, and *E* the fifth.

Suppose there is no match, as, for example, in

        *X*ι*'CAFYE'*
3   1   6   12   5

All the characters except the *Y* can be matched. For that the system returns 12. But since the number of characters in the left argument is only 11,

        ρ*X*
11

then apparently the function is set to return a position one higher than
the last one available in the left argument. If we were to try

     *X*ι*'CAXYXE'*
3   1   12   12   12   5

this time both the *X*'s and the *Y* result in 12. This returning of an index
number one greater than the number of components on the left is character-
istic of the dyadic iota when there is no match.

Another point of information about this function is that when characters
are repeated in the right argument, the index numbers aren't used up. For
example, if

     W←*'AARDVARK'*
     ρ*W*
8

and we ask where in *W* is *W* found,

     *W*ι*W*
1   1   3   4   5   1   3   8

the first letter in *AARDVARK* is matched against the left argument and *A* is
found first in position 1, so 1 is recorded. Then the second *A* is matched
and is found on the left again in position 1, giving us a second 1 in the
result. *R* is found in position 3 on the left and 3 is recorded, etc.
From this you can infer that a sequence like 1 2 3 4 5 6 7 8 would be
returned only if no letters were repeated.

What if the right argument happens to be a matrix?

     A←3 2ρι6
     A

  1   2
  3   4
  5   6
      B←3 1 4 2 5
      *B*ι*A*

  2   4
  1   3
  5   6

The shape of the result is the same as that of the right argument, but the
left argument can be only a vector.

Indexing

Back now to *X*, which contains

     X
ABCDEFGHIJK

If

        X ι ' CAFE '
3   1   6   5

converts the characters *CAFE* into an ordered set 3 1 6 5 (called a "mapping"), it is perfectly reasonable to ask if there is any way we can change the ordered set back into characters. In *APL* this is done by the indexing function, which is also referred to as "subscripting:"

        X[3 1 6 5]
CAFE

This expression is usually read as "*X* sub 3 1 6 5." Note that [ ] are used, not ( ). Any valid *APL* statement can be used for subscripting. For instance:

        X[X ι ' CAFE ']
CAFE
        X[2 5ρ3 1 8 9 4 2 10 6 7 5]

CAHID
BJFGE

The result has the shape of the expression in the brackets.

But if we try to execute

        X[X ι ' CAFYE ']
INDEX ERROR
        X[X ι ' CAFYE ']
        ∧

Clearly to avoid an error message the expression in brackets must refer only to left argument indices that exist. In the last example, since the character *Y* is not found in *X*, and *X* has 11 characters, if we were to ask for

        X[12]
INDEX ERROR
        X[12]
        ∧

the system can't answer the question, there being no twelfth position. This isn't quite the same situation we had in ranking, where the result returned for an unidentifiable right argument character was one more than the number of components in the left argument. In that case the response is the system's way of telling us that the character in question was not to be found on the left. Thus, the dyadic ι and indexing are inverse operations, provided that each component on the right is also to be found in the left argument.

Again let's look at

        X
ABCDEFGHIJK
        X[3 3 3 3]
CCCC

As with ranking, the index numbers aren't used up by being repeated. Note, however, that we cannot index an array which hasn't been specified:

```
      SAM[1 4]←10 20
RANK ERROR
      SAM[1 4]← 10 20
      ∧
```

In addition to having a different form from the other functions, indexing is unique in that it is the only function that can appear on the left side of the specification arrow. For example, suppose we want to change D in X above to the character $?$:

```
      X[4]←'?'
      X
ABC?EFGHIJK
```

and the substitution has taken place. More generally, components can be rearranged by indexing. The following illustration shows such a change:

```
      X[5 6]←X[6 5]
      X
ABC?FEGHIJK
```

If no indices are entered, every element of the array is respecified:

```
      X[ ]←'T'
      X
TTTTTTTTTTT
```

Both ranking and indexing can be used with numerical as well as literal arrays. For instance, say we are given the heights (in inches) of five students:

```
      L←51 63 60 62 59
```

What is the position of the student who is 63 inches tall?

```
      Lι63
2
```

If the third student's height has been entered incorrectly, and should be 61 instead of 60 inches, the change can be made easily by

```
      L[3]←61
      L
51   63   61   62   59
```

The height of the student who is 62 inches tall can be changed to 65 inches:

```
      L[Lι62]←65
      L
51   63   61   65   59
```

We haven't yet shown how arrays of rank 2 and higher can be indexed. This is deferred to chapter 28, following a general discussion of multidimensional arrays.

Compression

Another function similar in many respects to indexing is compression, used for picking out specific components of a vector. If in L again

```
      L
51   63   61   65   59
```

we wanted to get the second and third students, the expression

```
      L[2 3]
63   61
```

will do it. We can also select with the following operation:

```
      0 1 1 0 0/L
63   61
```

which can be read as the "0 1 1 0 0 compression of L." The same symbol, the slash /, is used for compression as for reduction, but the difference is that instead of having an operation symbol before the slash, the left argument consists solely of 0's and 1's. Where there is a 0 in the left argument, the corresponding element on the right isn't picked up. The only elements returned are in those positions where there is a 1 to match it on the left. This means that the lengths of both arguments must be the same.

To illustrate a practical use of compression, here is a problem in accounts. If A is a vector of accounts in dollars, say we want to select out those accounts that are overdrawn (negative):

```
      A←3 ¯4 5 0 ¯6
```

The instruction

```
      A<0
0   1   0   0   1
```

flags the culprits by producing a vector with 1's in the positions of the offenders and 0's elsewhere. This is made to order for the compression function:

```
      (A<0)/A
¯4   ¯6
```

and we have extracted from A

```
      A
3   ¯4   5   0   ¯6
```

only the negative components.

Keep in mind that the left argument must contain 0's and 1's only:

```
      2 3/5 6
DOMAIN ERROR
      2 3 / 5 6
          ^
```

Both arguments must have the same length, unless all or none of the components are desired. In this case we need only a single 1 or 0:

```
      A←'ABCDEF'
      1/A
ABCDEF
      0/A
      @
```

If the lengths don't agree, an error message results:

```
      1 0 1 0/A
LENGTH ERROR
      1 0 1 0 /A
              ^
```

In 1 CLASS there is a function called CMP which uses compression to
compare two scalar arguments for size and prints out a message stating
whether the left argument is less than, equal to or greater than the right
argument.

Use the COPY command to get it into your active workspace:

```
      )COPY 1 CLASS CMP
SAVED    15.02.39 07/29/69
```

Let's try it out on a few examples:

```
      3 CMP 5
LESS
      5 CMP 3
GREATER
      5 CMP 5
EQUAL
```

Here is what CMP looks like:

```
      ∇CMP[☐]∇
    ∇ A CMP B
[1]   ((A>B)/'GREATER'),((A=B)/'EQUAL'),(A<B)/'LESS'
    ∇
```

It doesn't return an explicit result (since we wouldn't be apt to have any
further use for the result). Notice the practical use for catenation here
operating on literals, not unlike line 2 of the function GEO3 on page 132.
Starting from the right on line 1, we pick up either all of the literal
vector LESS or none of it, depending on whether A is less than B. The
vectors EQUAL and GREATER are treated similarly and catenated. Since
only one of the three conditions can possibly hold at any one time, we are
actually catenating two empty vectors to a vector of literals to produce the
desired result.

Expansion

Just as compression gives us a way to get a subset of a vector, so there exists also in *APL* a function called <u>expansion</u> which allows us to insert additional components. To illustrate its use, specify

$A←'ABCDEFG'$

It has 7 components:

$ρA$
7

The symbol for expansion is \, the backward pointing slash, on the same key as the compression symbol in the lower right corner of the keyboard:

```
      1 0 1 0 0 1 1 1 1 1\A
A B  CDEFG
      1 0 0 1 0 1\323
323  0  0  323  0  323
      1 0 0 1 0 1\3 2 3
3  0  0  2  0  3
```

The examples show that where 0 appears in the left argument, a blank (for literals) or zero (for numeric arrays) is inserted in the result which otherwise is identical to the right argument. Scalars are extended to match the length of the nonzero part of the left argument.

Here is a summary of the conditions governing the use of this function:

If $C←A\backslash B$, then
(1) A must consist of all 0's and 1's
(2) $(+/A) ≡ ρB$
(3) $(ρC) ≡ ρA$

Thus, let B be a vector of five components:

$B←2$ ⁻5 7 ⁻9 1
$ρB$
5

Say we want to insert four values, 41 42 43 44 between ⁻5 and 7. One way to do this is to enter

$D←B[1\ 2],41\ 42\ 43\ 44,B[3\ 4\ 5]$
D
2 ⁻5 41 42 43 44 7 ⁻9 1

Another way is to expand B:

$D←1\ 1\ 0\ 0\ 0\ 0\ 1\ 1\ 1\backslash B$
D
2 ⁻5 0 0 0 0 7 ⁻9 1

and then respecify D:

```
      D[3 4 5 6]←41 42 43 44
      D
 2  ‾5  41   42   43   44   7  ‾9  1
```

As mentioned before for indexing, the compression and expansion functions will be applied to multidimensional arrays in chapter 28.

PROBLEMS

1. Drill. Specify $A←0$ ‾5 ‾8 6.2 15 ‾2 25, $B←1$ 0 0 1 0 1 1 and
   $C←'ABCDEFGHIJKLMNOPQRSTUVWXYZ ?'$

   $(2<\iota 5)/\iota 5$ $A[2\ 4\ 7]$ $A[\iota \rho A]$

   B/A $\rho A[2\ 4\ 7]$ $A[1]+A[2\ 3\ 4]×A[7]$

   $A[\rho A],B[‾2+\rho B]$ $1\ 1\ 0\ 1\backslash 'TWO'$ $A[\lceil /A\iota A]$

   $(3\ 2\ 7)[2\ 1\ 3]$ $A[8]$ $A[0\rho 3]$

   $A[3\ 6]←2E5\ 4E‾4$ $A\iota \lceil /A$ $B\backslash 2\ 3\ 4\ 5$

   $C[1\ 16\ 12\ 27\ 9\ 19\ 27\ 1\ 12\ 7\ 15\ 18\ 9\ 20\ 8\ 13\ 9\ 3]$

2. Specify $D←‾2.1\ 4\ 1.9\ 0\ ‾1\ ‾4\ ‾1.4\ .7\ 2.5\ 2$. Select from D those components which are

   A) less than .5   D) negative and greater than ‾1
   B) positive   E) equal to 2
   C) equal in magnitude to 4 F) less than 1 and greater than or
                                 equal to ‾2

3. Define a monadic function to insert the character ∘ between each pair
   of adjacent elements in a vector V.

4. For any arbitrary vector V write a function $INCR$ to compute increments
   between adjacent elements.

5. For mathematicians only: Obtain the area under the curve $Y=3X^2$ between
   X_1 and X_2 by breaking it up into rectangles of width I in that interval.
   Hint: First define F to compute $3×X*2$.

6. Write a program $WITHIN$ to select from a vector W those elements
   which lie within an interval R on either side of the average of W.

7. Write an APL expression to select those elements in a vector which are
   integers.

8. Define a function IN to tell what percent of the elements in a vector
   A lie within the interval $B±C$.

9. Construct an expression that selects the largest element in a three-
   element vector V and prints out a 1 if it exceeds the sum of the
   remaining two elements, 0 otherwise.

10. Show how to select the elements with even indices in a vector Y.

11. You are given a vector X whose components are all different and arranged
     in ascending order. Write a program to insert a given scalar S into the
     appropriate place in the sequence so that the result is still in ascend-
     ing order. Be sure that your function is able to handle the case where
     S is identical to some element in X.

12. What is the difference between

         A) $\iota A[2]$ and $(\iota A)[2]$ for some integer A
         B) $\rho M,\rho N$ and $(\rho M),\rho N$ for $M\leftarrow 1\ 2$ and $N\leftarrow 3\ 4$

13. Write an APL expression to pick up the last element of a vector V.

14. Why is $V[\bar{\ }1+\iota\rho V]$ not executable?

15. Write an APL expression which returns the index of the largest element
     in a vector W.

16. Define a function to remove all duplicate elements from a vector.

17. Write an APL expression to calculate the sum of the first eight
     components of a vector Q (or all of them if the number of components is
     less than eight).

18. Write a program $SELECT$ which takes two arguments and will print
     out that element in the left argument X whose position corresponds to
     the position of largest element in the right argument Y.

19. Construct APL expressions to insert for $V\leftarrow\iota N$ a zero

         A) between each two adjacent components of V
         B) before each even component of V
         C) after each odd component of V

20. Write a function returning an explicit result which finds all the fac-
     tors of a given integer N (i.e., the integers which divide evenly into
     N).

21. Write a program to convert a numeric literal with less than ten digits
     to a number, so that, for example, '1456' becomes 1456, and can be
     used like an ordinary number for further calculations.

22. Define a function $COMFACT$ to print a list of common factors, if any,
     of two integers A and B.

23. Define a monadic function which takes a literal argument and selects
     the longest word in it. Hint: Look for the longest set of consecutive
     non-blank characters.

CHAPTER 20:

Identity elements

Identity elements

In mathematics for a number of operations there is in the domain of elements associated with them a particular element that has a unique property. Specifically, in addition the number 0 added to any number results in the number itself:

        0+1
1
        3+0
3

Any element that behaves in this fashion is called an <u>identity</u> element for the operation in question. The mathematician defines the concept even more narrowly. In the example above, 0 acts as an identity element when it is on the left. Hence it can be thought of as a left identity for addition. Similarly, it is a right identity for addition. If an element is both a left and a right identity, it is often spoken of as "<u>the</u> identity element" for a particular operation. As we will see, many operations have no identity element, or have either a right or a left identity, but not both.

In APL there is a simple way to find identity elements where they exist. We can lead up to this with an example. Let B be the following vector:

   $B \leftarrow 5 \ ^{-}3 \ ^{-}2 \ 3 \ 0$

An obvious true statement is that the sum reduction of B is made up of the sum of the sum reduction of the elements of B that are negative and the sum reduction of those positive or 0, i.e.,

   $(+/B)=(+/(B<0)/B)++/(B\geq0)/B$
1

So far we haven't really said anything earthshaking. But what if B didn't have any negative elements? Then the sum reduction of these elements would be 0:

```
      B←5 3  2  3  0
      (+/B)=+/(B≥0)/B
1
      +/(B<0)/B
0
```

Let's examine the last two lines more closely. We compress B by selecting those elements of B which are negative. Since there are no such elements, the compression results in an empty vector:

```
      (B<0)/B
      @
```

and the sum reduction over this empty vector yields 0:

```
      +/(B<0)/B
0
```

But an empty vector can be represented in APL by ι0. Hence, the sum reduction over an empty vector should give us 0, and 0 is the identity element for addition:

```
      +/ι0
0
```

In exactly the same way, if we looked at the times reduction of B   we get

```
      (×/B)=(×/(B<0)/B)××/(B≥0)/B
1
```

a similar argument would then yield

```
      ×/ι0
1
```

which is the identity element for multiplication.

This suggests that the way to find the identity element for any standard scalar dyadic function (assuming the identity element exists) is to execute fn /ι0, where fn stands for some function. However, there are two precautions which need to be emphasized here. First, there is no indication as to whether the result is a left identity, right identity or both; and second, no warning is given of any restrictions, if indeed there are any, on the domain of the operation.

Here are a few additional examples that point up these restrictions:

```
      ÷/ι0
1
```

We can divide any number by 1 and return the original number, so 1 is a right identity for division. No left identity exists for this operation.

```
     ∧/ι0
1
     ∨/ι0
0
```

The logical functions ∧ and ∨ have both left and right identity elements, as examination of their operation tables shows (pages 26-27). But, if we were to take a function like <, no identity element exists over the entire domain of real numbers. If we restrict the domain to 0 and 1, then 0 is a left identity for <:

```
     </ι0
0
```

No such restriction helps in the case of the function ⋆:

```
     ⋆/ι0
DOMAIN ERROR
     ⋆/ι0
     ∧
```

A prepared drill exercise in *APL*

In chapter 9 the tutorial exercise *EASYDRILL* was introduced to give you practice in the *APL* functions discussed up to that point. We haven't yet exhausted all the functions so far implemented in the language, but, as before, it's worth taking a breather at this point to review what has been done. In the workspace 1 *APLCOURSE* there is another drill exercise called *TEACH*, which contains a larger variety of more difficult problems for you to work on.

Now load this workspace and execute *TEACH*. Indicate which functions you want practice in. Be sure at least this first time to include exercises in vectors of length 0 and reduction. Especially note the instructions pertaining to your responses for vectors of length 0 or 1. The format and way in which the problems are generated are the same as in *EASYDRILL*. You get three tries, then the answer is furnished and you are given another similar problem of the same kind. Typing *PLEASE* gives you the answer and another similar problem. Both *STOP* and *STOPSHORT* get you out of the exercise, but *STOP* gives you in addition a record of your performance. Continue practicing at this point and at any subsequent time as your needs require it and your schedule permits.

Below is a short sample practice session with *TEACH* .

```
     )LOAD 1 APLCOURSE
SAVED   11.07.53 09/01/69
     TEACH
ANSWER THE FOLLOWING QUESTION WITH Y FOR YES OR N FOR NO.
ARE YOU ALREADY FAMILIAR WITH THE INSTRUCTIONS FOR THIS
EXERCISE?
N
THIS IS AN EXERCISE IN SIMPLE APL EXPRESSIONS.
YOU WILL FIRST HAVE THE OPPORTUNITY TO SELECT THE FEATURES
YOU WISH TO BE DRILLED IN.  THE EXERCISE THEN BEGINS.  FOR
EACH PROBLEM YOU MUST ENTER THE PROPER RESULT.  ANSWERS
```

```
WILL CONSIST OF SCALAR INTEGERS IF EXERCISES WITH VECTORS
ARE NOT DESIRED; OTHERWISE ANSWERS WILL CONSIST OF
SCALARS OR VECTORS.   A VECTOR OF LENGTH ZERO REQUIRES THE
RESPONSE ι0, A VECTOR OF LENGTH ONE REQUIRES THE RESPONSE
,X WHERE X IS THE VALUE OF THE ELEMENT.   YOU HAVE THREE
TRIES FOR EACH PROBLEM.   TYPE STOP AT ANY TIME TO TERMIN-
ATE THE EXERCISE AND PRODUCE A RECORDING OF YOUR PERFORM-
ANCE.   TYPING STOPSHORT WILL TERMINATE THE EXERCISE BUT
WILL NOT PRODUCE A RECORD OF PERFORMANCE.   TYPING PLEASE
FOR ANY PROBLEM WILL LET YOU PEEK AT THE ANSWERS.
TYPE Y UNDER EACH FUNCTION FOR WHICH YOU WANT EXERCISE
SCALAR DYADIC FUNCTIONS
+-×÷*⌈⌊<≤=≥>≠!|∧∨⊛⍱⍲
      YY      YY
SCALAR MONADIC FUNCTIONS
+-×÷⌈⌊!|~
   Y  Y
TYPE Y IF EXERCISES ARE TO USE VECTORS, N OTHERWISE
Y
TYPE Y IF REDUCTION EXERCISES ARE DESIRED, N OTHERWISE
Y
TYPE Y IF VECTORS OF LENGTH ZERO OR ONE ARE DESIRED,
N OTHERWISE.
Y
MIXED DYADIC FUNCTIONS
ριι,∈⊥⊤/↑↓\⌽
YYY
MIXED MONADIC FUNCTIONS
ιρ,⌽
YY
                         ⌈/ ¯2  ¯5  4
□:
      4
                         ≠/,¯5
□:
      ,¯5
TRY AGAIN
□:
      ¯5
                         10>7
□:
      1
                         ⌊/,¯6
□:
      ¯6
                         6  4 ⌊ 3  ¯9
□:
      6 9
TRY AGAIN
□:
      PLEASE
ANSWER IS   3  ¯9
                         (ι0)⌊ι0
□:
      ι0
                         !  1  4
□:
      1  24
```

```
                7   1   5 ⌊ 7   1   5
⎕:
        7 1 5
                !  0   4
⎕:
        1 24
                >/,¯1
⎕:
        ¯1
                ÷⍳0
⎕:
        ⍳0
                ÷ 0.25  1
⎕:
        4 2
TRY AGAIN
⎕:
        4 1
                ¯1   9   ¯4 , 3   ¯2
⎕:
        ¯1 9 ¯4 3 ¯2
                (,3)⍴,1
⎕:
        1 1 1
                9   ¯5 ⌈ 9   ¯5
⎕:
        9 ¯5
                ⍳0
⎕:
        ⍳0
                ⌊/,2
⎕:
        STOPSHORT
```

PROBLEMS

1. Find the identity elements (if any) for the following dyadic functions:
   - ⋆ ⊛ ⌈ ⌊ | ! ⍟ = ≠ ≤ > ≥. Explain the results for ⌈ and ⌊.

CHAPTER 21:

Still more mixed functions

This chapter will be devoted to several more mixed functions that alter the order of the components of an array and enable us to make selections from among the components. Where the operations are applicable to arrays of higher rank than 1, discussion of the function syntax will be deferred until chapter 28.

Reversal

This mixed monadic function, the symbol for which is ϕ (upper shift O overstruck with upper shift M, reverses the order of the components of a vector:

```
      φ1 2 3 4
4   3   2   1
      φ'ABCDEFG'
GFEDCBA
```

Reversal of a scalar results in the same scalar:

```
      φ4
4
```

and, like logical negation, reversal is its own inverse:

```
      φφ'ABCDEFG'
ABCDEFG
```

Rotate

The symbol ϕ also has a dyadic use, and is called <u>rotate</u> or <u>rotation</u> when so employed. To get a feel for its syntax and how it operates, try

```
      2φ'ABCDEFG'
CDEFGAB
      4φ1 2 3 4 5 6 7
5   6   7   1   2   3   4
```

```
        0φ34 56 78
34    56   78
```

It rotates or shifts all the elements cyclically to the left. By a cyclic rotation is meant the following. Imagine our vector of literals arranged in closed loop, as below:

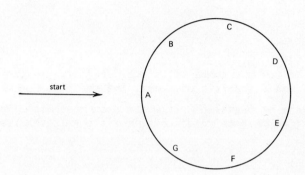

Rotating to the left is equivalent to a counterclockwise shift in position of all the elements, producing

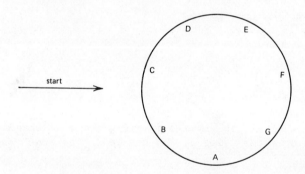

Since we will be using the same vector of literals repeatedly, let's represent it by H. It has seven components:

```
    H←'ABCDEFG'
    ρH
7
```

What happens if we rotate H seven places?

```
    7φH
ABCDEFG
```

The result is H itself, which shouldn't surprise you at all. What about rotation by a number greater than the number of components in the right argument, say eight?

$$8\phi H$$
$$BCDEFGA$$

which is equivalent to

$$1\phi H$$
$$BCDEFGA$$

and, in fact, $7|8$ gives the number of places shifted. In general, if H is the right argument and L the left argument, the shift is $(\rho H)|L$ places.

Can the left argument be negative? It would seem reasonable that a negative left argument ought to produce rotation to the right (clockwise). Let's try it and see:

$$^-2\phi H$$
$$FGABCDE$$

The characters are indeed moved to the right two places. Since the 7 residue of $^-2$ is 5,

$$7|^-2$$
5

then $^-2\phi H$ should be the same as $5\phi H$:

$$5\phi H$$
$$FGABCDE$$

Take and drop

The take function, which is the upward pointing arrow ↑ (upper shift Y), is a dyadic selection operator. See if you can tell from some examples how it works:

```
        V←8 5 3 9 ¯1 ¯4
        4↑V
8  5   3  9
        0↑V
        @
        8↑V
8  5   3  9   ¯1  ¯4  0  0
       ¯2↑V
¯1   ¯4
       ¯8↑V
0  0   8  5   3  9   ¯1  ¯4
       2 3↑5

     5   0  0
     0   0  0
```

If A is the left argument and is positive, ↑ selects the first A elements from the right argument. If A is negative, the last A elements are taken. When A is greater than ρV the result is V with sufficient 0's on the right or left to make a vector of length A. Note that with a vector left argument, the take function applied to a scalar returns an array whose shape is determined by the left argument and whose elements consist of 0's, except for the [1;1] element. (See also the restructure function ρ on page 126 for a comparison)

Drop, ↓, behaves in much the same way, except that A elements are dropped instead of selected:

```
      0↓V
8  5  3  9  ̄1  ̄4
      2↓V
3  9  ̄1  ̄4
      8↓V
@
      ̄3↓V
8  5  3
```

From these examples a general inference can be drawn that $A↑V$ is equivalent to $(A-\rho V)↓V$, provided that A isn't greater than ρV.

Membership

We have encountered a number of functions (logicals, relationals) that yield only 0's and 1's as results. Another function that behaves similarly is membership ϵ (upper shift E). Here is a set of numbers, 3 1 6 1. Which of these are members of the set 1 2 3 4 5?

What we are asking is really a series of questions which, in APL, could be stated as

```
      3=ι5
0  0  ï  0  0
      1=ι5
ï  0  0  0  0
      6=ι5
0  0  ö  0  0
      1=ι5
ï  0  0  0  0
```

the net result being the logical vector 1 1 0 1 as indicated by the diaereses. On the terminal this is

```
      3 1 6 1ε1 2 3 4 5
1  1  0  1
```

Clearly the shape of the result must be the same as that of the left argument. Both arguments may be arrays of any rank with this function.

Grade up and down

These two functions, by themselves, give the indices according to which we would have to select components of a vector to reorder the vector ascending (grade up) or descending (grade down). The symbols used are the upper shift H and G overstruck with upper shift M, for grade up and grade down, respectively. Here are some examples:

```
      V←8  5  3  9  ‾1  ‾4
      ⍋V
6   5   3   2   1   4
      ⍒V
4   1   2   3   5   6
```

In the grade up of V the first component, 6, tells us that the sixth element of V should be taken first; the second component, 5, tells us to take the fifth component of V next, etc., to reorder V in ascending fashion.

If the elements happen to be duplicates, the indices of the duplicates are treated in the same way as the vector is searched from left to right:

```
      W←3  2  4  6  3  3
      ⍋W
2   1   5   6   3   4
```

Since the result tells us the order of the indices that should be chosen to sort out the components ascending or descending, these functions give us a handy quick way to produce an actual reordering:

```
         V[⍋V]
‾4   ‾1   3   5   8   9
         V[⍒V]
9   8   5   3   ‾1   ‾4
```

Deal

The last mixed function to be considered in this chapter is the dyadic query, $?$, called <u>deal</u>, a few examples of which follow:

```
         3?8
3   7   4
         6?10
10   6   3   8   1   9
         6?6
3   5   2   4   1   6
         ‾2?6
DOMAIN ERROR
      ‾2?6
         ∧
         8?6
DOMAIN ERROR
      8?6
         ∧
```

A vector results, which has the same length as the magnitude of the left argument. If A is the left argument and B the right, $A?B$ generates a random selection of A integers with no duplication from the population ιB. Both arguments must be positive scalars or vectors of length 1, with $A \leq B$

Here is a practical application of some of these functions. Let's suppose
we are given the literal characters *THIS ONE* and we want to insert some
additional characters between the *S* and the *O*. This can be done by means
of a prepared function *INSERT* in 1 *CLASS*. Load 1 *CLASS* and display the
function *INSERT*:

```
      )LOAD 1 CLASS
SAVED   15.02.39 07/29/69
      ∇INSERT[□]∇
    ∇ R←N INSERT B;P;X
[1]    P←Bι'o'
[2]    X←(P-1)↑B
[3]    R←P↓B
[4]    R←((Nρ1),((ρX)ρ0),((ρR)-N)ρ1)\R
[5]    R[N+ιρX]←X
    ∇
```

INSERT is dyadic, with the left argument *N* being the position after which
the insertion is to be made. The right argument *B* is what is to be inserted,
with a small circle as shown to separate it from its follow-on:

```
      3 INSERT '?ω¯oABCDEFGH'
ABC?ω¯DEFGH
```

Thus, if *U* is specified by *THIS ONE* and we want to insert the literals
IS between *S* and *O*, then we should execute

```
      U←'THIS ONE'
      4 INSERT ' IS','o',U
THIS IS ONE
```

or

```
      4 INSERT ' ISo',U
THIS IS ONE
```

Look at the function again. In line 1 *P* is the position of the little circle
in the right argument *B*. Line 2 selects all the components in *B* up to
but not including the little circle and assigns them to *X*. In line 3 the
first *P* components of *B* are dropped and the rest stored in *R*. Line 4 resets
R by expanding it. The left argument of the expansion is built up by
taking *N* 1's followed by as many 0's as there are components in *X*, which
in turn is followed by as many 1's as the difference between the number of
components in *R* and *N*. Finally, line 5 inserts the message in place of
the 0's or blanks resulting from the expansion.

Some applications to cryptography

Because of the ease with which vectors of all sizes can be operated on,
APL is quite suitable for the development of schemes for coding information (cryptography). We will explore some of these to illustrate a few
practical uses of the functions introduced in this chapter and chapter 19.

Since we will need the alphabet repeatedly throughout this section, let's
store it under *ALF*:

```
      ALF←'ABCDEFGHIJKLMNOPQRSTUVWXYZ'
```

To start, here's a function which makes a simple random letter substitution for a message M:

```
      M←'TOBEORNOTTOBETHATISTHEQUESTION'
      ∇C←P SUBST M
[1]   ALF
[2]   ALF[P]
[3]   ' '
[4]   M
[5]   C←ALF[P[ALFιM]]∇
      P←26?26
      P SUBST M
ABCDEFGHIJKLMNOPQRSTUVWXYZ
WGMKRUYTBZHCNXFDJLPEVOAQSI

TOBEORNOTTOBETHATISTHEQUESTION
EFGRFLXFEEFGRETWEBPETRJVRPEBFX
```

The grade up function can be used to improve on the letter substitution by
transposing the letters according to the following scheme:

```
      ∇P TRANSP M
[1]   T←⍋(ρM)ρP
[2]   M
[3]   M[T]∇
      M←'SENDSUPPLIESTONEWLOCATIONATONCE'
      P TRANSP M
SENDSUPPLIESTONEWLOCATIONATONCE
ILSECNEOEAWDCLNNTTOOSENPUASTOPI
```

We will now introduce a further complication by using a "key" to be added
to the indices resulting from $ALFιM$, thus generating a new set of indices
for application to ALF:

```
      ∇K VIG M;C
[1]   N←ALFιM
[2]   M
[3]   C←26|N+(ρN)ρK
[4]   ALF[(ρN)ρK]
[5]   (ρM)ρ'‾'
[6]   ALF[C]∇
      K←1 2 3
      M←'ENEMYWILLATTACKATDAWNWITHTENDIVISIONS'
```

We will run into trouble here since the 26 residues of some of the new
indices may be 0. However, provision is made in APL for a shift to 0 in
the starting point for indexing:

```
      )ORIGIN 0              (remember to reset the origin to 1 when
WAS 1                         you are done)
```

This command also affects ranking, the index generator, roll, deal, grade
up and grade down. See also chapter 34 for a fuller discussion.

Now we can safely execute the function:

```
      K VIG M
ENEMYWILLATTACKATDAWNWITHTENDIVISIONS
BCDBCDBCDBCDBCDBCDBCDBCDBCDBCDBCDBCDB
-------------------------------------

FPHNAZJNOBVWBENBVGBYQXKWIVHOFLWKVJQQT
```

Our last illustration catenates an arbitrary string of literal characters P onto the front end of a message M and drops off the excess characters from the back end, so that the resulting character string Q is the same length as M. The indices produced by $ALF\iota Q$ are added to those from $ALF\iota M$ and the results reduced with the residue function as before:

```
      ∇P AUTO M;Q;R;S
[1]    R←ALF\iota Q←P,((ρM)-ρP)↑M
[2]    S←26|R+ALF\iota M
[3]    M
[4]    Q
[5]    (ρP)ρ'*'
[6]    (ρM)ρ'‾'
[7]    ALF[S]∇
      P←'GYLTZZY'
      P AUTO M
ENEMYWILLATTACKATDAWNWITHTENDIVISIONS
GYLTZZYENEMYWILLATTACKATDAWNWITHTENDI
*******
-------------------------------------

KLPFXVGPYEFRWKVLTWTWPGIMKTAAZQOPLMBQA
```

PROBLEMS

1. <u>Drill</u>. Specify $A←3\ 2\ 0\ {}^-1\ 5\ {}^-8$

$3\phi A$	$\phi 0,\iota 3$	$A[\Psi 0\ 1\ 0\ 1\ 0\ 1]$
$2\phi A[\iota 4]$	$2\phi\phi\iota 7$	$(\iota 4)\epsilon A$
$4↑A$	${}^-3↓A$	$(3↑A)\epsilon\iota 4$
$2↑{}^-3\phi A$	$A[\blacktriangle\blacktriangle A]$	$(\iota 6)=\blacktriangle A[\blacktriangle A]$

2. Use the membership function to identify and select the one-digit integer elements of a vector V.

3. Write an *APL* expression to determine if two sets of numbers, $S1$ and $S2$, have identical elements, except possibly for order.

4. You are given a vector of characters $S←'WE\ ARE\ \ \ ALL\ \ \ GOOD\ MEN\ '$ Write an *APL* expression to determine how many occurrences of the letters $ABCDEFGHIJKL$ are in S.

5. Use *APL* to rearrange the above character vector S so that the letters (including duplicates and blanks) are in alphabetical order.

6. Define a function to remove the extra blanks in S where they occur.

7. For an arbitrary numerical vector V which has been sorted in ascending
    order, show how to insert another vector $V1$ so as to preserve the
    ordering.

8. For a given numeric vector V of length N, write an APL expression
    that tests whether V is some permutation of the vector ιN (i.e.,
    every element of V is in ιN and vice versa).

9. Let C be a vector of characters. Construct an expression which
    replaces every X in C with a Y.

10. For a vector of eight components, construct two expressions for
    selecting the last three components. Use the compression function
    in one and the take function in the other.

11. Write a program to find the median of a set of numbers. (The
    median is defined as the scalar in the middle of the list after it
    has been sorted. When the number of elements is even, the arithmetic
    mean of the two middle elements is defined to be the median.)

12. Explain what each of the following expressions does:

    $$A[\blacktriangle\blacktriangle(\rho A)\rho 0\ 1]\qquad (A \text{ a vector})$$

    $$A\uparrow\blacktriangle?B\rho\lfloor/\iota 0\qquad (A \text{ and } B \text{ scalars})$$

13. Write a program to decode the message resulting from execution of
    the function $SUBST$ on page 156.

14. Modify the function VIG on page 156 to require two keys, KA and KB, of
    varying length, to be restructured and added on line 4. Let the
    function now take only the single argument M.

15. Define a function $VERNAM$ that modifies the indices resulting from
    $ALF\iota M$ (M is the message to be coded) by adding to them a vector V of
    M random numbers from 0 to 25. Reduce the result, as in VIG and
    $AUTO$, and apply it to ALF.

CHAPTER 22:

Number systems

Base value

It is a fact of life in our language that it is impossible to conceive of a number in the abstract without associating it with some concrete representation. Take the number 3, for instance. Can you think of the concept of threeness without imagining three objects or visualizing the number 3 in some system of notation, be it Roman numerals, exponential notation, base-2 notation, or whatever?

No matter how many different ways of depicting 3 we may come up with, they all stand for the same thing, this abstract notion of threeness. Yet, most of the time, we have no difficulty in recognizing the number if it is imbedded in a context which conditions our thinking along the right lines:

I I I	o o
	o
0.03E2	0003
3.00	00011

This last entry could be 11 in decimal notation but, because of the other more familiar ways of expressing 3 that preceded it, we would quite likely accept it as 3 in the binary system.

What it all boils down to is this: Just as a rose by any other name is still a rose and smells just as sweet, so in mathematics there are many ways to express the same number, and their value to us depends on what we are most used to and what form is most useful to us.

Thus far, in all our *APL* work, we have been using ordinary decimal notation. But many other systems are in common use. Mixed systems like clock time and number systems to the bases 2, 8, 16 are examples. In this chapter we will be examining how *APL* makes it possible for us to switch conveniently from one system to another.

Suppose, for instance, that we are in a room whose length is

$$3 \text{ yds} \quad 0 \text{ ft} \quad 1 \text{ inch}$$

How could we reduce this example of the English system of measurement at its worst, to a single unit, say, inches? If we were to do it by hand, we would probably set up something like the following:

$$\begin{array}{ccccc} 3 \text{ yds} & & 0 \text{ ft} & & 1 \text{ inch} \\ \underline{\times\ (12\times3)} & & \underline{\times\ 12} & & \underline{\times\ 1} \\ 108 & + & 0 & + & 1 = 109 \text{ inches} \end{array}$$

There is a dyadic function in APL that will make this conversion for us. It is called the <u>base value</u> or <u>decode</u> function, and its symbol is the upper shift B, $\bot$.   The right argument of $\bot$ is the vector to be converted, while the left argument is a vector whose components are the increments needed to make the conversion from one unit to the next. Since each of the components on the left can be thought of as acting somewhat like the base of a number system (called a "radix" by mathematicians), the left argument is usually referred to as the <u>radix vector</u>.

In a mixed number system like the one involving our length measurements of the room, the syntax of the function requires that the dimensions of both arguments be the same. There is one exception to this, namely, that either argument may be a scalar or vector of length 1, a case which will be considered shortly. For our particular problem, we'll use 1760 (the number of yds/mile) as the multiplying factor for the next increment, even though it won't be used:

```
      1760 3 12⊥3 0 1
109
```

As a matter of fact, any number will do in that position, as long as there is something there:

```
      0 3 12⊥3 0 1
109
      3 1⊥3 0 1
LENGTH ERROR
      3 1 ⊥ 3 0 1
        ∧
```

Here is another example, converting 2 minutes and 10 seconds to seconds:

```
      60 60⊥2 10
130
      0 60⊥2 10
130
```

We can formalize the action of the radix vector on the right argument concisely by letting $W[J]$ be the weighting factor that tells us what the increments should be from one unit to the next in our reduction. In our example of the room size, if A is the radix vector and B is the right argument, then $W[3]$ is 1, $W[2]$ is $A[3]\times W[3]$ or 12, $W[1]$ is $A[2]\times W[2]$ or 3×12. The result is equivalent to 36 12 1×3 0 1, or $+/W\times B$.

Ordinary length and time measurements are examples of mixed number systems. The base value function, however, works equally well for decimal or other fixed base number systems. For instance, suppose the following is a picture of the odometer reading (in miles) of a car:

This can be regarded as a scalar 3521 or a vector 3 5 2 1. If it is the latter and we want to convert it to the scalar number 3521 , then we can execute

          10 10 10 10⊥3 5 2 1
3521
          0 10 10 10⊥3 5 2 1
3521

The base value function can be applied to number systems other than decimal. Here is a binary counter:

```
+---+---+---+---+
| 0 | 1 | 0 | 1 |
+---+---+---+---+
```

This can be converted to a decimal number by

          2 2 2 2⊥0 1 0 1
5

But if the counter were to be interpreted as readings on an odometer:

          10 10 10 10⊥0 1 0 1
101

Clearly we need to know what the representation is in order to tell what a particular number stands for.

Here in summary form is the syntax for the base value function:

   (1) The right argument is the vector to be converted
   (2) The left argument is a vector (radix) of the same length
       stating the increment from each component to the next
   (3) The result is always a scalar
   (4) Exception: if either the left or right argument is a number
       repeated, it is sufficient to use a single component

The fourth point can be illustrated by the following:

          10⊥3 5 2 1
3521
          2⊥0 1 0 1
5
          10 10 10 10⊥5
5555

You should be able to see why we can't use a single component on <u>both</u> sides in the last example.

In 1 *CLASS* there is a prepared dyadic function called *BASE*. It is used in exactly the same way as ⊥ to demonstrate how the base value function works step by step. Let's try it in a sample problem:

```
     )LOAD 1 CLASS
SAVED  15.02.39 07/29/69
     10 BASE 0 1 0 1
INTERPRET AS 10   10   10 ⊥ 0   1   0   1
WEIGHTING VECTOR CALCULATIONS
COMPONENT 1 IS ×/10   10   10   OR   1000
COMPONENT 2 IS ×/10   10   OR   100
COMPONENT 3 IS ×/10   OR   10
COMPONENT 4 IS ×/   OR   1

+/1000   100   10   1 × 0   1   0   1   IS   101
```

The printout shows how the result 101 is arrived at through the use of
the weighting vector. Executing it with our room length problem, we have:

```
     1760 3 12 BASE 3 0 1
WEIGHTING VECTOR CALCULATIONS
COMPONENT 1 IS ×/3   12   OR   36
COMPONENT 2 IS ×/12   OR   12
COMPONENT 3 IS ×/   OR   1

+/36   12   1 × 3   0   1   IS   109
```

You can experiment with BASE yourself, using other right arguments and
radices.

Representation

Like so many of the other functions we've encountered so far in APL, there
is a function that "undoes" the work of the base value function, i.e.,
converts from a value to some predetermined representation. Appropriately,
it is called representation or encode, and its symbol is ⊤ (upper shift N).
Thus, if we execute

```
     2 2 2 2⊥0 1 0 1
5
```

then the function ⊤ brings back our initial argument:

```
     2 2 2 2⊤5
0   1   0   1
```

Here are our room length and odometer problems in reverse:

```
     1760 3 12⊤109
3   0   1
     10 10 10 10⊤3521
3   5   2   1
```

This latter example describes how 3521 would appear on a 4-position
odometer. How would 13521 appear on the same odometer?

```
      10 10 10 10⊤13521
3   5   2   1
```

We can draw an analogy here. It's like an odometer which reads only up to
9999 and then starts over from 0 again. In fact, in this case the right
argument has been reduced by 10*4 and

```
      (10*4)|13521
3521
```

What happens when we're not sure how many components are needed in the
radix vector, yet we don't want to lose anything, as was unfortunately the
case in the example above? Typing a zero as the left most component puts
everything left in the first component of the result, as shown below:

```
      0 10 10 10⊤43521
43   5   2   1
      0 60⊤130
2   10
```

The simulation *REP* in 1 *CLASS* does for ⊤ what *BASE* did for ⊥ in the
last section. Execute *REP* for these cases:

```
      10 10 10 10 REP 45321
COMPONENT 4 IS 10|45321 OR 1   AND   ⌊(45321-1)÷10 IS 4532
COMPONENT 3 IS 10|4532 OR 2    AND   ⌊(4532-2)÷10 IS 453
COMPONENT 2 IS 10|453 OR 3     AND   ⌊(453-3)÷10 IS 45
COMPONENT 1 IS 10|45 OR 5      AND   ⌊(45-5)÷10 IS 4

RESULT IS 5   3   2   1


      0 10 10 REP 13521
COMPONENT 3 IS 10|13521 OR 1   AND   ⌊(13521-1)÷10 IS 1352
COMPONENT 2 IS 10|1352 OR 2    AND   ⌊(1352-2)÷10 IS 135
COMPONENT 1 IS 0|135 OR 135    AND   REMAINING COMPONENTS ARE
   ZEROS
RESULT IS 135   2   1


      10 10 REP 3 4
RIGHT ARGUMENT MUST BE A SCALAR OR 1-COMPONENT VECTOR
      10 10⊤3 4
RANK ERROR
      10 10 ⊤ 3 4
            ∧
```

Both representation and base value yield some rather interesting results
when used with negative numbers and nonintegers. Here are a few illustrations, but you are advised to explore their uses on your own. You will find
the *BASE* and *REP* functions helpful here.

```
      ¯2 3 0⊥7 5 ¯4
¯4
      5 2 ¯6⊤487
4  1  1
      2.16⊥5 4 2
34.147445
```

PROBLEMS

1. Drill

    (3ρ40)⊥8 7 2   2⊥5 1 9 6   , 10⊥9 8 2 1 6

    1 ‾4.1 .8⊥1 2 3   7 8 9⊥7 8 9   3⊤5217

    3 3⊤5217   3 3 3⊤5217   (5ρ3)⊤5217

    (4ρ8)⊥‾14   1 4 6⊤345   2 4 5⊤78

2. Write APL expressions

    A) to convert 2 gallons, 8 quarts and 1 pint to pints
    B) to find the number of ounces in 3 tons, 568 pounds and 13 ounces

3. Find the

    A) base-8 value of 2 1 7 7
    B) base-2 value of 1 0 1 1 0 1
    C) base-3 representation of 8933
    D) base-5 representation of 4791

4. Earlier in the text the residue and floor functions were used to sepa-
    rate the integer and fractional parts of a number. Show how this
    separation can be done in a single step by using the encode function.

5. Write expressions that will show that ⊥ and ⊤ are inverses of each other
    (not, however, for all arguments).

    (For additional problems on ⊥ and ⊤, see end of chapter 23)

CHAPTER 23

Applications of base value and representation

Hexadecimal numbering system

In this chapter we will explore some of the possible uses for the functions ⊥ and ⊤, introduced before. One obvious application lies in the conversion of decimally represented information to another numbering system. The bases 2, 8 and 16 have been used for computers and, for our first illustration, let's build an algorithm to convert from the decimal to the hexadecimal (base-16) system.

Just as in our ordinary base-10 system, we require ten distinct symbols (0 1 2...9), so in the base-16 system 16 symbols are needed. Larger numbers are represented by adding positions on the left (provided, of course, we are talking about whole numbers and not fractions). For example, 10 is a two-position number, 9 being the largest number able to be represented by a single symbol.

In the hexadecimal system the symbols are 0 1 2...9 A .B C D E F. If you were to ask why the letters A...F, the most appropriate response would be "why not?" We need some single symbol for each of the numbers 10 through 15. New symbols could be invented or old ones used differently (like upside down or with a bar across them), but it really doesn't matter as long as they are used consistently.

A decimal system number can be represented in so-called expanded notation as follows:

$$\text{Number: } 6325$$
$$\text{Decimal Expansion: } 6\times10^3 + 3\times10^2 + 2\times10^1 + 5\times10^0$$

We can define a hexadecimal number in exactly the same way, except that powers of 16 instead of powers of 10 are involved:

$$\text{Number: } 1AF2$$
$$\text{Hexadecimal Expansion: } 1\times16^3 + 10\times16^2 + 15\times16^1 + 2\times16^0$$

which is equivalent to 6898 in decimal form.

In 1 *CLASS* there is a dyadic function *HEXA* which makes the conversion for us. The left argument is the number of positions we want to see represented, the right argument is the number to be converted:

```
      )LOAD 1 CLASS
SAVED  15.02.39 07/29/69
      3 HEXA 254
OFE
      2 HEXA 254
FE
      1 HEXA 254
E
```

Let's look at *HEXA*:

```
      ∇HEXA[□]∇
   ∇ R←N HEXA X
[1]    R←'0123456789ABCDEF'[1+(Nρ16)⊤X]
   ∇
```

$N\rho16$ generates a vector of N components, each of which is 16. If N is, say, 3, and X is 254, $(N\rho16)\top X$ is

```
      (3ρ16)⊤254
0   15  14
```

In expanded notation this is the same as

$$0\times16^2 + 15\times16^1 + 14\times16^0$$

and, on looking through the vector of literals 0 1 2...F, we see that since the 0 is in the first position, 1 in the second position, etc., it is necessary to add 1 to $(3\rho16)\top254$ to pick up the subscripts for the right characters:

```
      1+(3ρ16)⊤254
1   16  15
```

257 is a number which needs three positions in hexadecimal notation:

$$1\times16^2 + 0\times16^1 + 1\times16^0$$

Let's execute *HEXA* for this number, specifying first four and then two positions:

```
      4 HEXA 257
0101
      2 HEXA 257
01
```

We get a false impression if we don't specify sufficient positions. Incidentally, 0101 is a vector of characters:

```
      ρ4 HEXA 257
4
```

Do you see why?

Hexadecimal to decimal conversion

What about the reverse operation, converting from hexadecimal to decimal representation? Such a function, called DEC, exists already in 1 $CLASS$. We'll use it before displaying it. It is monadic and requires quotes for the argument:

        DEC '$0FE$'
254

It seems OK in this example, so let's display it:

        $\nabla DEC[\Box]\nabla$
      ∇ $R \leftarrow DEC$ H
[1] $R \leftarrow 16 \bot^{-}1 + $'$0123456789ABCDEF$'$\iota H$
      ∇

H represents the vector of literals in hexadecimal notation. The dyadic iota with H on the right picks up the positions of the corresponding characters in the left argument. Trying this out with $0FE$, we get

        '$0123456789ABCDEF$'ι'$0FE$'
1   16   15

which is one position too high to use as the right argument of $\bot$. Hence $^{-}1$ is added before the base value function is applied:

        $16 \bot 0$ 15 14
254

It should be clear why no left argument is needed in DEC. The base value function will automatically extend the scalar 16 in length to match the length of the right argument.

If we were to try DEC with undefined characters, say, WER, we get a result:

        DEC 'WER'
4336

but it is meaningless. To find out why, remember what the dyadic iota does for an element in the right argument not found on the left. It will produce the vector 17 15 17, and after adding $^{-}1$ to each component we have

        $16 \bot 16$ 14 16
4336

Now try

        DEC 5 $HEXA$ 321
321
        DEC 2 $HEXA$ 321
65

and DEC and $HEXA$ are inverse functions, provided that sufficient positions have been allowed.

Check protection

Another practical application is demonstrated by the function *CP*, which
fills in the space before a number with stars up to a predetermined position.
Its use for check protection should be evident. *CP*, which is in 1 *CLASS*,
is dyadic. The left argument is the total number of places to be filled up,
including the dollar amount, and the right argument is the amount of the
check. Here are a few examples:

```
      5 CP 301
**301
      5 CP 12345
12345
      5 CP 00301
**301
```

Let's look at *CP*:

```
      ∇CP[□]∇
    ∇ R←N CP X;P
[1]   R←'0123456789'[1+(Nρ10)⊤X]
[2]   P←⁻1+(R≠'0')ι1
[3]   R←(Pρ'*'),P↓R
    ∇
```

Line 1 makes a vector of characters out of X, the argument, and adds enough
0's in front to make ρR equal to N. Line 2 sets P as one less than the
index of the first nonzero character, while line 3 puts into R P copies of
* followed by all but the first P components of R.

PROBLEMS

1. Define a function to remove commas from a character vector consisting
    of digits and commas, and convert the result to a numerical vector.

2. Write an *APL* expression which determines whether or not, for a given
    three-digit number N, N is equal to the sum of the cubes of its digits.

3. Use ⊥ to write a dyadic function *EVAL* to evaluate at the point X a
    polynomial with coefficients C (descending powers of X). Compare with
    page 46.

4. For $M←'1234583'$, what are the differences between each of the fol-
    lowing expressions?

    $$M←⁻1+'0123456789'ιM$$

    $$M←10⊥⁻1+'0123456789'ιM$$

    $$M←10⊥0\ 1\ 2\ 3\ 4\ 5\ 6\ 7\ 8\ 9['0123456789'ιM]$$

5. It is a fact that a number N is divisible by 11 if the alternating sum
    of its digits is divisible by 11. Construct an expression that uses
    the encode function with this condition to test for divisibility by 11.

CHAPTER 24:

Branching

One of the more prominent features of most programming languages is the
concept of branching. Some of you who are familiar with other languages
may be wondering why this notion, which involves selection of only some
of the steps of a function or causes repeated execution under specified
conditions, hasn't yet been presented in this course. The reason is due
to the nature of *APL*, which makes it possible to solve many problems in
a more straightforward way without branching.

The branch instruction

Whenever an algorithm requires a decision to be made as to what the next
step should be, based on the results of some previous step, a branch is
generally called for. This is nothing more than an instruction to alter
the regular sequence of steps.

We can demonstrate how this can be done by using a function called *SORT* in
1 *CLASS*. The problem which *SORT* is designed to handle is a very simple
one: Rearrange the components of a vector (here 3 1 4 3 1 3 4) in ascending
order. Actually there isn't any need to write a function to do this, since
the grade up function can be used with subscripting to accomplish the same
thing very concisely (see page 154). But, at least, it will give us a feel
for how branching can be used.

Let's talk ourselves through the algorithm needed to solve the problem. The
first and most obvious step is to start with a clean sheet of paper. Next
we pick out the smallest value in the vector, see how many times it occurs,
and write it down that number of times. Then we would cross these off the
original vector, go back and pick out the smallest value from what's left
and repeat the process above until all the numbers are used up.

It isn't any great challenge to design a machine to go through the repeti-
tive steps, but it would need a safeguard built into it. We know when to
stop; the machine would have to be instructed, otherwise it would continue
its sequence of steps indefinitely.

This means that our algorithm would have to have a step which says in
effect "look each time through to see if any numbers are left in the
vector; if there are any, go on, if not, stop."

169

Now we are ready to build the function $SORT$. Since only one argument is required, let's make it monadic and return an explicit result. Here is the header:

$\nabla R \leftarrow SORT \ X$

To start with, R has nothing in it (corresponding to the clean sheet of paper). Thus, line 1 should be

[1] $R \leftarrow \iota 0$

The next step is to look for the smallest number in X, which is $\lfloor / X$.

But we need as many copies of it as there are in X. So what we require is really $(X = \lfloor / X) / X$ to select them. Since these are to be added onto R, we can set line 2 as follows:

[2] $R \leftarrow R , (X = \lfloor / X) / X$

We then look at what's left, which is the new X, namely, $(X \neq \lfloor / X) / X$:

[3] $X \leftarrow (X \neq \lfloor / X) / X$

This is as far as we can go, and now we have to repeat the process. In APL the instruction which directs the system to a step out of the normal sequence is the right pointing arrow →, found on the same key as the specification arrow ←. The arrow, which may be read as "go to" or "branch to," has to be followed by some value to complete the instruction. In this case

[4] $\rightarrow 2$

is the obvious step.

Unfortunately, we have neglected to tell the system when to stop, so it will loop around steps 2, 3 and 4 forever. One logical place for this checkpoint is just before step 2. Now what should it be? $0 = \rho X$ will yield a 1 if X is empty, a 0 if X is not. Our problem is how to write the complete statement so that this extra line will cause execution to fall through to the next line (i.e., continue cycling) or cease, depending on the state of X. An instruction which does this is

[1.5] $\rightarrow 0 \times \iota 0 = \rho X$

Here is how this works. If ρX is 0 (X is empty), then the instruction reads "branch to 0" ($0 \times \iota 1$ is 0). But there is no line 0 in the function, and we are in effect asking the system to leave the function and return to desk calculator mode. Branching to <u>any</u> line number which isn't in the function will do the same thing, namely, exit us from the function. Branching to line 0 is guaranteed to work, however, because no function, no matter how big, has a line 0. The header doesn't count as a line here, even though we refer to it as [0] in function editing.

What if X isn't empty? Then $0 \times \iota 0$ is a vector of length 0, and the instruction reads "branch to an empty vector." A reasonable interpretation might

consider this to be no branch at all, and indeed this is the way it is
used in *APL*. It simply causes execution to continue with the next statement.

$\times\iota$ is an interesting combination of *APL* functions. Its action is such
that when it occurs it can be read as "if," so that our line above can be
read "branch to 0 if *X* is empty." Incidentally, if the system is directed
to branch to a nonempty vector, only the first component is significant.

All these steps have been incorporated into the function *SORT*, and the
lines renumbered. Load 1 *CLASS* and display *SORT*:

```
      )LOAD 1 CLASS
SAVED   15.02.39 07/29/69
      ∇SORT[□]∇
    ∇ R←SORT X
[1]   R←ι0
[2]   →0×ι0=ρX
[3]   R←R,(X=⌊/X)/X
[4]   X←(X≠⌊/X)/X
[5]   →2
    ∇
```

Can you think of a simple way to use the compression function with branching
in line 2 to accomplish the same result?

Let's try *SORT* on a couple of vectors:

```
      SORT 5 3 2
2   3   5
      SORT 5 3 1 5 4 2
1   2   3   4   5   5
```

It seems to work satisfactorily, so we'll go on to a second example, the
function *CMP*, introduced earlier on page 141. Here is the original
version, which doesn't contain any branches and prints out *GREATER*, *EQUAL*
or *LESS* after comparing its two arguments:

```
      ∇CMP[□]∇
    ∇ A CMP B
[1]   ((A>B)/'GREATER'),((A=B)/'EQUAL'),(A<B)/'LESS'
    ∇
```

Comparing 3 and 5:

```
      3 CMP 5
LESS
```

Labels

An equivalent function which does involve branching is *CMPX*:

```
        ∇CMPX[□]∇
     ∇  A  CMPX  B
[1]     →BIGGER×ιA>B
[2]     →SMALLER×ιA<B
[3]    'EQUAL'
[4]     →0
[5]   BIGGER:'GREATER'
[6]     →0
[7]   SMALLER:'LESS'
     ∇
```

A new feature is used in *CMPX*, the colon on lines 5 and 7 as a separator. The name immediately to the left of the colon is called a <u>label</u>. In *CMPX* the label *BIGGER* appears on line 5. Branching to *BIGGER* is equivalent to branching to line 5, the value of the label being set as soon as function definition is completed.

Why use a label? It is convenient way to branch if there is any possibility that the function is to be later edited and lines added or deleted. For example, if line 1 tells us to branch to line 5 and we add a line between 1 and 2, line 5 would then be what line 4 is now, namely, a command to exit the function. So labels direct us to specific points in the function, rather than specific line numbers.

Labels are local constants and hence not known outside the function, as can be seen by inspection of the following list of variables, which is from 1 *CLASS*:

```
        )VARS
B         CIRCUIT  D         HELP     M        MILEAGE PREVIOUSTIME
SPL       STOP     TAB0      TAB1     TAB2     TAB3    X          Y
```

Having labels local instead of global avoids confusion among labels in different functions, and prevents the user from accidentally resetting the label outside the function. However, unlike local variables, they must <u>not</u> be listed in the header of the function. Also, they are automatically respecified each time function execution is initiated.

CMPX, which has the two labels *BIGGER* and *SMALLER*, will be used to show these features. Notice what happens when we put the label in the header:

```
        ∇CMPX[0□15]
[0]    A  CMPX  B

[0]    A  CMPX  B;BIGGER
[1]    ∇
        3 CMPX 2
VALUE ERROR
CMPX[1]  →BIGGER×ιA>B
         ∧
        →0                        (to remove the suspension)
```

In order to illustrate the behavior of the label when the function is suspended, let's edit *CMPX* to include a variable *R* which has no value assigned:

```
        ∇CMPX[ 0[]15]
[0]      A CMPX B;BIGGER
                  ///////
[0]      A CMPX B
[1]      [5.5]R∇
```

Now we'll execute the function for given values of A and B:

```
        3 CMPX 2
GREATER
VALUE ERROR
CMPX[6] R
        ^
```

BIGGER has a value assigned to it within this suspended function:

```
        BIGGER
5
```

Suppose we try to assign a value to BIGGER :

```
        BIGGER←3
SYNTAX ERROR
        BIGGER←3
        ^
```

The system prevents us from so doing while in suspension.

In addition, labels are found in the list of suspensions:

```
        )SIV
CMPX[6] *           A          B          BIGGER   SMALLER
```

Editing of a suspended function contains a few pitfalls, as can be seen
from the following display:

```
        ∇CMPX[ 1[]6]
[1]      →BIGGER×ιA>B
         //////6
[1]      →LARGER×ιA>B
[2]      [5[]6]
[5]      BIGGER:'GREATER'
         //////6
[5]      LARGER:'GREATER'
[6]      ∇
SI DAMAGE
        )SIV
        * A          B          BIGGER   SMALLER
        →1
        @
        →0
        @
        )SIV
        @
```

```
        3 CMPX 2
GREATER
VALUE ERROR
CMPX[6]  R
           ∧
        )SIV
CMPX[6]  *          A          B          LARGER   SMALLER
        →0
```

The message *SI DAMAGE* indicates that the state indicator command is not operating properly, as can be seen from the fact that *CMPX[6]* is missing from the printout below it.

Finally, here is another version of the same function. This one is called *CMPY*:

```
        ∇CMPY[□]∇
     ∇ A CMPY B
[1]     →4+2×SIGN A-B
[2]     'LESS'
[3]     →0
[4]     'EQUAL'
[5]     →0
[6]     'GREATER'
     ∇
```

Line 1 is the key here. It subtracts *B* from *A* and uses the function *SIGN* (page 72) to return 1, ‾1 or 0 depending on what comes out of the subtraction. The monadic signum function could be used in place of *SIGN* if we so desired. The result of *SIGN* is multiplied by 2 and 4 is added. Thus, if *A* is greater than *B*, *A-B* is positive and line 1 causes a branch to line 6. If *A* is less than *B*, we branch to line 2, while if *A=B*, we go to line 4, which is pretty sneaky, albeit effective way to go about it.

One last comment about branching. It is a powerful tool in defining functions. Branch if you must, but with a little extra care and ingenuity on your part, you will often find a way to eliminate the need for it.

Rules for branching

We may summarize the rules for branching in function definition as follows:

→   (any *APL* expression)

is

(1) INVALID if the expression results in other than a nonnegative integer or a vector whose first component (the only one which can cause a branch) is a nonnegative integer or a valid label.

(2) VALID if the expression results in

(a) an empty vector, which causes a branch to the next statement
(b) a nonnegative integer outside the range of statement numbers of the function, which causes an exit from the function
(c) a nonnegative integer inside the range of statement numbers of the function, which causes a branch to that line number

(d) a label, which causes a branch to that line of the function
on which the label is to be found

Examples of branch instructions

For the benefit of the reader, here is a list of different ways of writing
branch instructions in APL. Labels may be used in place of line numbers.
Also, the membership function and any appropriate logical or relational
function may be used in place of those listed.

(1) Branch unconditionally to a fixed point in the program:

$$\rightarrow 5$$
$$\rightarrow LABEL$$
$$\rightarrow 3 \times B + I \leftarrow I + 1$$

(2) Branch unconditionally out of the program:

$$\rightarrow 0 \quad \text{(or any nonexistent line number)}$$

(3) Branch to one of two possible lines:

$$\rightarrow (L1,L2)[1+X \geq Y]$$
$$\rightarrow ((X \geq Y),\sim X \geq Y)/L1,L2$$

(4) Branch to one of several lines:

$$\rightarrow ((X>Y),(X<Y),X=Y)/L1,L2,L3$$
$$\rightarrow I \phi L1,L2,L3,\ldots \quad (I \ IS \ A \ COUNTER)$$

(5) Branch to a given line or drop through to the next line:

$$\rightarrow (X \geq Y)/L1$$
$$\rightarrow (X \geq Y)\rho L1$$
$$\rightarrow L1 \times \iota X \geq Y$$
$$\rightarrow L1 \lceil \iota X \geq Y$$
$$\rightarrow (I \phi L1,L2,L3) \times \iota X \geq Y$$
$$\rightarrow L1 \times \iota X \geq I \leftarrow I+1$$
$$\rightarrow (X \geq Y)\rho \lfloor /L1,L2,L3$$
$$\rightarrow ((A<0),A>0)/L1,L2$$
$$\rightarrow L1 \ IF \ C$$

where IF is defined as follows for those users who prefer English in
their instructions:

$$\nabla A \leftarrow L1 \ IF \ C \qquad\qquad \nabla A \leftarrow L1 \ IF \ C$$
$$[1] \quad A \leftarrow C/L1 \nabla \qquad\qquad [1] \quad A \leftarrow C \rho L1 \nabla$$

It has the advantage of being able to handle vector arguments which $\times \iota$
can't, and will work with 0 or without it.

(6) Branch out of the program or drop through to the next line:

$$\rightarrow(X \geq Y)/0$$
$$\rightarrow(\vee/,X \geq Y)/0$$
$$\rightarrow 0 \times \iota X \geq Y$$

(7) Branch out of the program or to a specific line:

$$\rightarrow((X \geq Y),X<Y)/L1,0$$
$$\rightarrow L1 \times X \geq Y$$

(8) Branch to a given line and specify and/or display:

$$\rightarrow L1, \rho \square \leftarrow 'MESSAGE'$$
$$\rightarrow L1, \rho X \leftarrow 3 \quad 4\rho \iota 12$$

Finally, as a reminder, to remove a suspension, execute

$$\rightarrow$$
$$\rightarrow 0$$

and to branch to a particular point in a suspended program,

$$PROGRAM \ [9]$$
$$\rightarrow 12$$

PROBLEMS

1. Tell what each of the following commands does:

    A) $\rightarrow((5<W),5>W)/3 \ 2$

    B) $\rightarrow 3 \times \iota A = 8$

    C) $\rightarrow END \times Y>,R \leftarrow 1 \quad 1\rho 1$

    D) $\rightarrow(\vee/,B \epsilon C)/7$

    E) $\rightarrow(5 \ 0)[1+A>C]$

    F) $\rightarrow ^-1\uparrow\phi3 \ 4 \ 7 \ 9$

    G) $\rightarrow 8 \times \iota 0 \neq J \leftarrow J - 1$

    H) $\rightarrow 4 \times(|X) \geq I \leftarrow I + 1$

    I) $\rightarrow AGAIN \times \iota N = 2 \times 1\rho R \leftarrow 2 \quad 4\rho 5 \ 7 \ 1 \ 8$

2. Let T be a vector of "trash" characters, some of which may occur in the literal vector V. Define an APL function that will eliminate the trash from V.

3. Write a program to determine all three-digit numbers between P and Q such that if the final digit is eliminated, the result divides the original number.

4. Use branching to find the median of a set of numbers.   (See problem 11, chapter 21 for more information about the median.)

5. Define a dyadic function $DUPL$ that will locate all occurrences of some scalar N in a vector V and print out an appropriate message if the desired scalar is not present.

6. Design an APL function so that it ignores all nonscalar input and takes the square root of any scalar argument.

7. Take the opening two sentences of this chapter and define a function to sort them out alphabetically, eliminating all punctuation marks and blanks. Your output should list all the A's followed by the B's, etc.

8. The mode of a set of data is defined as the most frequently occurring number in the set. Write a program to find the mode.

9. The Fibonacci series is of the form 1 1 2 3 5 8 13..., where each term after the first two is the sum of the preceding two terms. Define a function which prints out N terms of the series.

10. Define a function which will produce a histogram of a vector A of nonnegative integers, i.e., the height of the histogram for $A[1]$ is $A[1]$, the height for $A[5]$ is $A[5]$, etc. Show how the histogram can be "cleaned up" by replacing the 0's with blanks and the 1's with $*$.

11. Use branching to construct a function which prints out an annual compound interest table. Design your function to produce three columns, the first to be the year, the second the value of the principal at the beginning of the year, and the third the interest accumulated during the year. Include appropriate column headings and round off each figure to the nearest cent.

CHAPTER 25:

Diagnostic aids

Until the last chapter, execution of defined functions was relatively straightforward, proceeding from one line to the next in order. But since we introduced branching, it is possible for the sequence of steps to become quite involved. At such times it is often desirable to be able to follow what is happening on certain lines during execution. And, if problems arise, knowledge of what occurs at each step may be a definite help to us in debugging the program.

APL provides two controls for tracing and stopping execution of defined functions. These will be examined and illustrated in the following sections.

Trace and stop controls

Our guinea-pig function will be *SORT*, which is in 1 *CLASS*:

```
        )LOAD  1  CLASS
SAVED   15.02.39  07/29/69
        ∇SORT[□]∇
     ∇  R←SORT X
[1]     R←ι0
[2]     →0×ι0=ρX
[3]     R←R,(X=⌊/X)/X
[4]     X←(X≠⌊/X)/X
[5]     →2
     ∇
```

The interesting lines here are 3 and 4. We can trace execution on them to see what has been put into *R* (line 3) and *X* (line 4) by the command

```
        TΔSORT←3  4
        @
```

TΔSORT is called the <u>trace vector</u> for the function *SORT*, and is set to trace lines 3 and 4. It will remain set to these lines in *SORT* until we remove it or change it. The trace lets us execute *SORT* and follow the progress of the trace. Here is an example:

```
        SORT 3 2 4 3 2 5
SORT[3] 2   2
SORT[4] 3   4   3   5
SORT[3] 2   2   3   3
SORT[4] 4   5
SORT[3] 2   2   3   3   4
SORT[4] 5
SORT[3] 2   2   3   3   4   5
SORT[4]
2   2   3   3   4   5
```

The first time through R receives $\iota 0$ and the vector 2 2, the smallest elements, while X is 3 4 3 5, which is what's left. The second time through 3 3 is added to R, and X has just 4 5 in it, etc.

If the next time we execute $SORT$ we want to change the trace vector, all that is necessary is to respecify $T \Delta SORT$. Without actually doing it at this point, what do you think should be specified if we want to drop the trace altogether?

Now let's look at the action of the stop control on $SORT$. It operates in much the same way as the trace, but has the effect of suspending the function just prior to the lines specified. For example, specify

```
        S∆SORT←ι5
        @
```

and execute

```
        SORT 3 2 3 2
```

```
SORT[1]
```

The response tells us where in the function we are suspended, the line number being the one to be executed next. This is confirmed by the state indicator:

```
        )SI
SORT[1] *
```

Since we are inside the function we might want to take a look at the values of the local and dummy variables, which are otherwise inaccessible to us. For instance:

```
        R
VALUE ERROR
        R
        ∧
```

We get a value error since $SORT$ is hung up just prior to line 1 and R hasn't been set yet. But X has already received a value:

```
        X
3   2   3   2
```

If we wanted to do so, X could be changed at this point by respecifying it. However, we'll continue with the execution of this function by using the branch command:

>   →1

SORT[2]

There is a stop on line 2 also, and in fact on every line in this function. Now we can get *R*:

>   *R*
>   @

No value error is returned here since on line 1 *R* was specified to be an empty vector, as shown by taking ρ*R* (remember we're still inside the function):

>   ρ*R*
0

Continuing, we get:

>   →2

SORT[3]
>   →3
SORT[3] 2   2

SORT[4]

The new value of *R*, 2 2, is printed out here because the trace is still set on lines 3 and 4. We could go on, but this should be enough to demonstrate how the stop works.

To turn it off, we respecify the stop vector as follows:

>   *S*Δ*SORT*←0
>   @

Since there is no line 0 (the header doesn't count in the numbering even though we can edit it by calling for [0]), the stop vector is no longer set. This is just like branching to line 0 to exit a function.

However, we are still suspended on line 4 of *SORT*:

>   )*SI*
SORT[4] *

Branching to line 4 continues the execution without any further suspensions but with the trace still on (we haven't taken it off yet):

>   →4
SORT[4] 3   3
SORT[3] 2   2   3   3
SORT[4]
2   2   3   3

This time we'll turn the trace off in the same manner as the stop:

        $T\Delta SORT\leftarrow 0$
        @

Now we try the state indicator

        $)SI$
        @

and we see that by having resumed execution in a function ($SORT$) which is completely executable and doesn't have any stops on it, we have removed the suspension.

$SORT$ can now be executed in the normal fashion:

        $SORT$ 2 3 4 1 2
1   2   2   3   4

It pays to be selective in setting the trace vector. For instance, suppose

        $T\Delta SORT\leftarrow \iota 5$

and we execute $SORT$:

```
        SORT  2  3  2  1  4  5
SORT[1]
SORT[2]
SORT[3]  1
SORT[4]  2    3    2    4    5
SORT[5]  2
SORT[2]
SORT[3]  1    2    2
SORT[4]  3    4    5
SORT[5]  2
SORT[2]
SORT[3]  1    2    2    3
SORT[4]  4    5
SORT[5]  2
SORT[2]
SORT[3]  1    2    2    3    4
SORT[4]  5
SORT[5]  2
SORT[2]
SORT[3]  1    2    2    3    4    5
SORT[4]
SORT[5]  2
SORT[2]  0
1    2    2    3    4    5
```

No useful information is obtained from the trace on lines 1, 2 and 5.

A final note—both the trace and stop control vectors can be used as a line or part of a line in a defined function, since they are valid APL instructions. See the function $TRACETIME$ on page 189 for an illustration.

Also, the trace and stop vectors are <u>not</u> variables and are deleted when the function for which they are set is deleted!

Recursion

Sometimes it is necessary for a function to appear on one of the lines of its own definition. When this happens, it is said to be <u>recursively defined</u>. Here is an example, a defined function to calculate factorials, and found in 1 *CLASS*. The function is called *FACT*, but before displaying it, let's look at the definition of N! in conventional notation:

$$N! = \begin{cases} \text{undefined for N not a nonnegative integer} \\ 1 \text{ if } N=0 \\ N \times (N-1)! \text{ if } N \neq 0 \end{cases}$$

By this definition 5! would be figured as

$$
\begin{aligned}
5! &= 5 \times 4! \\
&= 5 \times (4 \times 3!) \\
&= 5 \times (4 \times (3 \times 2!)) \\
&= 5 \times (4 \times (3 \times (2 \times 1!))) \\
&= 5 \times (4 \times (3 \times (2 \times (1 \times 0!)))) \\
&= 5 \times (4 \times (3 \times (2 \times (1 \times 1))))
\end{aligned}
$$

This is the recursive approach.

Now for the function *FACT*, which carries out a recursive calculation of a factorial:

```
      ∇FACT[□]∇
    ∇ R←FACT N;NM1
[1]    →0×ιN≠|LN
[2]    →6×ιN=0
[3]    NM1←N-1
[4]    R←N×FACT NM1
[5]    →0
[6]    R←1
    ∇
```

The local variable *NM1* stands for $N-1$ and is useful for tracing the function. Line 1 causes a branch to 0 if N is not a positive integer or 0. Line 2 branches to 6 if N is 0, at which point R is set to 1 (since !0 is 1). If N isn't 0 line 3 sets *NM1* while line 4 sets R to $N \times FACT$ $N-1$, which will itself result in execution of *FACT*. Each time the function comes to line 4, it gets deeper and deeper into successive levels of execution until N works its way down to 0. Then the system begins to work its way out to the surface again and finally exits on line 5.

Let's see if *FACT* 4 can be executed:

```
      FACT 4
24
```

This gives the same answer as !4 (since we set it up that way), but takes longer to execute:

```
      !4
24
```

If we set a trace on *FACT* , we can see how it develops. Lines 3, 4 and 6
are our best bets here for tracing:

```
        TΔFACT←3 4 6
        FACT 4
FACT[3] 3
FACT[3] 2
FACT[3] 1
FACT[3] 0
FACT[6] 1
FACT[4] 1
FACT[4] 2
FACT[4] 6
FACT[4] 24
24
```

The first time through line 3 sets *NM1* to be 3. But when execution drops
through to the next line, in order to execute *FACT* 4, *FACT* 3 has to be
calculated first. So the system cycles through the first three steps
again, and this time the trace on line 3 shows that *NM1* is 2. This will
continue until *NM1* is 0. At this point, when the system tries to calculate
FACT 0 it loops through steps 1 and 2 and branches to 6, yielding a 1.

Meanwhile, back on line 4 there finally is a value to put in *R*, namely, 1,
which is followed by 2, 6 and 24 in succession as the function works its
way out.

Now let's turn the trace off and set the stop control at 6 to explore
what's happening near the end of the function:

```
        TΔFACT←0
        SΔFACT←6
        FACT 4

FACT[6]
```

We are suspended just prior to line 6. The state indicator shows some
interesting results:

```
        )SI
FACT[6] *
FACT[4]
FACT[4]
FACT[4]
FACT[4]
```

Line 4 is listed four times as pending, which isn't surprising since we
are held up on that line that many times, each time getting deeper into
the function while waiting for *NM1* to reach 0.

We can get out by branching to line 6, which our previous trace shows we
won't encounter again:

```
      →6
24
```

If this is what we get into with an argument 4, what do you suppose would happen if we ask for *FACT* 50? This will take quite a while, and we may want to interrupt execution with the ATTN button before line 6 is reached:

```
      FACT 50
```

```
FACT[2]
```

We get a suspension on line 2. Let's see what the state indicator shows:

```
      )SI
FACT[2] *
FACT[4]
FACT[4]
FACT[4]
FACT[4]
FACT[4]
```

Execution of this list has been interrupted by the use of the ATTN button, since otherwise it would be apt to run on for some time.

What happens if we try to get out of this mess? If we branch to line 6, it might go on a lot longer while the system worked its way out. Branching to 0 will get us out, as indeed will typing → alone:

```
      →0
VALUE ERROR
FACT[4]  R←N×FACT N⍱1
              ∧
```

We get a value error because *FACT* hasn't been set yet. As a matter of fact (no pun intended!), any solution we come up with to get out, since branching to 0 didn't work (check this by executing)*SI* again), will be expensive if it doesn't involve destroying the function.

At this point the function is in a pretty sad state. We are suspended at great depth. The sequence of commands that will get us out is to first save the active workspace, then clear, and copy the saved workspace. *CONTINUE* is always available to us (CAUTION! don't use for long term storage), so we'll save into *CONTINUE*:

```
      )SAVE CONTINUE
8.58.14  04/03/70
      )CLEAR
CLEAR WS
      )COPY CONTINUE
SAVED    8.58.14  04/03/70
```

The *COPY* command copies all the global objects in *CONTINUE*, but won't copy suspensions. However, loading *CONTINUE* will bring along all the suspensions associated with the functions in *CONTINUE*. If we don't want to keep the function, the easiest way out would be to delete it with the *ERASE* command, or drop the entire workspace without saving it. These

alternatives may be unacceptable if the workspace and function are important to the user. Just remember that copying an entire workspace uses
up a considerable amount of CPU time.

PROBLEMS

1. Trace the execution of each of the functions developed in the problem
    section at the end of chapter 24, problems 2, 7 and 8.

2. The function below uses the Euclidean algorithm to get the greatest
    common divisor of the two arguments:

```
         ∇ Z←A GCD B
    [1]    Z←A
    [2]    A←A|B
    [3]    B←Z
    [4]    →A≠0
         ∇
```

    Enter the function GCD in your own workspace and trace its execution
    for A←75 and B←105.

3. ACK is a function constructed for the purpose of proving that nonprimi-
    tive recursive functions do exist, and is named after its creator (see
    Communications of the ACM, page 114, Vol. 8, No. 2, February, 1965).
    Follow the execution of ACK with the trace and stop controls:

```
         ∇ R←I ACK J
    [1]    →(0=I,J)/ 4 3
    [2]    →0,R←(I-1) ACK I ACK J-1
    [3]    →0,R←(I-1) ACK 1
    [4]    R←J+1
         ∇
```

    Use small values for I and J.

CHAPTER 26:

Miscellaneous APL functions

This chapter will be concerned with two groups of functions, one of which is helpful in a wide variety of mathematical algorithms, while the other gives information about the state of the *APL* system.

<u>Circular functions</u>

The operator symbol for this group is the large circle ○ (upper shift *O*). With one exception the functions are all dyadic, the left argument being one of the integers ‾7 to 7 and the right argument a scalar or vector (expressed in radians for the trigonometric functions):

0○*X*	$(1-X*2)*.5$
1○*X*	sine *X*
2○*X*	cosine *X*
3○*X*	tangent *X*
4○*X*	$(1+X*2)*.5$
5○*X*	hyperbolic sine of *X* (sinh *X*)
6○*X*	hyperbolic cosine of *X* (cosh *X*)
7○*X*	hyperbolic tangent of *X* (tanh *X*)
‾1○*X*	arcsin *X*
‾2○*X*	arccos *X*
‾3○*X*	arctan *X*
‾4○*X*	$(‾1+X*2)*.5$
‾5○*X*	arcsinh *X*
‾6○*X*	arccosh *X*
‾7○*X*	arctanh *X*

There is a monadic function which, strictly speaking, doesn't belong in this group, but is included for completeness:

○*X*	$X\times PI$

To get *PI* itself, execute

```
      ○1
3.141592654
```

The inverse (arc) functions return only the principal value of the angle:

```
      3○2
¯2.185039863
         ¯3○¯2.185039863
¯1.141592654
      3○1
1.557407725
         ¯3○1.557407725
1
```

so that the resultant of an expression like

```
      ¯3○3○0
0
```

will be the same as the right argument only if the angle lies in the proper quadrant. These are from -PI÷2 to +PI÷2 for the sin and tan, and from -PI to +PI for the cos function. Further details can be obtained from any standard text on trigonometry.

The functions can be shown to satisfy the usual trigonometric identities, a few of which are illustrated here:

```
      (3○ι5)=((1○ι5)÷2○ι5)
1   1   1   1   1
```

which corresponds to the identity

$$\tan X = (\sin X)/\cos X$$

in conventional notation, and

```
      (((1○4)*2)+(2○4)*2)=1
1
```

analogous to

$$\sin^2 X + \cos^2 X = 1$$

The hyperbolic functions are defined in conventional notation as follows:

$$\sinh X = \frac{e^X - e^{-X}}{2} \qquad \cosh X = \frac{e^X + e^{-X}}{2} \qquad \tanh X = \frac{\sinh X}{\cosh X}$$

This can easily be demonstrated on the terminal:

```
      5○3.8
22.33940686
      ((*3.8)-*-3.8)÷2
22.33940686
      6○2
3.762195691
      ((*2)+*-2)÷2
3.762195691
```

```
      7○6
0.9999877117
      (5○6)÷6○6
0.9999877117
      (((6○4.4)*2)-(5○4.4)*2)=1
1
```

This last example is one of the fundamental hyperbolic identities:

$$\cosh^2 X - \sinh^2 X = 1$$

In addition to their uses in problems involving the trig functions, to those who are familiar with the calculus the value of having a complete set of circular functions readily available will be obvious. For instance, to name just a few possibilities:

$$\frac{d}{dx} \sin X = \cos X$$

$$\frac{d}{dx} \arccos X = \frac{-1}{\sqrt{1-X^2}}$$

$$\int \frac{dx}{\sqrt{1+X^2}} = \operatorname{arcsinh} X + C$$

$$\int \operatorname{sech}^2 X dx = \tanh X + C$$

I-beam functions

The functions in this group are called I-beam because the symbol used, formed by overstriking ⊥ and ⊤, looks like the cross-section of an I-beam. They are monadic and defined only for certain integer arguments, each of which gives information about some current aspect of the *APL* system. Wherever clock times are involved, they are given in sixtieths of a second.

The first of these functions is I19, which gives the total time the user's keyboard has been unlocked in the current session:

```
      I19
38230
```

Another is I20:

```
      I20
3126710
```

Your result for this function, as indeed for all the I-beam functions, probably will be different from what is shown in the sample executions in this section. I20 gives the time of day. To represent it in a more meaningful fashion we'll use the representation function:

```
      60 60 60 60TI20
14   28   46   45
```

In our discussion of niladic headers in chapter 11, the example function
TIME was given. We have now reached the point where we can open it up
and see how it is constructed:

```
      )LOAD 1 CLASS
SAVED  15.02.39 07/29/69
      TIME
02:29:00 PM EASTERN
      ∇TIME[⎕]∇
    ∇ TIME;T
[1]      T← 2 12 60 60 60 ⊤⍳20
[2]      T←4ρT
[3]      T[2]←T[2]+12×T[2]=0
[4]      T←100⊥T
[5]      T←10,(2,6ρ10)⊤T
[6]      ('0123456789:'[1+T[3 4 1 5 6 1 7 8]]),' ',('AP'[1+T[2]]),
         'M EASTERN'
    ∇
```

Of course, this result could be off, since the time is set by the system
operator. However, the elapsed time between two events is fairly accurate.
Line 1 of *TIME* takes the current time, represents it in a mixed number
system, and assigns it to the local variable T. The 2 on the left stands
for the two time segments AM or PM. Line 2 throws away the last component
of T (sixtieths of a second), while the next line takes $T[2]$, which is
hours, and modifies it so that 0:05 is printed as 12:05. Lines 4 and 5
give the value of T in the base 100 and then extend it out. The last
line picks up the different components to give the display shown in the
result.

There is a function called *TRACETIME* that traces what is happening on
each line. It is niladic and can be executed simply by typing the name:

```
      TIME
02:31:09 PM EASTERN
      TRACETIME
TIME[1] 1   2   31   15   15
TIME[2] 1   2   31   15
TIME[3] 2
TIME[4] 1023115
TIME[5] 10  1   0   2   3   1   1   5
TIME[6] 02:31:15 PM EASTERN
```

Here is the function displayed:

```
      ∇TRACETIME[⎕]∇
    ∇ TRACETIME
[1]      T∆TIME←⍳6
[2]      TIME
[3]      T∆TIME←⍳0
    ∇
```

The trace control is first set on line 1, then *TIME* is called for, and
finally the trace is removed after execution.

I21 gives the CPU time since sign-on:

          I21
3

To find out how much CPU time has been used up to execute a particular function, all that is necessary is to take the difference in I21 before and after execution. This will be utilized later in a function called *CPUTIME* .

I22 gives the number of bytes still unassigned in the active workspace. Since each workspace has only a limited amount of storage, it is quite possible that we may not have enough space to store everything we want. For example:

          Y←ι10000
WS FULL
          Y←ι10000
             ∧

How much room is there? Each *APL* literal character uses up 1 byte, while each integer (up to 2*31) takes 4 bytes, except for 0 and 1, which require 1/8 byte. 8 bytes are needed for all other numbers.

At present, in the active workspace, we have

          I22
14932

bytes left. Now get a clean workspace and execute the function again:

)CLEAR
CLEAR WS
          I22
31868

which is the number of available bytes per workspace in this *APL* system. Some additional space is taken up in the management of the workspace. Before going on, this is a good time to remind you that a considerable amount of storage may be eaten up by suspended functions, so that it pays to find out what is wrong and remove the suspension.

Let's now reload 1 *CLASS* and look at I23 :

)LOAD 1 CLASS
SAVED 15.02.39 07/29/69
          I23
19

I23 gives the number of users currently on the system, including the *APL* operator, so that you can judge when a good time would be to get on the system if you have some heavy computing to do.

I24 gives the sign-on time:

          I24
3083695

so the total elapsed time since sign-on (in sixtieths of a second) is
(I20)-I24 .

I25 gives the current calendar date, with the day, month and year run
together:

```
      I25
42870
```

We can make it look more like a proper entry by executing

```
      100 100 100⊤I25
4  28  70
```

I26 furnishes the current value of the line counter. If no functions are
suspended, then I26 is 0, as in the present case:

```
      I26
0
```

If a function is suspended, it gives the number of the line on which the
most recent suspension occurred, and corresponds to the top entry of)SI .
It is also useful in branch instructions where it is desired to move ahead
N statements. This can be done by entering

```
      →N+I26
```

I27 is another listing of suspensions, giving just the line numbers to be
found currently under)SI :

```
      I27
      @
```

Here is an example combining a number of these functions. Display the function *TIMEFACT*:

```
      ∇TIMEFACT[□]∇
    ∇ TIMEFACT N;S
[1]    CPUTIME
[2]    ''
[3]    S←!N
[4]    CPUTIME
[5]    S←×/⍳N
[6]    CPUTIME
[7]    S←FACT N
[8]    CPUTIME
[9]    S←FACTLOOP N
[10]   CPUTIME
    ∇
```

This function obtains the factorial of *N* four different ways (lines 3, 5, 7
and 9) and uses the function *CPUTIME* to print out elapsed CPU time for
each execution.

Let's now look at *CPUTIME*:

```
        ∇CPUTIME[□]∇
     ∇ CPUTIME
[1]     0 60 60 60 T0⌈(I21)-PREVIOUSTIME
[2]     PREVIOUSTIME←I21
     ∇
```

All it does is subtract from the current CPU time, I21 , PREVIOUSTIME (a global variable) and represent it in a mixed number system. Then PREVIOUSTIME is updated by being set to the current value of the CPU time. If we attempt to use CPUTIME without setting PREVIOUSTIME we would get an error message, but PREVIOUSTIME has already been set:

```
        PREVIOUSTIME
0
        CPUTIME
0   0   0   19
```

Here is FACTLOOP :

```
        ∇FACTLOOP[□]∇
     ∇ R←FACTLOOP N
[1]     R←1
[2]     →0×ιN=0
[3]     R←R×N
[4]     N←N-1
[5]     →2
     ∇
```

It is monadic, sets R to 1 on line 1, and allows us to exit the function if N is 0 (line 2). Line 3 resets R to $R×N$, line 4 reduces N by 1, then loops back to line 2, etc. By setting R to 1 at the beginning, this also works for $N=0$.

Now try FACTLOOP 5:

```
        FACTLOOP 5
120
```

which is the same as

```
        !5
120
```

In examining the amount of time required for each of the algorithms in TIMEFACT, the first appearance of CPUTIME is used to clear out PREVIOUSTIME so that, in effect, we start from scratch after the initial line of the printout.

Let's try TIMEFACT 20 :

```
        TIMEFACT 20
0   0   0 11

0   0   0   1
0   0   0   1
0   0   0 51
0   0   0 31
```

!N and ×/ιN both require 1/60 seconds, while the recursive *FACT* and the iterative *FACTLOOP* need 51/60 and 31/60 seconds of CPU time, respectively. The amount of time required will, of course, differ from one system to another, so that your results will not necessarily be similar to those above.

TIMEFACT 50 shows the differences even more dramatically:

```
      TIMEFACT 50
0   0   0   3

0   0   0   1
0   0   0   3
0   0   2   5
0   0   1  17
```

I26 and I27 have some additional uses in connection with suspended functions. To illustrate these, do *FACT* 50 and suspend it with the ATTN button right after the return:

```
      FACT 50

FACT[3]
```

To see where we are:

```
      )SI
FACT[3] *
FACT[4]
FACT[4]
FACT[4]
FACT[4]
FACT[4]
FACT[4]
FACT[4]
```

and again ATTN is used to interrupt the list. We are obviously pending on line 4. But at what depth?

One way to get a picture of this which doesn't take quite so much time and room is to call for I27 :

```
      I27
3   4   4   4   4   4   4   4   4   4   4   4   4   4   4   4   4   4
    4   4   4   4   4   4   4   4   4
```

But it's a lot neater to ask for

```
      ρI27
28
```

to see how many lines there are in the listing.

While we're at it, we are still suspended on line 3:

```
      I26
3
```

so we'll remove the suspension by calling for

$\quad\quad\quad\rightarrow I26$
$3.04140932E64$

which is the same as !50.

$I28$ gives the type of terminal being used: 1 for correspondence terminals, 2 for all BCD terminals (except the IBM 1050), and 3 for the IBM 1050.

$I29$ gives the current user number. As an example, here is a function that only user number, say, 1421 can access:

```
        ∇FORYOUONLY
[1]     →(1421)≠I29)/0                    (This function is locked with
[2]     'THIS IS THE MESSAGE'∇            ∇.  See page 265 for discussion)
```

PROBLEMS

1. Drill

10○1 2	01÷180	20○1
180÷01	40ι3	30‾30ι5
‾201○○1÷2	‾10ι01	‾1 ‾201 10.5

2. Construct a table of sines of angles from 0 to $PI\div2$ radians in steps of $PI\div20$ radians.

3. Use the function $CPUTIME$ to compute the difference in computing time for calculating 2!10 and $(!10)\div(!2)\times!8$. See chapter 4 for a discussion of the algorithm.

4. Show that the following identity holds:

$$COS\ 2X = COS^2X - SIN^2X$$

5. Use $I25$ to construct a function that will express a date as MM/DD/YY.

6. Define a dyadic function $TIME$ whose arguments are scalars. The left argument X may be either 12 or 24, and the right argument Y may assume values 1, 2, or 3. The function is to furnish the time in either a 24-hour or 12-hour system, printing hours, minutes, and seconds if Y is 3, hours and minutes only if Y is 2, and hours only if Y is 1. Times are to be truncated with no rounding off if the value of the dropped seconds or minutes is 30 or more. Midnight is to be expressed as 00.

7. Use reduction to express the identity

$$SIN^2X + COS^2X = 1$$

Compare your version of the identity with that on page 187.

CHAPTER 27:

Multidimensional arrays

Except for some earlier applications of the dimension, restructure, and
ravel functions, just about all of our work has been with scalars and
vectors. Many of the other functions studied so far can take as arguments
arrays of rank higher than 1. In addition, there are a number of useful
functions specifically designed to make possible the manipulation of such
multidimensional arrays. These will be taken up in this and the next
few chapters.

Review

Our start will be a two-dimensional table which lists the number of
purchases made of three items, A, B, and C, during four successive weeks:

	A	B	C
week 1	1	2	0
2	1	3	2
3	3	4	2
4	3	3	0

This data is truly two-dimensional, since each entry in the table needs
two coordinates to specify it properly: the week and the item.

We can build this table with the restructure function but, before doing
so, execute $CLEAR$ so that we'll be able to operate in a fresh workspace:

)CLEAR
CLEAR WS

The twelve entries in the table will be stored in V. Note the row by row
order:

        V←1 2 0 1 3 2 3 4 2 3 3 0
        ρV
12

195

Since the table itself has four rows and three columns, we need

        4 3ρ V

    1   2   0
    1   3   2
    3   4   2
    3   3   0

This table will be used frequently in the chapter and, to save time, let's put it in M:

        $M \leftarrow 4$ 3ρ V

ρM gives the structure of the table:

        ρM
4   3

and, of course, M is the table itself:

        M

    1   2   0
    1   3   2
    3   4   2
    3   3   0

Dyadic operations on matrices

There are a number of things we can do to manipulate the components of M. For instance, we can increase each component by 2:

        2+M

    3   4   2
    3   5   4
    5   6   4
    5   5   2

or divide it by 3:

        $M \div 3$

    0.3333333333   0.6666666667   0
    0.3333333333   1   0.6666666667
    1   1.333333333   0.6666666667
    1   1   0

If we had another matrix of the same size, the two could be added or multiplied or what have you, component by component. Rather than define another matrix, we'll use M itself:

```
      M+M

 2    4    0
 2    6    4
 6    8    4
 6    6    0
      M×M

 1    4    0
 1    9    4
 9   16    4
 9    9    0
```

Note that this latter example is <u>not</u> ordinary matrix multiplication (to be covered in a later chapter). It is an extension of our earlier rules for multiplying two vectors, component by component. In fact, the rules developed on page 13 with scalar and vector arguments for all standard scalar dyadic functions hold equally well for matrices.

But why stop there? If they hold for matrices, why not for arrays of rank 3 and higher? This is indeed the case, the only stipulation being that the arrays have to have the same dimensions and rank. If you were to violate this rule and try to perform dyadic operations on some matrices by hand, you will quickly see the necessity for it.

There is one exception to this. Just as a scalar can be used as one of the arguments along with a vector, the scalar being automatically extended to match the length of the vector, so scalars can be used with higher dimensional arrays in exactly the same way. Our first two examples on the last page, $2+M$ and $M\div 3$, show this clearly. All of which leads us to an interesting conclusion. Scalars are 1-component arrays of rank 0; hence, the entire set of rules can be boiled down to:

$$\text{any-dimensional array} \longleftarrow \left(\text{any-dimensional array}\right) \circ \left(\text{any-dimensional array}\right)$$

with the array restrictions on dimension and rank previously stated and allowing the combination scalar-higher rank array on the right. ∘ here stands for any standard scalar dyadic function.

Monadic operations on matrices

Matrices (and other arrays of higher rank) can also be used as arguments for standard scalar monadic functions. Here are the subtract and factorial of M:

```
      -M

 ¯1   ¯2    0
 ¯1   ¯3   ¯2
 ¯3   ¯4   ¯2
 ¯3   ¯3    0
```

!M

1	2	1
1	6	2
6	24	2
6	6	1

Just as with the standard scalar dyadic functions, so a single rule suffices for the standard scalar monadics, keeping in mind that the shape of the result is the same as that of the argument:

$$\begin{array}{c} \text{any-dimensional} \\ \text{array} \end{array} \longleftarrow f \left(\begin{array}{c} \text{any-dimensional} \\ \text{array} \end{array} \right)$$

f being any standard scalar monadic function.

Operations along a single dimension

In a two-dimensional table such as M, we might conceivably be interested in several sets of sums (in a vector there is only one possible sum) obtained along either of two directions. For example, the total amount of each item bought over the four week period and the total number of all items sold weekly can be gotten by summing over the rows and columns:

		A	B	C	sum over items purchased
week	1	1	2	0	3
	2	1	3	2	6
	3	3	4	2	9
	4	3	3	0	6
sum over 4 weeks		8	12	4	grand sum 24

the grand total being

        8+12+4
24

which should be the same as

        3+6+9+6
24

Now look at +/M :

        +/M
3   6   9   6

It's the same as the sums over the items purchased. What about the sums over the four-week period? This brings up the question of how we specify which coordinate of a multidimensional array we want to sum over, a problem which, for obvious reasons didn't arise when we were dealing only with vectors.

Let's go back to M. Its structure is 4 3, four rows and three columns, so $+/M$ is really the sum over the last coordinate, which is the dimension along which we have three components. In APL this can be also done with

```
        +/[2]M
3   6   9   6
```

and, by analogy, the other set of sums is

```
        +/[1]M
8   12   4
```

It isn't necessary to specify [1] for reduction over the first coordinate. An alternate instruction which does this is ⌿, which is formed by overstriking the reduction and subtract symbols:

```
        +⌿M
8   12   4
```

However, for a three-dimensional array, neither ⌿ or / alone will produce reduction over the second coordinate, and it still is necessary to type /[2]

Now we made M by restructuring V:

```
        V
1   2   0   1   3   2   3   4   2   3   3   0
```

Summing, we get

```
        +/V
24
```

and

```
        +/[1]V
24
```

there being only one coordinate associated with a vector. The conclusion we can draw is that when no coordinate is specified, the last one is assumed.

What if we try to sum over a nonexistent coordinate?

```
        +/[3]M

    1   2   0
    1   3   2
    3   4   2
    3   3   0
```

This results in M itself. Similarly,

```
        +/[2]V
1   2   0   1   3   2   3   4   2   3   3   0
```

gives V. Now we can explain why we get the same sort of response for a scalar:

```
      +/5
5
```

The sum is over the last coordinate, none being specified. But there is no last coordinate (in fact, none at all, this being a scalar). Hence, the argument itself is returned.

For our final exercise, suppose we want to find out what the row and column averages are, or in general averages across any coordinate. The techniques to be developed here will be recognized by those with a background in statistics as having applicability, with just a bit more sophistication, to such procedures as analysis of variance.

In M the averages are

	A	B	C	week averages
week 1	1	2	0	1
2	1	3	2	2
3	3	4	2	3
4	3	3	0	2
item averages	2	3	1	

Each of the sums over the first coordinate was divided by the number of components in that direction, four, and each of the sums over the second coordinate was divided by three. Note that this is the same as the order and magnitude of the dimension vector, 4 3.

There is a function called $MEAN$ in 1 $CLASS$ that will compute these averages for us. Let's first copy it and then display it:

```
      )COPY 1 CLASS MEAN
SAVED    15.02.39 07/29/69
      ∇MEAN[□]∇
   ∇ R←K MEAN X
[1]    R←(+/[K] X)÷(ρX)[K]
   ∇
```

It is dyadic, the left argument K being the coordinate of the array X over which we are averaging. The function takes a given coordinate of X and divides the sum over that coordinate by the number of components comprising that sum, as explained above.

Let's try it on M. Here are the averages over the first and second coordinates:

```
      1 MEAN M
2   3   1
      2 MEAN M
1   2   3   2
```

The overall average is

        1 *MEAN* 2 *MEAN* M
2

If you try 2 *MEAN* 1 *MEAN* M, you'll find it won't work.   Do you see why
this is so?

PROBLEMS

1. <u>Drill</u>.   Specify $S \leftarrow 4$ $5 \rho \phi \iota 20$, $T \leftarrow 4$ $5 \rho \iota 20$, $U \leftarrow 2$ 3 $4 \rho \iota 24$

    $S+T$ $S \leq T$ $\lceil / \lceil / \lceil / U$

    $2 \times S + T \div 2$ $+/[2]T$ $\lceil /, U$

    $S \lfloor T$ $+ \neq T$ $\times \neq U$

    $3 | T$ $4 \div T$ $+/+/[1]T$

2. Write an *APL* expression to select N different random elements from
    a matrix M.

3. Show how to add a scalar N to each element in the even columns of a
    matrix M.

4. The matrix $GR3$ contains the grade records (A, B, C, D and F) of 25 stu-
    dents in a class, with the first row listing the number of A's received
    by each student, the second row the number of B's, etc.   Each course
    represented in the matrix is three credits.   A similar matrix $GR2$
    records grades for two-credit courses, and $GR1$ for one-credit courses.
    Write a program to calculate the grade point average for each student
    and for the class.   (The grade point average is computed by multiplying
    4 times the number of A credits, 3 times the number of B credits, etc.,
    adding them up, and dividing by the total number of credits earned.)

5. Write an *APL* expression to construct a 4 4 matrix made up of random
    integers in the range 1 to 100 .

6. You are given five vectors $V1-V5$ of invoices from fifteen customers.
    The first represents bills under 30 days old, the second 30-59 days
    old, the third 60-89 days, etc.   All entries with a given index are
    associated with the same customer.   Write a program that will .
    (1) construct a matrix of these invoices with each vector $V1-V5$ occupy-
    ing a single row; (2) print the total amount of receivables in each
    category and separately for each customer, with an appropriate message;
    (3) print the grand total of all receivables with an identifying message;
    and (4) identify which customers 1-15, if any, have invoices outstanding
    more than 59 days (at which time they become overdue).

CHAPTER 28:

Extensions of mixed functions to
multidimensional arrays

This chapter will be devoted to a study of the effects of various standard and mixed functions on multidimensional arrays. Although there are some functions operating on arrays that haven't yet been introduced, a discussion of them will be deferred to chapters 29-31.

Reversal

Since it is easier sometimes to see what is happening with characters, we'll first specify a matrix X of literals as follows:

        $X \leftarrow 3 \ 4\rho 'ABCDEFGHIJKLM'$

Here is X:

        X

$ABCD$
$EFGH$
$IJKL$

The reversal of this matrix is

        ϕX

$DCBA$
$HGFE$
$LKJI$

It reverses along the last coordinate and, in this respect, acts just like $+/M$ in the last chapter, where the reduction took place over the last coordinate if none was specified. Hence, ϕX is equivalent to $\phi[2]X$:

        $\phi[2]X$

$DCBA$
$HGFE$
$LKJI$

and, to get reversal over the first coordinate, we should execute

        $\phi[1]X$

IJKL
EFGH
ABCD

As in reduction, the functions reversal and rotation (see next section), operate over the first coordinate by overstriking the large circle with the subtract sign $\ominus$:

        $\ominus X$

IJKL
EFGH
ABCD

What do you suppose would happen if we tried $\phi[3]X$ or any nonexistent coordinate? Try it and see.

Rotation

This operation too takes place over the last coordinate unless one is speci-fied. Thus:

        $1\phi X$

BCDA
FGHE
JKLI

This is equivalent to

        $1\phi[2]X$

BCDA
FGHE
JKLI

while rotation over the first coordinate can be obtained by

        $1\phi[1]X$

EFGH
IJKL
ABCD

or

        1⊖X

EFGH
IJKL
ABCD

Here is X again for comparison:

        X

ABCD
EFGH
IJKL

There is another more general way to use rotation, in which we can
specify in vector form in the left argument how we wish to rotate each
component of a given coordinate. For example, suppose we want to move
the first row leftward one position, the second row leftward three positions and the third row two positions to the left. This can be done with

        1 3 2ϕ[2]X

BCDA
HEFG
KLIJ

The [2] isn't needed here for the reason stated previously. To do something
along the first coordinate, we need four components in the left argument:

        0 1 2 3ϕ[1]X

AFKD
EJCH
IBGL

and

        0 1 2 3⊖X

AFKD
EJCH
IBGL

Thus, the left argument is either a scalar or a vector whose dimension is
the same as the number of components in the coordinate over which the
rotation is to take place. Here are some examples operating on an array
of rank 3, TAB3 :

```
      )LOAD 1 CLASS
SAVED  15.02.39 07/29/69
      TAB3

  111   112   113
  121   122   123
  131   132   133
  141   142   143

  211   212   213
  221   222   223
  231   232   233
  241   242   243
      1ϕTAB3

  112   113   111
  122   123   121
  132   133   131
  142   143   141

  212   213   211
  222   223   221
  232   233   231
  242   243   241
      ( 2 3ρι3)ϕ[2]TAB3

  121   132   143
  131   142   113
  141   112   123
  111   122   133

  221   232   243
  231   242   213
  241   212   223
  211   222   233
      ( 2 4ρι3)ϕ[3]TAB3

  112   113   111
  123   121   122
  131   132   133
  142   143   141

  213   211   212
  221   222   223
  232   233   231
  243   241   242
      2 4ρι3

  1   2   3   1
  2   3   1   2
```

These latter two illustrations need careful examination in order to see what is happening. For instance, look at the last example, in which the rotation is over the third coordinate. The left argument is, itself, a matrix. Picking out a couple of these entries at random, the element 3 in the second row, second column of $2\ 4\rho\iota3$ tells us to rotate the second row, second plane of $TAB3$ by three positions (which leaves it unchanged). The element 1 in the first row, fourth column causes the fourth row, first plane to rotate one position to the left. By trying out a few additional examples yourself, you should be able to see how the left argument determines the rotation of the array.

Compression and expansion

As you might expect, the left argument must have as many 1's and 0's as the number of components in the coordinate over which compression occurs. Here is an example in which the third component of the second coordinate is elided. We will use the literal matrix X defined below:

        $X\leftarrow3\ 4\rho'ABCDEFGHIJKLM'$
        $1\ 1\ 0\ 1/[2]X$

ABD
EFH
IJL

To remove the second row, we can compress over the first coordinate:

        $1\ 0\ 1/[1]X$

$ABCD$
$IJKL$

Once more, compression and expansion over the first coordinate can be obtained by overstriking with the subtract sign:

        $1\ 0\ 1\neq X$

$ABCD$
$IJKL$

If in X we want to insert something between, say, the third and fourth components on each row, we can use expansion over the second coordinate:

        $1\ 1\ 1\ 0\ 1\backslash[2]X$

$ABC\ D$
$EFG\ H$
$IJK\ L$

while to get a row of blanks between the second and third rows, we execute

        1 1 0 1\[1]X

ABCD
EFGH

IJKL

or

        1 1 0 1⍀X

ABCD
EFGH

IJKL

What about compression and expansion over arrays of rank 3? *TAB*3 again
will be our specimen array:

        1 0/[1]*TAB*3

    111   112   113
    121   122   123
    131   132   133
    141   142   143
        1 0 1/[3]*TAB*3

    111   113
    121   123
    131   133
    141   143

    211   213
    221   223
    231   233
    241   243
        1 1 1 0 1\[2]*TAB*3

    111   112   113
    121   122   123
    131   132   133
      0   0   0
    141   142   143

    211   212   213
    221   222   223
    231   232   233
      0   0   0
    241   242   243

In 1 *CLASS* there are several prepared functions that provide the capability
for catenating rows and columns to multidimensional arrays. Before
looking at them, let's see if we can first define the problem clearly.
We are given the matrix *X*:

```
        X←2 4ρ2 5 3 1 4 2 3 3
        X
```

```
  2   5   3   1
  4   2   3   3
```

and we want to add a third row 9 8 7 7 or a fifth column 12 15. The first function to be used is ROWCAT, which is displayed below:

```
        ∇ROWCAT[□]∇
      ∇ R←X ROWCAT V
[1]     R←(1 0 +ρX)ρ(,X),V
      ∇
```

V is the row to be added. It is catenated to the ravel of X, and the new vector thus formed is restructured to give the desired result. It doesn't pay to use the trace on this function since there is only one line. We can, however, execute the function by hand, step by step, as follows after putting a stop on line 1:

```
        V←9 8 7 7
        S∆ROWCAT←1
        X ROWCAT V
```

```
ROWCAT[1]
        X,V
RANK ERROR
        X,V
        ^
```

We aren't permitted to catenate vectors to matrices. Continuing, with X raveled:

```
        (,X),V
  2   5   3   1   4   2   3   3   9   8   7   7
        1 0+ρX
  3   4
        →1
```

```
  2   5   3   1
  4   2   3   3
  9   8   7   7
```

Adding 1 0 to ρX has the effect of changing the structure to accommodate an additional row. Now we can remove the stop on ROWCAT:

```
        S∆ROWCAT←0
```

Adding a column is some what more difficult. Here is COLCAT1:

```
        ∇COLCAT1[□]∇
      ∇ R←X COLCAT1 V
[1]     R←(((ρX)[2]ρ1),0)\X
[2]     V←((ρX)[1],1)ρV
[3]     V←(((ρX)[2]ρ0),1)\V
[4]     R←R+V
      ∇
```

On line 1 X is expanded with a column of 0's on the back end. The assumption here is that X and V consist of numbers only. If you go through the algorithm you will see why it won't work with characters. Line 2 restructures V, the vector to be catenated, as a matrix with as many rows as X and one column. The effect of line 3 is to expand V with as many columns of 0's tacked on the front end as correspond to the original structure of X, and line 4 completes the picture by adding componentwise the results of lines 1 and 3.

We'll use the same X as before, with W as shown for extra components:

```
      X

 2   5   3   1
 4   2   3   3
      W←12 15
      X  COLCAT1  W


 2   5   3   1   12
 4   2   3   3   15
```

To understand better how this works, let's put a trace on each line:

```
      T∆COLCAT1←ι4
      X  COLCAT1  W
COLCAT1[1]
 2   5   3   1   0
 4   2   3   3   0
COLCAT1[2]
 12
 15
COLCAT1[3]
 0   0   0   0   12
 0   0   0   0   15
COLCAT1[4]
 2   5   3   1   12
 4   2   3   3   15

 2   5   3   1   12
 4   2   3   3   15
      T∆COLCAT1←0
```

Line 1 added an extra column of 0's on the right, while line 2 made a matrix with two rows and one column out of W. Line 3 expanded the restructured W by adding sufficient 0's on the front end to make the resulting matrix the same dimensions as the expanded X of line 1. The last line added the results of lines 1 and 3.

Indexing

To illustrate indexing on multidimensional arrays, we'll first define a vector of four components:

```
        V←'ABCD'
        ρV
4
```

Earlier we saw that we could pick out components by appropriate indices, as, for instance

```
        V[2 4 3]
BDC
```

The problem is a bit more complicated for an array of higher rank. Take X, which is still in storage:

```
        X

    2   5   3   1
    4   2   3   3
```

To specify an element of the array requires two numbers, one to tell the column and the other the row on which the element is located. Say, for example, we want the element in the second row and fourth column, which is 3. The way to get it in APL is to type

```
        X[2;4]
3
```

The semicolon is used here as a separator between coordinates.

More than one element can be specified at a time, like the second and fourth components of the second row:

```
        X[2;2 4]
2   3
```

or the elements of the second column:

```
        X[1 2;2]
5   2
```

There is a shorthand way of specifying all the elements along a particular coordinate, namely by not typing any components of the coordinate in question. For example, our last problem could be written as

```
        X[;2]
5   2
```

while to get all the elements of the first row type

```
        X[1;]
2   5   3   1
```

This implies that to get all of X, we need

        $X[;]$

    2   5   3   1
    4   2   3   3

which is a bit wasteful, perhaps, but consistent.

The same rules hold for a three-dimensional array. $TAB3$ should still be
in the active workspace, so let's use it:

        $TAB3$

    111   112   113
    121   122   123
    131   132   133
    141   142   143

    211   212   213
    221   222   223
    231   232   233
    241   242   243

You have probably already noticed that the elements are arranged so that
if we took the 10 10 10⊤ of any component, we would get its position.   For
example, 143 is

            first plane   fourth row   third column
                 1   4   3

Thus,

        $TAB3[2;;2]$
212   222   232   242

will get us all the elements in the second column of the second plane.
From what we've done so far it follows that the number of semicolons needed
is one fewer than the rank of the array.

We had mentioned in an earlier chapter that subscripting could be used
on the left of the specification arrow (see page 139).   This works with
higher rank arrays as well as vectors, as shown by the following examples:

        X

    2   5   3   1
    4   2   3   3
        $X[2;3]\leftarrow90$
        X

    2   5   3   1
    4   2   90 3
        $X[1;]\leftarrow X[1;]\times2$
        X

    4   10 6   2
    4   2   90 3

Now we are ready to consider a much shorter algorithm for adding a column to a matrix:

```
      ∇COLCAT2[□]∇
   ∇ R←X COLCAT2 V
[1]    R←(((ρX)[2]ρ1),0)\X
[2]    R[;(ρR)[2]]←V
   ∇
```

Line 1 expands X exactly as in $COLCAT1$ by adding a column of 0's at the back end, while line 2 respecifies the last column of R as the components of V.

Let's put a trace on this function and execute it. We still have X available, and to it we'll catenate a column consisting of the elements 8 7:

```
      T∆COLCAT2←1 2
      X

   4   10    6    2
   4    2   90    3
      X COLCAT2 8 7
COLCAT2[1]
   4   10    6    2    0
   4    2   90    3   ‾0
COLCAT2[2] 8   7

   4   10    6    2    8
   4    2   90    3    7
```

The trace shows the 0's added on line 1 to build up the matrix, while on line 2 the 0's are respecified as 8 and 7, respectively.

$COLCAT2$ works equally well with characters, but we'll remove the trace first, since the blanks added on line 1 won't show anyway:

```
      T∆COLCAT2←0
      Y←2 4ρ'ABCDEFGHIJKL'
      Y

ABCD
EFGH
      Y COLCAT2 '?*'

ABCD?
EFGH*
```

Now, look back at $COLCAT1$ on page 208. Do you see why characters can't be used in this function?

Take and drop

The take and drop functions applied to multidimensional arrays work in the same fashion as with vectors, except that the elements of the left argument refer to what is to be taken or dropped along each coordinate. For example:

```
      TAB3

111   112   113
121   122   123
131   132   133
141   142   143

211   212   213
221   222   223
231   232   233
241   242   243
        1 3 ¯2↑TAB3

112   113
122   123
132   133
```

Here the first element of the first coordinate (i.e., the first plane) is taken, and within the first plane the first three rows and last two columns. Another illustration is

```
      1 ¯1 2↓TAB3

213
223
233
```

which drops the first plane (leaving only the second), the last row and the first two columns.

Membership

As pointed out on page 153, the membership function works with arrays of any rank, but the result always has the shape of the left argument:

```
      R←2 4ρ,TAB3
      R

111   112   113   121
122   123   131   132
      TAB3

111   112   113
121   122   123
131   132   133
141   142   143

211   212   213
221   222   223
231   232   233
241   242   243
        2 4ρTAB3

111   112   113   121
122   123   131   132
```

```
        TAB3∈R
```

```
  1 1 1
  1 1 1
  1 1 0
  0 0 0
```

```
  0 0 0
  0 0 0
  0 0 0
  0 0 0
        R∈TAB3
```

```
  1 1 1 1
  1 1 1 1
```

PROBLEMS

1. **Drill.** Specify $A \leftarrow 3$ $5\rho\iota15$, $B \leftarrow 3$ $3\rho'ABCDEFGHI'$, $C \leftarrow 2$ 3 $4\rho,A$

   $A[;2\ 5]$ $+\not/C[1\ 2;2;3]$ $B[1;2\ 3]$

   $C[1;2\ 3;]$ $A[1\ 3;\iota4]$ $2\ 2\ 2\uparrow\phi C$

   $^-1\ 1\ 2\downarrow\ominus C$ $1\ 0\ 1\ 1\backslash[2]C$ $1\ 0\ 1\not/B$

   $1\ 1\ 1\ 1\ 0\ 1\backslash A$ $0\ 1/[1]C$ ϕA

   $\ominus A$ $3\ 1\ 2\phi A$ $^-1\ ^-2\ 2\phi B$

   $^-1\ ^-2\ 2\ 1\ 1\ominus A$ $,\phi B$ $1\ 3\ 3\phi3\ 1\ 1\ 2\ 4\phi[1]A$

2. Make the first row of B (prob. 1) equal to the third column.

3. Define a function that will delete a given name from a matrix of names A, or print out an appropriate message if the name is not in the matrix.

4. What is the difference between $M[1;2]$ and $M[,1;,2]$?

5. Starting with a matrix $M \leftarrow 3$ $4\rho\iota4$, produce another matrix R whose shape is 3 3 4 and made up of the columns of M. Use only indexing.

6. A magic square of order n is one made up of the integers 1 through n^2. The sums over each row, column, and diagonal are the same. One way to construct the squares of odd order is to start with a matrix of the right size, made up of the successive integers ordered rowwise. Then set up a vector of n successive integers with 0 in the middle to rotate the matrix successively over the last and first coordinates. Define a monadic function MS to do this.

7. Write an APL function to make a matrix out of two vectors $V1$ and $V2$, using $V1$ as the first column and $V2$ as the second.

CHAPTER 29:

Transposition

By transposition is meant the interchanging of elements along two coordinates. This wasn't introduced in the last chapter along with the other
functions mainly because it operates meaningfully on multidimensional arrays
only. The transpose function may have one or two arguments. These will be
considered separately below.

Monadic transpose

If X is the matrix specified below,

        $X \leftarrow 3 \ 4\rho'ABCDEFGHIJKLMN'$
        X

$ABCD$
$EFGH$
$IJKL$

then by the transposition of X is meant an interchange of rows and columns
such that the element whose indices are $[J;K]$ ends up in the $[K;J]$ position for all J and K values possible. The APL function which will do this
for us is the monadic <u>transpose</u>, formed by overstriking the large circle
with the backward pointing slash:

        ϕX

AEI
BFJ
CGK
DHL

The first row of X has become the first column of the transpose of X, etc.

What happens when we apply the transpose function to a vector?

        $V \leftarrow 2 \ 5 \ 1$
        ϕV
2   5   1

Nothing has changed. The same is true for a scalar, incidentally. But we
see something a little more interesting when we work with a three-dimensional
array. Our old standby, *TAB*3 , is always handy, so let's work with it:

```
      )LOAD 1 CLASS
SAVED   15.02.39 07/29/69
      TAB3

  111   112   113
  121   122   123
  131   132   133
  141   142   143

  211   212   213
  221   222   223
  231   232   233
  241   242   243
      ρTAB3
2   4   3
```

Note the dimensions of *TAB*3, two planes, four rows, three columns. Here
is what the transpose does to *TAB*3; and, while we're at it, *TAB*2:

```
      ⍉TAB3

  111   121   131   141
  112   122   132   142
  113   123   133   143

  211   221   231   241
  212   222   232   242
  213   223   233   243
      ρ⍉TAB3
2   3   4
      ⍉TAB2

  3    7    6    1
  1   10    9    6
  7    4    1    7
      ρ⍉TAB2
3   4
      ρTAB2
4   3
```

Only the last two coordinates are interchanged and, as a matter of fact,
this is always the case for all multidimensional arrays.

Dyadic transpose

The monadic transpose doesn't help us to interchange other than the last
two coordinates. For this the dyadic transpose is useful. Its left argument is a vector specifying the new positions of the original coordinates.
Here is an example:

```
    1  3  2⍉TAB3
```

```
111    121    131    141
112    122    132    142
113    123    133    143

211    221    231    241
212    222    232    242
213    223    233    243
```

This is identical with the monadic transpose of *TAB*3. What it says is to leave the first coordinate alone and interchange the other two. Not so trivial is

```
    2  1  3⍉TAB3
```

```
111    112    113
211    212    213

121    122    123
221    222    223

131    132    133
231    232    233

141    142    143
241    242    243
```

The dimensions of the result are 4 2 3. Notice that the third coordinate, representing the number of columns, is unchanged, the elements in each of the original columns remaining in the same column but not necessarily in the same order rowwise and planewise after transposition. More formally, if an arbitrary element in *TAB*3 has indices $[I;J;K]$, then its new position in the result is $[J;I;K]$ for the example above. For instance, the indices of 232 in *TAB*3 are $[2;3;2]$, and after transposition in the result they are $[3;2;2]$. Let's apply dyadic transposition to a two-dimensional object, the matrix *T*:

```
    T←3 5⍴⍳15
    T
```

```
 1     2     3     4     5
 6     7     8     9    10
11    12    13    14    15
    1  2⍉T
```

```
 1     2     3     4     5
 6     7     8     9    10
11    12    13    14    15
```

The 1 2 transpose of a matrix doesn't change it at all, and the 2 1 transpose

```
      2 1⍉T

1    6    11
2    7    12
3    8    13
4    9    14
5   10    15
```

is the same as the monadic transpose.

What about

```
      1 1⍉T
1    7    13
```

This gives the components along the major diagonal of T:

```
      T
```

```
  1    2    3    4    5
  6    7    8    9   10
 11   12   13   14   15
```

The result is made up of those elements of T whose row and column indices are the same. If this puzzles you, there is a simulation of the dyadic transpose called TRA, in 1 $CLASS$:

```
      )LOAD 1 CLASS
SAVED  15.02.39 07/29/69
      T←3 5⍴⍳15
      1 1 TRA T
GIVEN R←1  1 ⍉ X;  THEN  ⍴⍴R  IS  ⌈/1  1  OR  1
   AND  R[I]  IS  X[I;I]
GIVEN ⍴X  IS  3  5  THEN
   I  RUNS FROM 1 TO 3  BECAUSE  ⌊/3  5  IS  3

⍴R  IS  3
```

Here are a few more examples with $TAB3$:

```
      2 1 1TRA TAB3
GIVEN R←2  1  1 ⍉ X;  THEN  ⍴⍴R  IS  ⌈/2  1  1  OR  2
   AND  R[I;J]  IS  X[J;I;I]
GIVEN ⍴X  IS  2  4  3  THEN
   I  RUNS FROM 1 TO 3  BECAUSE  ⌊/4  3  IS  3
   J  RUNS FROM 1 TO 2

⍴R  IS  3  2
      2 1 1⍉TAB3

111  211
122  222
133  233
```

```
        1  2  1 TRA TAB3
GIVEN R←1  2  1 ⍉ X;   THEN  ⍴⍴R   IS   ⌈/1  2  1   OR  2
    AND  R[I;J]  IS  X[I;J;I]
GIVEN  ⍴X  IS  2  4  3   THEN
    I  RUNS FROM 1 TO 2   BECAUSE   ⌊/2  3  IS  2
    J  RUNS FROM 1 TO 4

⍴R  IS  2  4
        1  2  1⍉TAB3


   111   121   131   141
   212   222   232   242
        1  1  1 TRA TAB3
GIVEN R←1  1  1 ⍉ X;   THEN  ⍴⍴R   IS   ⌈/1  1  1   OR  1
    AND  R[I]  IS  X[I;I;I]
GIVEN  ⍴X  IS  2  4  3   THEN
    I  RUNS FROM 1 TO 2   BECAUSE   ⌊/2  4  3  IS  2

⍴R  IS  2
        1  1  1⍉TAB3
111   222
```

But

```
        1  1  3⍉TAB3
DOMAIN ERROR
        1  1  3 ⍉TAB3
               ∧
        1  1  3 TRA TAB3
LEFT ARGUMENT MUST BE A DENSE SET OF INTEGERS STARTING AT 1
```

By a dense set of integers is meant one with no gaps.

The syntax of the dyadic transpose with arrays of rank 3 and higher can get a little messy, but with the aid of the prepared function TRA you ought to be able to get a feel for the set of rules under which it operates.

A transformation mnemonic

You have probably noticed by this time that the appearance of the symbols ⌽, ⊖ and ⍉ is related to the kind of transformation which results when they are applied to certain arrays. Specifically, let's apply them to a matrix M←3 4⍴⍳12:

```
     M

   1    2    3    4
   5    6    7    8
   9   10   11   12
        ⌽M

   4    3    2    1
   8    7    6    5
  12   11   10    9
```

⊖M

```
9   10   11   12
5    6    7    8
1    2    3    4
```
    ⌽M

```
1   5    9
2   6   10
3   7   11
4   8   12
```

In each case the overstruck line, |, - or \, represents the axis about which the transformation occurs.

PROBLEMS

1. Drill.   Specify M←3 4ρι10, N←2 3 4ρι24

    1 1⌽M   2 1 3⌽N   ⌽2 1⌽M

    1 1 2⌽N   ⌽⌽⊖M   ⌽M

    ρ2 1 3⌽N   1 2 1⌽N   ⌽⌽M

2. For the matrix B (Problem 1, chapter 28), write an APL expression to obtain the diagonal that runs from the upper right to the lower left.

3. Define a function DIAG that takes as its right argument a matrix M whose elements are positive integers, and forms a number out of the diagonal elements, i.e., 3 2 2 9 becomes 3229 .

4. Define a column-catenating function which transposes the rows and columns and uses ROWCAT (in 1 CLASS) to perform the catenation.

5. Write a one-line function to produce a table of three columns listing N, the factorial of N, and the reciprocal of N for the integers 1 through N.

6. S is an operation table for some APL function ∘. Write an expression that returns a 1 if the function is commutative, 0 otherwise.

7. Execute the following instructions and explain in your own words what they do:

$$B←⌽A←ι 25$$
$$⌽3 25ρA ,B ,A ×B$$

What tentative conclusion can be drawn from the data in the table?

CHAPTER 30:

Generalized outer product

Up to now we have been somewhat limited in the ways in which we could
generate arrays of rank >1, although we have studied a number of operations
which act to change the array once it is structured. In this chapter and
the next we shall look at two additional functions that will not only
expand our capability of producing arrays of all shapes, but also enable
us to define more compactly many of the functions we have already worked
with.

We will begin by introducing a problem that involves a large number of
multiplications. It asks that we compute the taxes to be paid for items
costing varying amounts and taxed at three different rates:

```
                            tax rates
                      .01    .02    .05
                     ┌────────────────────
                 1   │  -      -      -
                 2   │  -      -      -
    $ costs      3   │  -      -      -
                 4   │  -      -      -
                 5   │  -      -      -
```

The result desired is the matrix which is obtained by getting all possible
products of costs and rates. You can see that if the cost and tax rate
vectors had large numbers of components or noninteger components, this
procedure could involve a lot of work.

Outer product

APL has a function which operates on arrays in precisely the way needed
to fill in the table above. It is called the <u>outer product</u>. To illustrate
it, let the left argument be the vector of costs A and the right argument
the tax rates B:

```
      A←ι5
      B←.01×1 2 5
      B
0.01   0.02   0.05
```

The outer product is

```
      A∘.×B
```

```
0.01            0.02            0.05
0.02            0.04            0.1
0.03            0.06            0.15
0.04            0.08            0.2
0.05            0.1             0.25
```

which is read "A null dot times B." The little circle, called null, is the upper shift J. Clearly it gives all possible products of the left and right arguments and signifies that we want the outer product with respect to A and B.

Any standard scalar dyadic function can be used after the period in place of ×. For instance:

```
      A∘.+B
```

```
1.01            1.02            1.05
2.01            2.02            2.05
3.01            3.02            3.05
4.01            4.02            4.05
5.01            5.02            5.05
```

Notice that the shape or dimension of the result is the catenation of the shapes of the two arguments. In this case it is 5,3 or 5 3.

The outer product enables us to do a variety of things. For example, an addition table can be generated by

```
      A∘.+A
```

```
2   3   4   5   6
3   4   5   6   7
4   5   6   7   8
5   6   7   8   9
6   7   8   9  10
```

and the subtraction table by

```
      A∘.-A
```

```
0  ‾1  ‾2  ‾3  ‾4
1   0  ‾1  ‾2  ‾3
2   1   0  ‾1  ‾2
3   2   1   0  ‾1
4   3   2   1   0
```

Some of the patterns obtainable are interesting. Here is the identity matrix of order 4 (so-called because when matrix multiplication is used with any other 4 4 matrix *M* and the identity matrix, the result is *M*):

        (ι4)∘.=ι4

    1 0 0 0
    0 1 0 0
    0 0 1 0
    0 0 0 1

If = with the outer product gives the identity matrix, can you guess what ≠ will result in?

Finally, here are two others that yield matrices of all 0's and 1's:

        (ι5)∘.<ι5

    0 1 1 1 1
    0 0 1 1 1
    0 0 0 1 1
    0 0 0 0 1
    0 0 0 0 0
        (ι5)∘.≤ι5

    1 1 1 1 1
    0 1 1 1 1
    0 0 1 1 1
    0 0 0 1 1
    0 0 0 0 1

It isn't necessary that both arguments be vectors. One could be a matrix and the other a vector to give a three-dimensional array. In fact, this is where *TAB3* came from:

)LOAD 1 CLASS
    SAVED   15.02.39 07/29/69
        TAB3

    111   112   113
    121   122   123
    131   132   133
    141   142   143

    211   212   213
    221   222   223
    231   232   233
    241   242   243

Construction of multidimensional arrays

Follow the buildup of *TAB3* from scratch:

```
      W←10 20 30 40∘.+⍳3
      W

11    12    13
21    22    23
31    32    33
41    42    43
      ⍴W
4   3
      Z←100 200∘.+W
      Z

111   112   113
121   122   123
131   132   133
141   142   143

211   212   213
221   222   223
231   232   233
241   242   243
```

Z is identical to $TAB3$. It doesn't matter what the ranks of the left and right arguments are. The dimension of the result is still the catenation of the dimensions of the arguments.

Let's try building $TAB3$ another way:

```
      U←100 200∘.+10×⍳4
      U

110   120   130   140
210   220   230   240
      ⍴U
2   4
      Y←U∘.+⍳3
      Y

111   112   113
121   122   123
131   132   133
141   142   143

211   212   213
221   222   223
231   232   233
241   242   243
```

Again Y is the same as $TAB3$.

Scanning

The next concept to be considered in this chapter is scanning. If we were to start with a vector, say, 1 2 3 4, there may be times when we might want to get a record of the cumulative sums (or products) from left to right along the components of the vector.   In this case it would be 1 3 6 10.

There is in 1 *CLASS* a prepared monadic function *SUMSCAN* which does this for us:

```
      )LOAD 1 CLASS
SAVED   15.02.39 07/29/69
      SUMSCAN 1 2 3 ,4
1   3   6   10
```

Let's see how *SUMSCAN* is constructed:

```
      ∇SUMSCAN[□]∇
    ∇ R←SUMSCAN V
[1]    →4×ι1=ρρV
[2]    'ARGUMENT MUST BE A VECTOR'
[3]    →0
[4]    R←+/((ιρV)∘.≥ιρV)×(2ρρV)ρV
    ∇
```

Line 1 tells us to branch to 4 if the argument is a vector, otherwise drop through to line 2 where an appropriate message is printed out, followed by an exit from the function on line 3.   Line 4 causes a $2\rho\rho V$ restructure of V (for this example $2\rho\rho V$ is $2\rho 4$ or 4 4) which is

```
      V←ι4
      (2ρρV)ρV

  1   2   3   4
  1   2   3   4
  1   2   3   4
  1   2   3   4
```

This is then multiplied component by component by

```
      (ιρV)∘.≥ιρV

 1 0 0 0
 1 1 0 0
 1 1 1 0
 1 1 1 1
```

to give

```
      ((ιρV)∘.≥ιρV)×(2ρρV)ρV

  1   0   0   0
  1   2   0   0
  1   2   3   0
  1   2   3   4
```

which is then summed over the second coordinate.

Graphing

Our last topic has to do with the use of the outer product to build up a simple-minded but instructive graphing function. To begin, define

```
      Y←ϕX←¯5+ι9
      X
¯4  ¯3  ¯2  ¯1  0  1  2  3  4
      Y
4  3  2  1  0  ¯1  ¯2  ¯3  ¯4
```

Because there is a 0 as the middle element in X and Y, their outer product will produce 0's only along the "axes" of the matrix:

```
      M←Yo.×X
      M
```

¯16	¯12	¯8	¯4	0	4	8	12	16
¯12	¯9	¯6	¯3	0	3	6	9	12
¯8	¯6	¯4	¯2	0	2	4	6	8
¯4	¯3	¯2	¯1	0	1	2	3	4
0	0	0	0	0	0	0	0	0
4	3	2	1	0	¯1	¯2	¯3	¯4
8	6	4	2	0	¯2	¯4	¯6	¯8
12	9	6	3	0	¯3	¯6	¯9	¯12
16	12	8	4	0	¯4	¯8	¯12	¯16

The next step is to replace the 0's with some character, say, +, and everything else with blanks. One way to do this is to use the array to index a suitable character vector:

```
      ' +'[1+0=M]
```

```
        +
        +
        +
        +
+++++++++
        +
        +
        +
        +
```

Since the horizontal axis is somewhat out of scale (one character space isn't as wide as a line space), we will adjust our "graph" as follows:

```
      (18ρ1 0)\' +'[1+0=M]


            +
            +
            +
            +
 + + + + + + + + +
            +
            +
            +
            +
```

Suppose now we wish to plot on this set of axes a number of points (X, Y), where $Y \leftarrow X+1$. Our axes are made up of literal characters, so that the points themselves would have to be represented as literals in order to include them. It is more interesting, however, to go back to our original outer product, which is numeric, and superimpose the desired set of points F on it before converting to characters:

```
      F←Y∘.=X+1
      F
```

```
0 0 0 0 0 0 0 1 0
0 0 0 0 0 0 1 0 0
0 0 0 0 0 1 0 0 0
0 0 0 0 1 0 0 0 0
0 0 0 1 0 0 0 0 0
0 0 1 0 0 0 0 0 0
0 1 0 0 0 0 0 0 0
1 0 0 0 0 0 0 0 0
0 0 0 0 0 0 0 0 0
```

F produces a matrix of 1's where the points are. We next add the matrices F and $1+2×0=M$. You should be able to see why multiplication by 2 is necessary if you execute the next step without doing so.

```
      F+1+2×0=M
```

```
1   1   1   1   3   1   1   2   1
1   1   1   1   3   1   2   1   1
1   1   1   1   3   2   1   1   1
1   1   1   1   4   1   1   1   1
3   3   3   4   3   3   3   3   3
1   1   2   1   3   1   1   1   1
1   2   1   1   3   1   1   1   1
2   1   1   1   3   1   1   1   1
1   1   1   1   3   1   1   1   1
```

Finally, our expanded plot is

```
PLOT←(18ρ1 0)\' o+o'[F+1+2×0=M]
PLOT
```

```
        +       o
        +     o
        +   o
        o
+   +   +   o   +   +   +   +   +
        o       +
      o         +
    o           +
                +
```

Now that we have built up the algorithm for the plot routine, we can incorporate it into a defined function, GRAPH :

```
      ∇ Z←GRAPH
[1]     Z←((2×ρX)ρ 1  0)\'  o+o'[F+1+2×0=(φX)o.×X]
      ∇
```

F and X must be set before the function is executed:

```
X← ̄5+ι9
F←(φX)o.=X+1
GRAPH
```

```
        +         o
        +       o
        +     o
        o
+   +   +   o   +   +   +   +
      o         +
    o           +
  o             +
                +
```

Plotting functions can get quite complex when it is desired to include such
amenities as labeling of the axes, provision for changing the scale of the
plot, and rounding off the computed values for the coordinates, since the
printer can't type characters between lines and spaces.

APL provides a useful set of plotting routines in 1 PLOTFORMAT. Since
instructions for the use of this workspace are quite complete (type
DESCRIBE after loading), practice in the functions is left as an exercise
(see problem 9).

PROBLEMS

1. **Drill.** Specify $A \leftarrow \iota 4$, $B \leftarrow 2\ 3\rho 'ABCDEF'$, $C \leftarrow 'ABD'$, $D \leftarrow 3\ 1\rho\iota 3$

   $A \circ . \div \phi A$ $A \circ . \lceil 2\phi A$ $1\ 0\ 0\ 1\ 1 \circ . \lor 0\ 1\ 0\ 1\ 1$

   $C \circ . = B$ $1\ 3\ 9 \circ . > D$ $1\ 2\ 3 \circ . \mid \iota 5$

   $D \circ . \times A$ $1\ 0 \circ . \land 1\ 0$ $(\iota 5) \circ . * 0\ 1\ 2\ 3$

2. Use the outer product to generate the following tables:

   A) Sines and cosines of angles from 0 to PI at intervals of $PI \div 6$
   B) Logarithms of the integers 1 through 10 for a vector B of different bases
   C) Occurrences of the vowels $AEIOU$ in the character string S
   D) Squares and square roots of the integers 1 through 10

3. What is the shape of the result when the outer product is used to add the elements of a vector of length 4 to the components of a 2 2 matrix?

4. Define a function $DIST$ that computes the rounded off (nearest integer) distances between any two cities whose X and Y coordinates are given in a matrix L. Assume ρL is $N,2$ and the cities are all located north and east of the origin of the coordinate system.

5. Write an APL expression to find the number of occurrences of each of the letters $ABCDEFG$ in the word $CABBAGE$. Compare your answer with that given for problem 4, chapter 21.

6. Construct expressions which will give the sum and carry digits for addition of two numbers in any system with base $B < 10$. Using these results, write a function to generate an addition table of a set of integers INT in base B.

7. Write a program to multiply two polynomials together. Assume their coefficient vectors $C1$ and $C2$ are arranged in descending order of powers of X.

8. Use the function $GRAPH$ (page 228) for each of the following:

   A) $Y \leftarrow \mid X \leftarrow {}^{-}5 + \iota 9$

   B) $Y \leftarrow {}^{-}5 + X * 2$

   C) $Y \leq X + 1$

   D) $(Y \leq X + 1) \land Y \geq 3 - \mid X$

   E) $Y \leq 3 \mid X$

9. Execute the following instructions in order:

```
Y←φ¯13+ι25
R←(0=(¯3×Y)∘.+(2×X)-2)∨0=(2×Y)∘.+X-8
R
```

Explain the resulting display.

10.   After loading 1 *PLOTFORMAT* execute each of the following:

A) `X←ι20`
    `Y←X*2`
    `Z←2×X*2`
    `40 60 PLOT Y VS X`
    `40 60 PLOT Y AND Z VS X`

B) `X←1,50×ι7`
    `Y←÷X`
    `20 30 PLOT Y VS X`
    `20 30 PLOT Y[1+ι7] VS X[1+ι7]`

C) `X←0(0,ι36)÷18`
    `Y←10X`
    `Z←20X`
    `70 PLOT Y AND Z VS X`

D) (For Y and Z defined as in part C)

    `Y AND Z`
    `Y VS X`

11.   In 1 *CLASS* is a function *DFT* which can be used to format the
       output of a calculation in *APL*. Its left argument is a vector
       of two elements, the first of which determines the maximum width
       of the field to be printed and the second, the number of places
       to the right of the decimal point. The right argument is the
       data to be formatted. Execute 10 5 *DFT X AND Y* after copying
       AND from 1 *PLOTFORMAT* and specifying $X←÷ι10$ and $Y←X*.5$.

CHAPTER 31

Generalized inner product

In the last chapter we examined a function called <u>outer product</u> which formed all possible combinations of the two arguments, using some standard scalar dyadic function. This operation, however, doesn't result in what in mathematics is called ordinary matrix multiplication.

For those not familiar with it, here is an example which illustrates the use of such matrix multiplication. We have three men who are engaged in buying four items, A, B, C and D. The cost and tax on each item are given. If we know how much each man bought, what is the total cost and total tax per man? In tabular form:

			cost/unit	tax/unit
	A		4	.05
	B		2	.06
item	C		1	.01
	D		1	.02

man	item	A	B	C	D	cost/unit	tax/unit
1		2	3	0	1	(1–1)	(1–2)
2		0	2	1	4	(2–1)	(2–2)
3		1	1	2	1	(3–1)	(3–2)

What we want are the entries to go into the dotted table, whose boxes are numbered as shown above. Let's see how we can figure them out. To get the total cost for each man, we would multiply the numbers of the various items purchased by their respective costs, add them up, and put the results in the appropriate boxes. For man 1 this is

$$(2x4)+(3x2)+(0x1)+(1x1) \quad \text{or} \quad 15$$

This will go in box 1-1. The total tax for man 1 can be obtained similarly and placed in box 1-2:

$$(2x.05)+(3x.06)+(0x.01)+(1x.02) \quad \text{or} \quad .3$$

What goes in box 3-1, to take one more example, can be gotten by

$$(1x4)+(1x2)+(2x1) \div (1x1) \quad \text{or} \quad 9$$

The completed table looks like this:

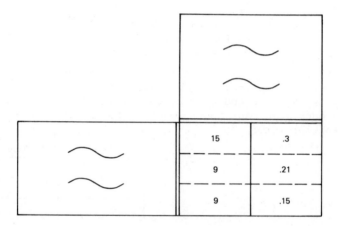

Note that the first dimension of the result is the same as the first dimension of the left matrix, and the second dimension of the result is the same as the second dimension of the right matrix. In addition, the inner two dimensions (second dimension of the left argument and first dimension of the right argument) must be the same in order to make possible this new kind of "multiplication," if we may be permitted to use the term in a somewhat different sense from its customary arithmetic meaning.

Inner product

To show how this operation can be performed on the terminal, let's build these matrices from their elements. First, we'll define the left matrix:

```
      A←3 4ρ2 3 0 1 0 2 1 4 1 1 2 1
      A
```

```
 2   3   0   1
 0   2   1   4
 1   1   2   1
```

The right argument B is

```
      B←4 2ρ4 .05 2 .06 1 .01 1 .02
      B
```

```
 4                    0.05
 2                    0.06
 1                    0.01
 1                    0.02
```

and the desired result, which is known as matrix multiplication, is formed by executing

```
      A+.×B
```

```
 15                   0.3
  9                   0.21
  9                   0.15
```

Why use three symbols for this common operation? Very simple: for the +
and × any standard scalar dyadic functions can be substituted. The reason
+ and × are used here is that these are the two operations needed to get the
result matrix, the products first and then the sums. There is also a
pattern to the way the elements are combined. For example, the element of
the result which goes into box 3-2 (the third <u>row</u> second <u>column</u> of the
result) is obtained by operating in the fashion described with the third
<u>row</u> of the left matrix and the second <u>column</u> of the right matrix. Such a
sequence of three symbols, f.g, f and g being any standard scalar dyadic
functions, is called an <u>inner product</u>. It is <u>not</u> the same as $A\circ.+B$ or
$A\circ.×B$ and in this case can't even be compared with $A×B$ since the latter
operation is possible only when the two matrices are the same size, and
the multiplication is carried out between corresponding elements only. The
inner product, $Af.gB$, operates on array arguments of many shapes with the
dimension of the result in each case (except for scalars) being
$(\bar{}1\downarrow\rho A),1\downarrow\rho B$. Here are some additional examples involving scalars and
vectors:

```
      10+.×3 2 8
130
      1 2 3 4+.*0 1 2 3
76
      2 1 6+.×3 2ρι6
35   44
      (3 4ρι12)+.=ι4
4    0   0
```

        (2 3 4⍴⍳24)+.-4 2⍴⍳8

 ⁻6 ⁻10
 10   6
 26 22

 42 38
 58 54
 74 70

Applications of the inner product

Here is another problem, this time involving distances between cities on a map.   The diagram shows not only the intercity distances but also the directions in which they are measured:

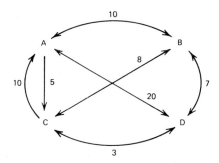

Notice that the distances are not necessarily the same in both directions between any two cities.   This is to allow for the most general case where the roads may be one-way and not laid out parallel to each other.   We can summarize the diagram in the form of a mileage table:

to

		A	B	C	D
	A	0	10	5	20
from	B	10	0	8	7
	C	10	8	0	3
	D	20	7	3	0

Such a table is provided in 1 *CLASS*   under the name *MILEAGE* :

)LOAD 1 CLASS
SAVED   15.02.39 07/29/69

MILEAGE

```
 0    10    5    20
10     0    8     7
10     8    0     3
20     7    3     0
```

Believe it or not, the longest two leg trips from any city to any other city passing through some intermediate city is given by

MILEAGE⌈.+MILEAGE

```
40    27    23    20
27    20    15    30
23    20    16    30
20    30    25    40
```

The longest trip from A to B is 27 miles (A-D-B), from B to C 15 miles (B-A-C), etc.

Why does this work? Let's arrange the matrices for the inner product in the same form that our earlier problem was:

The longest trip from B to C is represented by the contents of box 23. This is formed by operating with the second row of the left matrix and the third column of the right matrix. It requires adding 10 and 5, and taking the greater of that sum and the sum of 0 and 8, which is 15, then taking the greater of 15 and the sum of 8 and 0, which is still 15, and finally taking the greater of 15 and the sum of 7 and 3, which is 15 again.

There are many other interesting combinations and possible uses, only a few of which will be considered. For instance, the shortest two-leg trip is

MILEAGE⌊.+MILEAGE

```
 0    10    5    8
10     0    8    7
10     8    0    3
13     7    3    0
```

Notice that the shortest trip from, say, A to C, is 5 miles, which is A to
A to C or A to C to C. We are allowed this possibility because there are
entries (they happen to be all 0's) in the mileage table from A to A and C
to C on the major diagonal of *MILEAGE*:

        MILEAGE

```
    0   10    5   20
   10    0    8    7
   10    8    0    3
   20    7    3    0
```

One way to be protected from such a sneaky result is to put arbitrarily
large numbers along the major diagonal. This can be done without destroying or rewriting *MILEAGE* as follows:

        F←MILEAGE
        T←1000×(ɩ4)∘.=ɩ4
        T

```
  1000      0      0      0
     0   1000      0      0
     0      0   1000      0
     0      0      0   1000
```
        F←F+T
        F

```
  1000     10      5     20
    10   1000      8      7
    10      8   1000      3
    20      7      3   1000
```

Now we get for the shortest two-leg trips

        FL.+F

```
   15   13   18    8
   18   14   10   11
   18   10    6   15
   13   11   15    6
```

and, this time, the shortest such trip from A to C is 18 miles (A-B-C).
Application of this operation a second time would give the shortest three-
leg trip:

        FL.+FL.+F

```
   23   15   11   20
   20   18   14   13
   16   14   18    9
   21   13    9   18
```

We can continue this process ad nauseam, but there is a prepared function in
1 *CLASS* called *AGAIN* that will do it for us. Let's display it:

```
        ∇AGAIN[□]∇
     ∇ AGAIN
[1]     T←T⌊.+F
     ∇
```

It is niladic and simply respecifies T as $T⌊.+F$. If we set T equal to F, the first time we execute $AGAIN$ we will get the shortest two-leg trip, the next time the shortest three-leg trip, etc.:

```
     T←F
     T
```

1000	10	5	20
10	1000	8	7
10	8	1000	3
20	7	3	1000

```
     AGAIN
     T
```

15	13	18	8
18	14	10	11
18	10	6	15
13	11	15	6

```
     AGAIN
     T
```

23	15	11	20
20	18	14	13
16	14	18	9
21	13	9	18

The next example is one in circuit design. Imagine a circuit with six components connected as follows:

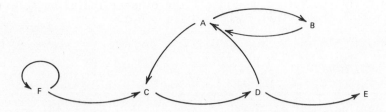

A, B, C, D, E and F are some kind of functional units which can be either energized or not. The circuit works this way: if C is energized, after a certain increment of time D is energized, and after another increment of time E is energized; if A is energized, after an increment of time C and B are energized, etc. F is the oddball unit here. Once it is energized it stays on permanently, but unless we start with F on there is no way to turn it on. E is a terminus. It doesn't turn anything on.

...ion can be summarized in a matrix, with 1 standing for ... connection from the unit named on the left to the one ...he top:

		to				
	A	B	C	D	E	F
A	0	1	1	0	0	0
B	1	0	0	0	0	0
C	0	0	0	1	0	0
from D	1	0	0	0	1	0
E	0	0	0	0	0	0
F	0	0	1	0	0	1

This matrix is available as a variable called $CIRCUIT$ in 1 $CLASS$:

        $CIRCUIT$

```
0 1 1 0 0 0
1 0 0 0 0 0
0 0 0 1 0 0
1 0 0 0 1 0
0 0 0 0 0 0
0 0 1 0 0 1
```

We can set up a vector X with six components (one for each unit in the circuit) and let 1 signify that the unit is turned on initially. For example, if only A is on, we specify X as

        $X \leftarrow 1\ 0\ 0\ 0\ 0\ 0$

What units are on after one increment of time? From the matrix it appears that B and C will be turned on and all the others, including A, will be off. The result should therefore be 0 1 1 0 0 0.

This can be achieved by

        $X \vee . \wedge CIRCUIT$
0   1   1   0   0   0

After another increment of time:

        $0\ 1\ 1\ 0\ 0\ 0 \vee . \wedge CIRCUIT$
1   0   0   1   0   0

and A is back on (due to the loop between A and B) with D also on.

To step this through several increments of time there is a function RUN in 1 $CLASS$. Let's display it:

```
      ∇RUN[□]∇
    ∇ NETWORK RUN STATUS;COUNT
[1]    COUNT←0
[2]    COUNT
[3]    STATUS
[4]    STATUS←STATUSv.∧NETWORK
[5]    COUNT←COUNT+1
[6]    →2
    ∇
```

The left argument is *NETWORK* , the matrix which describes the circuit connections, while the right argument *STATUS* represents the initial conditions. *COUNT* is a local variable which is set to 0 on line 1 and displayed on line 2. Line 3 prints out the current status of the circuit components. This is updated on the next line and the counter upped on line 5. The final line causes a branch to 2.

Does this program look a bit peculiar to you? It should. There is no safeguard in it to turn it off once it starts, and it will run forever! The proper thing to do would be to put a line in it that will cause execution to cease once *COUNT* reached a certain value. Since there is no such check, we'll let it go and manually interrupt execution with the ATTN button.

We'll start by turning on only A:

```
      X←1  0  0  0  0  0
      CIRCUIT RUN X
0
1   0   0   0   0   0
1
0   1   1   0   0   0
2
1   0   0   1   0   0
3
1   1   1   0   1   0
4
1   1   1   1   0   0
5
1   1   1   1   1   0
6
1   1   1   1   1   0
7
1   1   1   1   1   0
```

RUN[3]

Execution has been manually interrupted, as discussed above, and we are suspended on line 3:

```
      )SI
RUN[3] *
```

F will never turn on, no matter how many runs we make. A glance at the original circuit shows why.

COUNT is up to 10, the printout having lagged behind execution:

        COUNT
10

Ordinarily we can't get a value for *COUNT*, it being a local variable, but remember that we are still in the function as a result of the suspension.

Let's now remove the suspension:

        →0
)*SI*
        @

The few examples shown barely begin to cover the wide range of possible applications of the inner product. After you have gained a reasonable proficiency in *APL* you should be able to think up many more.

PROBLEMS

1. <u>Drill</u>. Specify $A←3\ 4\ 5$, $B←4\ 3\rho\iota10$, $C←3\ 4\rho\phi\iota7$

   $A+.=A$ $A\wedge.>C$ $B\times.=A$

   $B\times.-C$ $A\vee.\neq B$ $C|.-B$

   $B\vee.<C$ $3+.\times B$ $(\varphi C)\lceil.+A$

2. A) For two vectors A and B of the same length, and the conformable matrices M and U $(U←(\iota N)\circ.\leq\iota N)$ give a meaning to each of the following: $A\wedge.=B$, $M\wedge.=B$, $A+.\neq B$, $(M=0)\wedge.\geq U$, $A\times.\star B$
   B) For a logical square matrix N, what is the significance of $R←N\vee.\wedge N$?
   C) For the conformable matrices C and D, what is the meaning of $C+.=D$ and $C\lceil.LD$?

3. Redo each of the following problems using the inner product:

   A) problem 7, chapter 8
   B) problem 4, chapter 10
   C) problem 21, chapter 19
   D) problem 5, chapter 24

4. Write a program to evaluate at various points X a polynomial with coefficients C. Assume the terms of the polynomial are arranged in ascending order of powers of X. Use the inner product in your algorithm. (See also problem 3, chapter 23, and problem 7, chapter 30)

5. For a character matrix M, each of whose rows contains a name, write a function to alphabetize the names and place them in a new matrix A. Assume each name is entered in the form *JONES ANNABELLE* and $(\rho M)[2]=16$. One blank will separate the first and last names, and any spaces left over will be blanks on the right. The sort is to be on the last names, with first names sorted within them.

6. The Jones Computing Systems Corporation reimburses its employees for travel on company business at the rate of 14 cents per mile for the first 75 miles, 10 cents per mile for the next 50 miles and 6 cents per mile for all mileage in excess of 125. Define a monadic function which uses the inner product to compute mileage allowances for employees.

7. Use the inner product to write an expression which will simulate $10\perp M$ along the rows of M, where $M \times 3 \quad 3\rho\iota 9$. Your expression should produce the vector 123 456 789 .

8. Redo the cosine function (page 67) using the inner product.

CHAPTER 32:

Two applications of APL

There are a number of uses for APL in the branch of mathematics known as matrix algebra. Since this text is a teaching introduction to the language, only one of these will be considered, the solution of a set of exactly determined simultaneous linear equations.

For those who have forgotten their high school algebra, simultaneous linear equations are of the form (in conventional notation)

$$\begin{cases} aX + bY + cZ + \ldots = k_1 \\ dX + eY + fZ + \ldots = k_2 \\ \qquad\qquad \vdots \end{cases}$$

the problem being to find values of the variables X, Y, Z.... that satisfy all the equations. a, b, c, ...k_1, k_2... are numerical constants.

We will approach it with a numerical example. Suppose that in three successive weeks, we bought a number of different items A, B and C, spending the amounts listed:

		total cost	A	B	C
week	1	$1.10	4	6	0
	2	.59	3	2	2
	3	.78	1	3	4

What are the per unit costs of the various items?

The answer happens to be $.05 for A, $.15 for B and $.07 for C. Let's work back from the answer to see how we can solve similar problems. From our previous work with the inner product, we ought to be able to get the vector of total costs from the number of items matrix and the unit cost vector (try this for yourself). we'll call the total costs vector D, the matrix of the number of each item purchased X, and the unit cost vector B. Our trouble is that in a real problem we would know X and D but not B.

Before proceeding, here is a quick review of some elementary facts about matrices. M, N, P, Q and R are matrices of the appropriate size, and = is used in the conventional sense here. $+.\times$ means the usual inner product (here matrix multiplication). All of these facts you may verify on the terminal:

(1) If $M=N$, then $(R+.\times M)=R+.\times N$

(2) $(M+.\times(N+.\times P))=(M+.\times N)+.\times P$

(3) If Q has an inverse, $INV\ Q$, then $(\cdot(INV\ Q)+.\times Q)=I$ where I is the identity matrix

(4) $(M+.\times I)=(I+.\times M)=M$

The third point introduces a new concept, that of a matrix inverse. This is really not much different from the other kinds of inverses we have encountered thus far. For example, adding the additive inverse to a number resulted in the identity element for addition:

```
R←ι10
0=R+-R
1  1  1  1  1  1  1  1  1  1
```

and for multiplication:

```
1=R×÷R
1  1  1  1  1  1  1  1  1  1
```

$-R$ here is the additive inverse and $÷R$ the multiplicative inverse. So the inverse of a matrix is one which, when it multiplies M (matrix multiplication, not component by component), yields the identity matrix; shown here for 4 4 matrices:

```
(ι4)∘.=ι4

1  0  0  0
0  1  0  0
0  0  1  0
0  0  0  1
```

If $M+.\times INV\ M$ results in I, then $INV\ M$ is said to be a right inverse. Ditto for $((INV\ M)+.\times M)=I$, as a left inverse. If the same matrix is both a left and a right inverse of M, then M must be square (why?), and $INV\ M$ is referred to as the inverse of M. From this point on, $INV\ M$ will be used in this latter sense.

Now getting back to our problem, with the dimensions underneath as shown, we had

$$D \ \leftarrow \ X+.\times B$$
$$3 \quad 3\times 3 \quad 3$$

We want to find B. Using a dotted line to indicate that both sides are equivalent statements, the sequence of steps we will take is the following:

$(INV\ X)+.\times D$ | $INV\ X+.\times(X+.\times B)$ rule 1

$(INV\ X)+.\times D$ | $((INV\ X)+.\times X)+.\times B$ rule 2

$(INV\ X)+.\times D$ | $I+.\times B$ rule 3

$(INV\ X)+.\times D$ | B rule 4

The last line is our conclusion, that $B\leftarrow(INV\ X)+.\times D$

There is a prepared function in 1 *CLASS* called *INV* which acts as above, as well as the data for this problem. It requires a knowledge of matrix algebra beyond the scope of this text to explain how one can calculate matrix inverses, so *INV* will not be displayed:

```
      )LOAD 1 CLASS
SAVED   15.02.39 07/29/69
      X

  4   6   0
  3   2   2
  1   3   4
      D
1.1   0.59   0.78
      INV X

 ‾0.03846153846    0.4615384615   ‾0.2307692308
  0.1923076923    ‾0.3076923077    0.1538461538
 ‾0.1346153846     0.1153846154    0.1923076923
      (INV X)+.×D
0.05   0.15   0.07
```

The set of equations in our problem has as many equations as unknowns. There may be times when we have too many equations or not enough. You will find techniques for handling these and other variations in standard texts in matrix algebra and numerical analysis.

Some elementary examples from the calculus

The definition of the slope of a straight line (see problem 6, chapter 7) is of little value if the function we are considering is nonlinear. We can, for example, still use this definition to get an "average" slope over a modest-sized interval, but it is only an approximation.

In calculus courses it is shown that the slope of a function at a particular point P is the limiting value of the average slope over an interval encompassing the given point as the size of the interval becomes vanishingly small:

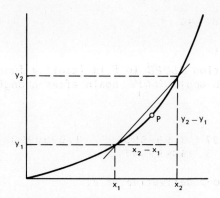

In the figure above, the average slope for the interval shown is
$(Y_2-Y_1) \div (X_2-X_1)$. By reducing the size of the interval about P, this
average approaches the instantaneous value of the slope at the point P, and
in the limit is the value of the derivative of the function at P.

APL can be used to obtain numerical values for the slopes (derivatives) of
functions, provided, of course, that the derivatives exist. As an example,
let's define a quadratic function F as follows:

```
        ∇R←F X
[1]     R←2×X⋆2∇
```

Using our previous definition of the slope, we'll set up a dyadic function
SLOPE which will allow us to choose intervals of varying size in the
computation:

```
        ∇R←I SLOPE X
[1]     R←((F X+I)-F X)÷I∇
```

Here are some executions of SLOPE with different intervals:

```
        X←ι10
        1 SLOPE X
6   10   14   18   22   26   30   34   38   42
        .1 SLOPE X
4.2   8.2   12.2   16.2   20.2   24.2   28.2   32.2   36.2
      40.2
        .01 SLOPE X
4.02   8.02   12.02   16.02   20.02   24.02   28.02   32.02
       36.02   40.02
        .0001 SLOPE X
4.0002   8.0002   12.0002   16.0002   20.0002   24.0002
         28.0002   32.0002   36.0002   40.0002
        1E¯6 SLOPE X
4.000001999   8.000001999   12.000002   16.00000199
         20.000002   24.00000199   28.000002   32.00000199
         36.00000199   40.000002
```

Those readers familiar with the calculus will understand why these last
results are nearly identical with

      $2 \times 2 \times X$
4   8   12   16   20   24   28   32   36   40

for the function F defined previously.

Since the result of applying the function $SLOPE$ to F is itself a function namely, $2 \times 2 \times X$ we ought to be able to apply $SLOPE$ again after changing

      $\nabla F[1]R \leftarrow 2 \times 2 \times X \nabla$
      $1E\bar{}6 \; SLOPE \; X$
4   4   4   3.999999997   3.999999997   3.999999997   3.999999997
      3.999999997   3.999999997   3.999999997

This execution corresponds to the second derivative of F.

Our final example is one in which we compute the area bounded by the curve, the X-axis and the ordinates at X_1 and X_2 (see problem 5, chapter 19):

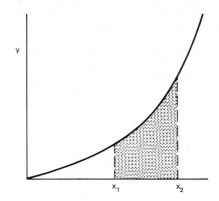

An obvious solution is to break up the cross-hatched area into rectangles of uniform width I,

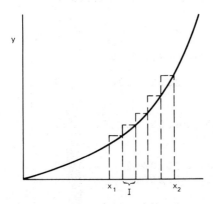

find an expression for the area of the "typical" rectangle, add up the areas and then decrease I to get a better approximation. The function $AREA$ does this for us. X is a two-component vector whose elements are X_1 and X_2 as shown in the diagram.

```
      ∇R←I AREA X
[1]   R←I+.×F X[1]+I×ιL(X[2]-X[1])÷IV
```

Again, those with a calculus background will recognize this as the numerical equivalent of

$$\int_{x_1}^{x_2} f(x)\,dx$$

Before applying the function, let's change F back:

```
      ∇F[1]R←2×X*2∇
      .1 AREA X
4.97
      .01 AREA X
4.6967
      .001 AREA X
4.669667
      .0001 AREA X
WS FULL
AREA[1] R←I+.×F X[1]+I×ιL(X[2]-X[1])÷I
```

Note that as the number of points which we use to evaluate the area increases, sooner or later we'll run out of storage space for the intermediate results in the algorithm, as indicated by the ws full message. Can you think of a way to "stretch" your available storage for greater precision?

PROBLEMS

1. Use the function $SLOPE$ to investigate the slope of the curve represented by $Y←*X$ for different points X. Compare your slopes with $*X$.

2. Find the inverse of the identity matrix.

3. Use INV to solve the following system of equations:

$$\begin{cases} 2X+Y+3Z=10 \\ 4X+3Y-Z=13 \\ 2X+Y-4Z=3 \end{cases}$$

4. In algebra it is shown that for the system of equations

$$\begin{cases} aX+bY=c \quad \text{(conventional notation)} \\ dX+eY=f \end{cases}$$

the application of Cramer's rule gives as solutions

$$\begin{cases} X=(ce-bf)÷(ae-bd) \\ Y=(af-cd)÷(ae-bd) \end{cases}$$

Write an APL program to solve by Cramer's rule a given set of two linear equations and print the message $NO\ UNIQUE\ SOLUTION$ if ae-bd=0. Then define a function $SOLVE$ which uses INV to solve the equation.

5. Nearly every calculus book ever printed has a problem similar to the following: A farmer has 300 feet of fencing material which he wants to use to enclose as large a rectangular area as possible. One side of the property to be enclosed is a relatively straight stretch of river, and needs no fencing. How should the fence be put in? (To solve this problem, set up an expression for the area, apply the slope function to it, and see where the slope is 0. This corresponds to a maximum point on the graph of area vs the variable representing the length of one side).

6. Use the function $AREA$ to find the area bounded by the curve represented by $Y \leftarrow \div X$, the X-axis, and the ordinates at $X = 1$ and $X = 2$. Compare your answer with ⊛2.

CHAPTER 33:

Input and output

We have been doing a considerable amount of computing without having to pay
too much attention to the problems of input and output. And for a good
reason—our work has been of a highly interactive nature. We fed information to the system and the system either responded or put things into storage
for us, to be recalled at some later time.

Nevertheless, there comes a time when we need to take a look at some of
the more specialized forms of input and output, especially as they appeared
in the drill exercises and some of the prepared functions. These features
are the basis for this chapter.

The quad

In 1 *CLASS* there is a function called *SD* which calculates the standard
deviation. Here it is:

```
      )LOAD 1 CLASS
SAVED   15.02.39 07/29/69
      ∇SD[□]∇
    ∇ SD;X;N
[1]    'ENTER OBSERVATIONS'
[2]    X←□
[3]    →0×ι0=ρX
[4]    'NUMBER OF OBS:';□←N←ρX
[5]    X←X-(+/X)÷N
[6]    'STANDARD DEVIATION'
[7]    ((+/X*2)÷N-1)*0.5
[8]    →1
    ∇
```

It is niladic and does not return an explicit result. Going through the
function, we find that line 1 prints out the message *ENTER OBSERVATIONS*
This is followed on line 2 by the local variable *X*, which is specified
by the quad (upper shift *L*) or box. The effect of this line is that when
control is on line 2, the output that appears on the paper is □: and causes
the system to wait until you have given it some input and pressed RETURN.
The input is then stored in *X*. Line 3 branches to 0 if 0=ρ*X*, i.e., if
an empty vector is entered. It is a signal in this function that we are

finished. Line 4 introduces another new feature, mixed output. It prints out *NUMBER OF OBS*: followed by the number of observations entered (ρX is stored in *N*, put into the box and printed out). The semicolon is used here in *APL* for such mixed output because characters can't be catenated to numbers. Line 5 subtracts from each component of *X* the average, and stores it in *X*. After a message *STANDARD DEVIATION* is printed (line 6), the calculation is carried out on the line 7 and printed, following which control is returned to line 1, and the program loops through the steps once more.

Let's try this a few times to see how it works:

```
        SD
ENTER OBSERVATIONS
[]:
        1 2 1 2 1 2 1 2
8
NUMBER OF OBS:8
STANDARD DEVIATION
0.5345224838
ENTER OBSERVATIONS
[]:
```

Note the 8 just prior to the line giving the number of observations. The reason for this is that on line 4 of the function, in executing from right to left, ρX was put into *N* and *N* in turn into []. Whenever the quad appears to the <u>left</u> of the specification arrow, the system interprets this as a command to print out the value of whatever is to the right of the arrow. So the right hand side of line 4 really does two things: It stores the length of the vector *X* in the local variable *N* for subsequent use on lines 5 and 7 and causes a printout of the length at the same time. Since in going from right to left the box is encountered first, the contents are printed out first, before the literal message, and then reprinted following the message. We will edit the function a little later to remove this undesirable feature.

Any valid *APL* expression can be entered:

```
[]:
        8ρ1 2
8
NUMBER OF OBS:8
STANDARD DEVIATION
0.5345224838
ENTER OBSERVATIONS
[]:
```

(Now we'll try)

```
[]:
        []←8ρ1 2
1   2   1   2   1   2   1   2
8
NUMBER OF OBS:8
STANDARD DEVIATION
0.5345224838
ENTER OBSERVATIONS
[]:
```

Since the quad appears just to the left of the arrow in this input, it causes an immediate printout of 8ρ1 2 and then proceeds with execution of the function.

Escaping by simply pressing RETURN and not entering anything is not enough. The system has to have some input, and only if an empty vector is entered is it possible to escape:

```
□:
      ι0
```

Let's now open up the function to remove the extra quad.   We'll use detailed editing on line 4:

```
      ∇SD[4□10]
[4]    'NUMBER OF OBS:';□←N←ρX
              //
[4]    'NUMBER OF OBS:';N←ρX∇
```

Now executing SD once more, it appears to be OK:

```
      SD
ENTER OBSERVATIONS
□:
      10ρ1 2

NUMBER OF OBS:10
STANDARD DEVIATION
0.5270462767
ENTER OBSERVATIONS
□:
         ' '
         @
```

Incidentally, as the last input shows, another way to enter an empty vector is to type ''.   Do you remember why this works?

This function has introduced three new features: (1) the use of the semi-colon for mixed output; (2) the quad to the left of the specification arrow; and (3) a quad to the right of the specification arrow which returns □: on the paper, skips a line and waits for any valid *APL* expression to be typed in as input.   The contents of the quad in the last case can be put into storage by an expression like $X←□$ which makes input available for future use in the function (or outside if X is a global variable).

SUB is another function that utilizes the quad.   Before displaying it we'll try it out a few times:

```
      SUB
3-3
□:
      0
THATS RIGHT
10-5
□:
      6
```

```
5+□=10
TRY AGAIN
10-5
□:
(RETURN)
□:
(RETURN)
□:
(RETURN)
□:
        5
THATS RIGHT
5-0
□:
        5
THATS RIGHT
14-10
□:
        HELP
○○○○○○○○○○○○○○    TAKE AWAY
○○○○○○○○○○○
14-10
□:
        4
THATS RIGHT
19-7
□:
        19-7
THATS RIGHT
11-9
□:
        11-9
THATS RIGHT
1-0
□:
        11-10
THATS RIGHT
11-8
□:
```

Note that giving no input to the program and just pressing RETURN (top of this page) won't get you out. Also observe the responses of the program under different conditions, and the fact that any *APL* expression can be used as input.

Let's now interrupt the function to get out. Since the input box will accept any *APL* expression,)*CLEAR* or)*LOAD* will get us out, but only at the expense of destroying the active workspace. We'll use the stop vector and then remove the suspension:

[]:
      SΔSUB←ι100

SUB[5]
)SI
SUB[5] *
      →0
      SΔSUB←0

Here is *SUB*:

      ∇SUB[[]]∇
    ∇ SUB
[1]   P←?20
[2]   P←P,⁻1+?P+1
[3]   P[1];'-';P[2]
[4]   A←[]
[5]   →OOK×ιA=-/P
[6]   →NP×ιA=HELP
[7]   →0×ιA=STOP
[8]   P[2];'+[]=';P[1]
[9]   'TRY AGAIN'
[10] →3
[11] OOK:'THATS RIGHT'
[12] →1
[13] NP:(P[1]ρ'∘'),'   TAKE AWAY'
[14] P[2]ρ'∘'
[15] →3
    ∇

On line 1 a random number from 1 to 20 is generated and stored in P. This
is then respecified by catenating to P a second random number from 0 to P.
Line 3 prints out mixed output, the first random number followed by the subtract sign and the second random number. Line 4 prints a box to accept
input, while line 5 causes a branch to 11 if the answer is correct and
prints the message *THATS RIGHT*, otherwise we drop through to 6. If
HELP is typed, line 6 branches to 13, and if *STOP* is typed, we exit the
function.

Assuming an incorrect answer and neither *HELP* nor *STOP* are entered, lines
8, 9 and 10 restate the problem and tell us to *TRY AGAIN*, and we start
over on line 3 with the same problem. If the problem is answered correctly
this time and we get to line 11, we branch to 1 and get a new problem to do.

Typing *HELP* brings us to line 13 where $P[1]$ copies of the small circle
followed by some spaces and the words *TAKE AWAY*, followed in turn by
$P[2]$ copies of the small circle on the next line and a restatement of the
problem are printed out, and we cycle through the same problem once again.

HELP and *STOP* in this exercise are global variables with rather unlikely
values attached to them to make them as student-proof as possible:

      HELP
2.718281828
      *1
2.718281828

```
        STOP
15.15426224
        **1
15.15426224
```

Being global they appear on the list of variables for 1 *CLASS*:

```
        )VARS
B         CIRCUIT  D        HELP     M         MILEAGE PREVIOUSTIME
SPL       STOP     TAB0     TAB1     TAB2      TAB3    X         Y
```

To see if *STOP* works, we'll call for *SUB* again:

```
        SUB
11-1
□:
        10
THATS  RIGHT
14-6
□:
        STOP
        @
```

and we get out of the program as anticipated.

Additional uses of the quad

Don't get the impression from the previous illustrations that the quad can be used only within defined functions. Here, for example, are some more ways in which the quad can be utilized for the display and input of information. Keep in mind that at all times, though it may be used to the left of the specification arrow, the quad is <u>not</u> a variable, and no values go into storage as a result of its use in this manner.

```
        □
□:
        15.27×8-42
‾519.18
        A←5 15 ‾2 ‾6 0
        A[□←(+/(A∘.≥A)-□←(X∘.>X)∧□←A∘.=A)ιX←ιρA]

  1  0  0  0  0
  0  1  0  0  0
  0  0  1  0  0
  0  0  0  1  0
  0  0  0  0  1

  0  0  0  0  0
  0  0  0  0  0
  0  0  0  0  0
  0  0  0  0  0
  0  0  0  0  0
  4   3  ‾5   1   2
 ‾6  ‾2   0   5   15
```

The last example uses the quad to display intermediate results, and helps us to understand how a messy expression such as the one just given works.

Here are some additional examples of the quad used as an input indicator on the right of the specification arrow:

```
        R←□
□:
        64
        R
64
        R+□÷10
□:
        16
65.6
        T←□
□:
        'THE CAT IN THE HAT'
        T
THE CAT IN THE HAT
```

The quad can also be used in a branch command (see page 176 at the end of chapter 24):

```
        →8,ρ□←'THIS MESSAGE WILL BE PRINTED'
```

Finally, when a system command is entered as input with the quad, the quad will disappear if the command replaces the active workspace or signs off, and will reappear after saving or when execution is resumed after loading or signing on again (if)CONTINUE had been executed). It also appears in the state indicator if)SI is entered as input.

The quote-quad

In the last program we were rather generous in allowing any APL expression as input. What if we want an exact predetermined answer? An example of such a program is given by ADD :

```
        ∇ADD[□]∇
      ∇ ADD
[1]     □←P←? 10 10
[2]     →0×ι0=ρA←,⍞
[3]     →WRONG×ι~∧/A∈'0123456789'
[4]     A←10⊥¯1+'0123456789'ιA
[5]     →1×ιA=+/P
[6]     'TRY AGAIN'
[7]     →2
[8]   WRONG:'?????????????'
[9]     →2
      ∇
```

This contains a quad with a quote overstruck. The effect of this is to make whatever is typed in accepted literally. This includes even system commands like OFF, CLEAR, etc., so it's vital that an appropriate means of escape from the function be planned.

After two random numbers are generated and printed out by being assigned to the box, line 2 exits us if an empty vector is entered. There is a branch to 8 if any character other than 0-9 is inputted. Line 4 takes the literal representation of the input, converts it to decimal representation, and puts it in *A*. This is then matched against the correct answer on line 5. If correct, we get another problem; if not, the message *TRY AGAIN*. Here is a sample execution:

```
        ADD
8    10
18
8    3
8+3
????????????
R E W
????????????
11
1    8
)CLEAR
????????????
(escape is effected by entry of a return)
```

Note that no quad is printed out. The typeball simply moves over to the left margin when literal input is called for, and the keyboard is unlocked.

Another function that accepts literal input is *SPELL* :

```
        SPELL
3
THREE
THATS RIGHT
5
FIV
TRY AGAIN
5
FIVE
THATS RIGHT
8
STOP
        ∇SPELL[□]∇
    ∇ SPELL
[1]     N←¯1+?10
[2]     N
[3]     ANS←⍞
[4]     →0×ι∧/(4ρANS)='STOP'
[5]     →CORRECT×ι∧/(5ρANS,'      ')=SPL[N+1;]
[6]     'TRY AGAIN'
[7]     →2
[8]  CORRECT:'THATS RIGHT'
[9]     →1
    ∇
```

A random number from 0 to 9 is selected, assigned to *N*, and printed on lines 1 and 2. Line 3 accepts the input and puts it in *ANS*. The next line compares the first four characters of the input with *STOP*. If they match,

we're out. If not, we drop through to line 5 where the first five characters of *ANS* are compared with the (*N*+1)th row of *SPL* :

        SPL

ZERO
ONE
TWO
THREE
FOUR
FIVE
SIX
SEVEN
EIGHT
NINE

If they match, we branch to line 8, where *THATS RIGHT* is printed out and
followed by another problem. Otherwise we get the message *TRY AGAIN* and
recycle through the problem.

SPL is actually a 10-row 5-column matrix with blanks on the end where
needed to fill up the five columns. We can show how such a matrix can
be built by executing

        W←10 5ρ'*ONE TWO THREEFOUR* '
        W

ONE
TWO
THREE
FOUR
ONE
TWO
THREE
FOUR
ONE
TWO

Two problems occur in connection with the function *SPELL* . One difficulty
in designing such a function is that as it is now set up, any characters
beyond the first five aren't checked on line 5. This leads to anomalies
like

        SPELL
9
NINE RT
THATS RIGHT
3
STOP

Another real problem is that we have built in no means of escape, except by
typing *STOP*. An additional avenue of escape from such a program will be
discussed further on in this chapter.

Extensions of the quote-quad

As with the quad, the quote quad can also be used by itself:

```
        Z←⍞
SIMON SAYS
        Z
SIMON SAYS
        LIT←⍞
HE WON'T GO
        LIT
HE WON'T GO
        ⍴LIT
11
```

Escape from an input loop

It sometimes happens that in spite of our best efforts, we may be caught in an endless loop and not know how to get out, or, what is worse, the function is poorly designed and has no way out. Shutting the terminal off won't help us, since when we sign on again we will be right back where we were before, because the *CONTINUE* workspace is automatically removed.

APL provides two escape mechanisms for such situations. Those functions calling for numeric input (□) can be gotten out of by typing →, while escape from those which require literal input (⍞) can be achieved by entering *O* backspace *U* backspace *T*, forming the overstruck character *⍝*.

PROBLEMS

1. Define a function that will give multiplication drill of integers *?N* for some argument *N* in the header. Have your function print out a message *TRY AGAIN* for wrong answers. Use *STOP* as a global variable for escape from the function.

2. Modify your answer to the above problem so that three tries are allowed, after which the correct answer is printed out and another problem is posed.

3. Add a further refinement to the multiplication drill so that when *HELP* is typed, the answer to the problem is given as *X*[1] rows of *X*[2] stars each, with an appropriate message and a repetition of the problem. *X* is the vector of random integers generated in the problem.

4. For a final feature, modify your function for problem 3 to print out the amount of time required to get the correct solution.

5. Replace the message *TRY AGAIN* on line 6 of *SPELL* with a statement Telling what the answer is.

6. Define a function *ENTER* that will take the literal spelling of numbers, like those in *SPL* , and put them in successive rows of a 20-column matrix. Exit from the function will be effected by entering an empty vector.

CHAPTER 34:

Miscellaneous APL commands and features

This chapter will be a catch-all for the remaining *APL* commands and features.

The commands *ORIGIN*, *WIDTH*, *DIGITS*

These system commands affect the active workspace and travel with it when it is saved. *ORIGIN,* sets the origin for indexing on arrays and all operations which depend on the index. Two origins are available, 0 and 1. Here is the command and its effect on the iota and indexing functions:

```
      )ORIGIN 0
WAS 1
      ι5
0  1  2  3  4
      ALF←'ABCDEFGHIJK'
      ALFι'CAFE'
2  0  5  4
      ALF[2 0 5 4]
CAFE
      4?4
3  0  2  1
```

Other array operations not shown here will be similarly changed. For instance, in a workspace set to origin 0 the normal transpose 2 1⍉*M* (*M* is some array) would have to be 1 0⍉*M*. Branching would be affected also, as, for example, in the case of →3×ι*A*=*B* , but this could be compensated for by calling for →3⌈ι*A*=*B* , which works for either origin (why?), or by increased use of labels.

To tell what the origin is in a workspace all we need do is execute

```
      ι1
0
```

Clearly the origin is 0, for an origin of 1 would call for a response of 1. Finally, to reset the origin, execute

```
      )ORIGIN 1
WAS 0
```

and we are back to normal:

```
      ι5
1   2   3   4   5
```

The *WIDTH* command works in much the same fashion, and sets the width of the printed line as specified by the integer (between 30 and 130) following the command:

```
      )WIDTH 30
WAS 120
      100ρ'0123456789'
0123456789012345678901234567890
      012345678901234567890123
      456789012345678901234567
      8901234567890123456789
```

This command won't change the margin settings on the terminal, nor the length of the input lines, but every line of output will be no longer than the width specified.

We'll now reset the width to its normal value:

```
      )WIDTH 120
WAS 30
```

The *DIGITS* command sets the number of significant places in the numerical output to some number between 1 and 16:

```
      )DIGITS 5
WAS 10
      1÷7
0.14286
      )DIGITS 10
WAS 5
      1÷7
0.1428571429
      )DIGITS 16
WAS 10
      1÷7
0.1428571428571428
      )DIGITS 20
INCORRECT COMMAND
      )DIGITS 10
WAS 16
```

The actual calculations aren't affected, only the output as printed.

The workspace *WSFNS*

In library 1 is a workspace called *WSFNS* , which you should now load:

```
      )LOAD 1 WSFNS
SAVED  23.45.54 07/07/69
      )FNS
DELAY   DIGITS   ORIGIN   SETLINK WIDTH
      )VARS
DESCRIBE
```

Execute *DESCRIBE* to see how the functions in this workspace are used:

```
      DESCRIBE
```

THE FUNCTIONS ORIGIN, WIDTH, AND DIGITS ARE EACH
SIMILAR TO THE COMMAND OF THE SAME NAME, EXCEPT THAT EACH IS
A FUNCTION RATHER THAN A COMMAND AND MAY THEREFORE BE USED
WITHIN OTHER FUNCTIONS.   EACH HAS AN EXPLICIT RESULT WHICH
IS THE PREVIOUS VALUE OF THE RELEVANT SYSTEM PARAMETER.

FOR EXAMPLE, THE FOLLOWING FUNCTION:

```
       ∇F X
[1]    X←ORIGIN X
[2]    G
[3]    X←ORIGIN X∇
```

WILL EXECUTE THE FUNCTION G WITH WHATEVER INDEX ORIGIN IS
SPECIFIED BY THE ARGUMENT OF F, AND WILL RESTORE THE INDEX
ORIGIN TO THE VALUE THAT IT HAD BEFORE THE EXECUTION OF F.

THE FOLLOWING FUNCTIONS ARE ALSO AVAILABLE:

<u>SYNTAX</u>   <u>DESCRIPTION</u>

Z←SETLINK X   *SETS THE VALUE OF THE LINK IN THE CHAIN OF*
                NUMBERS GENERATED IN THE USE OF THE ROLL AND
                DEAL FUNCTIONS.   THE EXPLICIT RESULT PRODUCED
                BY SETLINK IS THE PREVIOUS VALUE OF THE LINK.

                THE RESULTS PRODUCED BY THE ROLL AND DEAL
                FUNCTIONS ARE NOT THE LINKS THEMSELVES, BUT
                RATHER SOME FUNCTION OF THEM.   THE LENGTH OF
                THE CHAIN (BEFORE REPETITION) IS 2*31.

DELAY X   *DELAYS EXECUTION FOR X SECONDS.*

Here are some examples:

```
      X←WIDTH 30
      40ρ'0123456789'
01234567890123456789012345678 9
      0123456789
      X
120
      WIDTH X
30
```

```
      X←ORIGIN 1
      X
1
      ι3
1   2   3
      X←ORIGIN 0
      ι3
0   1   2
      ORIGIN X
0
      ι3
1   2   3
```

When the function is called for, the most recently set value is given, and
it is then reset to the original value, as stated in *DESCRIBE* above. The
function *DIGITS* works in the same way:

```
      X←DIGITS 5
      1÷3
0.33333
      X
10
      DIGITS X
5
      1÷3
0.3333333333
```

Groups

The command *GROUP* collects all but the first of the names that follow it
and stores them under the first name. Any object, including names of other
groups and even nonexistent global objects can be a member of a group, but
the group name can't be the same as that of a global object in the workspace.
The *COPY* and *ERASE* commands can be used with groups to make it easier to
move or delete a collection of related global objects. For some examples
we'll use functions and variables from 1 *CLASS*:

```
      )LOAD 1 CLASS
SAVED  15.02.39 07/29/69
      )WIDTH 60
WAS 120
      )FNS
ADD       AGAIN    AVG      AVG1     AVG2     AVG3     AVG4      AVG5
BASE      C        CMP      CMPX     CMPY     COLCAT1  COLCAT2
COLCAT3 COS        COSINE   CP       CPUTIME CP1       DEC
DELAY    DESCRIBE           DFT      DICE     E        FACT
FACTLOOP           GEO2     GEO3     HEXA     HY       HYP
INSERT   INV       MEAN     PI       RECT     REP      REVERSE
ROWCAT   RUN       S        SD       SETVARIABLES      SIGN      SORT
SPELL    SQRT      STAT     STATISTICS        SUB      SUMSCAN TIME
TIMEFACT           TRA      TRACETIME
```

```
      )VARS
B         CIRCUIT D        HELP      M         MILEAGE PREVIOUSTIME
SPL       STOP     TAB0    TAB1      TAB2      TAB3     X         Y
      )GROUP STAT ADD AGAIN AVG
NOT GROUPED, NAME IN USE
      )GROUP BAKER ADD AGAIN AVG
      @
```

The movement of the typeball six spaces over constitutes the system's
response to a successful grouping.

To list the members of the group, type

```
      )GRP BAKER
ADD       AGAIN    AVG
```

The group may be respecified in the same way as for a variable:

```
      )GROUP BAKER AVG1 AVG2 BOO WRONG HELP SOWHAT
      @
      )GRP BAKER
AVG1      AVG2     BOO       WRONG     HELP      SOWHAT
```

It may be enlarged by typing

```
      )GROUP BAKER BAKER SORT
      )GRP BAKER
AVG1      AVG2     BOO       WRONG     HELP      SOWHAT   SORT
```

and removed by entering an empty vector after the group name (or erasing):

```
      )GROUP BAKER
      @
      )GRP BAKER
      @
```

Having removed the group *BAKER* (it could also be removed with the *ERASE*
command, but this removes the members as well as the group itself, in contrast with the above command, which just disperses the group), let's define
two additional groups *ABLE* and *COVER*, one of which will include the
other:

```
      )GROUP ABLE PI RECT REP OOK SAY
      @
      )GROUP COVER ABLE TAB3 Y
      @
```

The names of all the groups in the active workspace can be listed by the
command

```
      )GRPS
ABLE      BAKER    COVER
```

The restrictions on group names are the same as those applying to functions
and variables, and a partial listing can be obtained by following the

command by a letter of the alphabet.

Message commands

The last set of system commands is that concerned with communication
between terminals (including the operator). Messages of importance to all
connected users begin with *PA!* which, contrary to public opinion, does
not stand for "political announcement."

Although messages can be received ordinarily only when the receiving keyboard is locked and not in the middle of function execution, such public
address messages can interrupt at any time. They come from the system
recording terminal, and are distinguished from routine messages from the
operator, which begin with *OPR:*

There are four message commands available to the user. Each is followed
by one line of text of length not exceeding 120 spaces:

> *)OPR   MESSAGE*

This prints out the message at the operator's terminal, prefixed by your
port number and *R*, indicating that a reply is expected, and then locks your
terminal until a reply is received. The ATTN button will unlock the keyboard
before the reply, if desired.

> *)MSG   PORT NUMBER AND MESSAGE*

This command must be followed by a port number and text, and will send a
message to the designated port. (To get the port numbers associated with
connected users, ask for *)PORTS* followed by the user code.) The message
will print out at the receiving terminal, along with the port number of the
sending terminal and the prefix *R* to indicate that a reply is expected.

As before the keyboard remains locked until a reply is received.

> *)MSGN   )OPRN*

These are the same as *)MSG* and *)OPR* except that no reply is expected and
the keyboard unlocks after transmission is completed. In all cases the
word *SENT* is printed at your terminal when transmission is complete.

Security features for user protection

APL makes available to each user a number of safety features that restrict
access to parts of the system. One of these has already been introduced,
the password associated with a user number. It can be changed at sign-off
by

> *)SIGN-OFF COMMAND:NEWPASSWORD*

or simply discontinued by following the sign-off command with a colon.

Another is a workspace lock, which follows the workspace name and is
separated from it by a colon. This lock must be included with the workspace when loaded. The lock remains in effect unless it is changed

when the workspace is saved again. As with the sign-off command,
a save followed only by a colon removes the lock. Also, workspaces
which are locked are listed when)*LIB* is called for, but the locks aren't
included for obvious reasons, and the locked workspaces aren't identified
as such in the listing. Should you be so unfortunate as to forget what
the lock name is, there isn't any way for you to retrieve the workspace
in question. About all you can do with it is to drop it.

Individual functions can also be locked by overstriking the opening and/or
closing dels with the tilde: ⍫. This is useful for sealing up functions
which contain proprietary information or things like classroom exercises
which a teacher doesn't want students to be able to see. Functions locked
in this manner are forever buried and inaccessible (see below) even to the
one who inserted it.

Locking a function isn't quite as bad as we may have made it sound in the
previous paragraph, however, since the function is still available for
every kind of use save two: it can't be displayed or edited. In fact, even
copying is possible, but the copy is likewise subject to the same restrictions as the original.

Earlier we touched on how names of functions and variables can be made up.
There is considerable freedom in choosing such names in that any sequence
of characters alphabetic (including underlined letters) and numeric except
blanks can be used, as long as the first character is alphabetic. *APL*
recognizes only the first 11 for workspace names, the first 8 for passwords
or locks, and the first 77 for all others, which is hardly likely to cramp
any user's style! Only the first 4 characters, incidentally, are significant for system commands, any additional ones being included only to make
it easier to remember.

Fuzz

Whenever a command is executed in *APL* calling for a comparison of two
numbers, since the number of significant figures in *APL* calculations isn't
infinite, there is a question as to how close two numbers must be in order
to be considered equal. The allowable discrepancy is about $1E^{-}13$, and is
called _fuzz_. Try some of the relationals or other functions dependent on
comparisons of two numbers, using as arguments numbers differing by less
than the fuzz, to illustrate these limitations. (Also see problem 9,
chapter 9.)

PROBLEMS

1. Execute each of the following in turn and observe the behavior of the
    arrays generated:

)LOAD 1 CLASS
        Y←ι10
)ORIGIN 0
        TAB3[0;2;1]
        Yι4 5 6
)DIGITS 5

```
            ÷TAB3
            )WIDTH 60
            )FNS J
            )LOAD 1 WSFNS
            X←DIGITS 6
            ÷ι7
            X
            DIGITS X
            ÷ι7
```

2.   Why is the expression $A[\iota N]$ independent of the index origin?

3.   Execute $\iota0$ and $\iota1$ with $)ORIGIN$ 0.   Are they vectors?   Of what size?

4.   Send a message to your own port number.   (This is useful when you want to be assured of getting an intelligent response!)

5.   Specify $A\leftarrow9.222222222222222$, $B\leftarrow9.222222222222227$, $C\leftarrow\iota10$ and execute $A=B$, $A\epsilon B$, $A-B$, $C[3.000000000000008]$.   Account for the responses.

6.   Rewrite the function SUB (page 253) using $ORIGIN$ in 1 $WSFNS$ before generating the second random number on line 2.

7.   Practice forming groups out of the functions and variables in 1 $CLASS$ List the groups and their members.

Appendix
Summary of APL notation

This section will be a summary of all *APL* function symbols with their names and the appropriate references in the preceding pages. System commands will not be included here since they were covered in chapters 15 and 34.

Omission of references to the use of some standard scalar dyadic functions with arrays of rank greater than 1 does not necessarily mean that the syntax of the function doesn't allow it, but simply that no specific examples or discussions were included. Where they occur, f and g stand for any standard scalar dyadic functions.

Function symbol	Monadic (M) Dyadic (D)	Name	References to arrays of rank 0,1	rank >1
<	D	less than	25	
≤	D	less than or equal	25	
=	D	equal	26	
≥	D	greater than or equal	25	
>	D	greater than	25	
≠	D	not equal	25	
∨	D	logical OR	27	
∧	D	logical AND	26	
⍱	D	logical NOR	27	
⍲	D	logical NAND	27	
−	M	arith. negation	50	197
−	D	subtraction	7	
+	M	additive identity	55	
+	D	addition	6,9	196
÷	M	reciprocal	51	
÷	D	division	7,11	196
×	M	signum	56	
×	D	multiplication	7,11	197
?	M	roll (query)	55	
?	D	deal (query)	154	
∈	D	membership	153	213
ρ	M	size (dimension vect)	116	117
ρ	D	Restructure	126	127
~	M	logical NOT (NEGATION)	52	
↑	D	take	152	213

Function symbol	Monadic (M) Dyadic (D)	Name	References to arrays of rank 0,1	rank >1
↓	D	drop	153	213
ι	M	index generator	113	
ι	D	index of (ranking)	136	
○	M	pi times	186	
○	D	circular functions	180	
φ,⊖	M	reversal	150	202,203
φ,⊖	D	rotate	150	203,204
⍉	M	transpose	215	215
⍉	D	transpose		216
*	M	exponential	51	
*	D	power	15	
⍟	M	natural logarithm	51	
⍟	D	logarithm to a base	17	
⌈	M	ceiling	52	
⌈	D	maximum	18	
⌊	M	floor	53	
⌊	D	minimum	18	
⍋	M	grade up	154	
⍒	M	grade down	154	
!	M	factorial	50	198
!	D	combinations	21	
[]	M	indexing	138	210
⊥	D	decode (base value)	160	319
⊤	D	encode (representation)	162	319
⌶	M	I-beam functions	188-191	
|	M	absolute value	51	
|	D	residue	23	
,	M	ravel	124	125
,	D	catenate, laminate	122	208,317
f/	D	reduction	37,200	198,199
/,⌿	D	compression	140	206
\,⍀	D	expansion	142	206
∘.f	D	outer product	222	224
f.g	D	inner product	233	233
⌹	D	matrix divide		316

Miscellaneous *APL* symbols

Symbol	Name	References
⁻	negative	7
←	specification	30
→	branch	169
_	underline	32
∇	del	63
⍫	locked function	265
Δ	delta	178(trace),179(stop)
'	quote	130
□	quad	63(disp),249(inp),254(out)
⍞	quote-quad	255,258
( )	parentheses	44(grouping),33(sys com)

Symbol	Name	References
;	semicolon	210(indexing),89(fn header) 250(mixed output)
:	colon	4(password),172(labels)
A	lamp (comment)	9
E	exponential notation	16
.	decimal point	6
v	correction indicator	8
^	error indicator	7
/	char deletion (in edit)	83

Answers to problems

Some of the problems will have more than one solution given. This will generally occur when there exist different, but sound, alternate approaches to the solution. The proposed solutions, because they are keyed to the functions presented up to that point in the text, will not always be the most concise or elegant possible, with the drill problems occasionally returning error messages. For this reason, certain solutions will have references to functions to be introduced at a later point in the text, and which will simplify the task of defining the function or expression needed to solve the problem.

Chapter 2
1.
```
            6  8  2  4+3  9  1  1
   9    17   3   5
            1  0  9  8-4  2  2  3
  ‾3   ‾2   7   5
            3-‾1  ‾56.7  0  ‾.19
  4    59.7   3    3.19
            3  4×1  2  3
  LENGTH ERROR
            3  4  ×  1  2  3
                   ∧
            5  4  3×6
  30    24   18
            2 ‾‾ 3
  SYNTAX ERROR
            2 ‾‾ 3
            ∧
```

Reminder: the negative sign is a mark of punctuation, not a function
```
            1  2  8÷1  2  0
  DOMAIN ERROR
            1  2  8  ÷  1  2  0
                      ∧
            10÷10  5  2  1
  1    2    5    10
```

```
          ‾2 0 .81+15 6 ‾5
    13  6  ‾4.19
3.          155 89 45×1.25 .50 .25
    193.75  44.5  11.25
4.          59.50 72.50 79.50 83.00÷1263 2016 1997 3028
    0.04711005542  0.03596230159  0.03980971457  0.02741083223
```

Chapter 3
```
1.          3⌈3 7 ‾10.8 2 0
    3  7  3  3  3
            1 9 ‾5 ‾2⌊0 6 4 3
    0  6  ‾5  ‾2
            5 ‾1 52⌈6
    6  6  52
            1⊕1
    1
            2*.5 .333 .25 .2
    1.414213562  1.25962998  1.189207115  1.148698355
            3*4 2 1 0 ‾5
    81  9  3  1  0.004115226337
            10⊕1 2 3 4 5
    0  0.3010299957  0.4771212547  0.6020599913  0.6989700043
            2 3 4 5 6⊕2
    1  0.6309297536  0.5  0.4306765581  0.3868528072
            2⌊0 5 ‾8
    0  2  ‾8
            ‾2⊕25
DOMAIN ERROR
            ‾2⊕25
             ∧
Both arguments must be greater than 0, and if the left argument is
1, the right argument must be 1 also.
            ‾2*.5
DOMAIN ERROR
            ‾2*0.5
             ∧
            1⊕55
DOMAIN ERROR
            1⊕55
             ∧
            ‾8*.3333333333333
DOMAIN ERROR
            ‾8*0.3333333333333
             ∧
Try adding a few more 3's on the right and reexecuting.
            10⊕0
DOMAIN ERROR
            10⊕0
             ∧
            1*0 1 10 100 1000
    1  1  1  1  1
            ‾7.11E4÷9.45E‾3
    ‾7523809.524
```

$$21.268E1+4.56E^-2$$
212.7256
$$8.2E0×7.9E^-3+56$$
459.26478

2.

	$1E0$		$1E^-1$
1		0.1	
	$1E1$		$1E^-2$
10		0.01	
	$1E6$		$1E^-4$
1000000		0.0001	
	$1E9$		$1E^-5$
1000000000		$1E^-5$	
	$1E10$		$1E^-6$
$1E10$		$1E^-6$	

3.   15 20 18 32 29⌊18 20 15 10 49
    15   20   15   10   29

4.   10⊛1÷C
    This is a bit ahead of the game in that we haven't said anything yet
    about order of execution, where multiple operations occur in a single
    expression. See chapter 8 for more details.

Chapter 4

1.   1 9 8|3 4 6
    0   4   6
            $^-$3 $^-$2 $^-$1|3
    0   1   0
            0|1 2 3
    1   2   3
            3|$^-$3 $^-$2 0 1 2 3
    0   1   0   1   2   0
            1|3.4 $^-$2.2 .019
    0.4   0.8   0.019
            0 1 2 3 4!3 4 5 6 7
    1   4   10   20   35
            4!3 4 5 6 7
    0   1   5   15   35
            $^-$2 4 $^-$5|8   13   3.78
    0   1   3.78

2.   The 5| any integer is in the set 0 1 2 3 4, which is in S. Note
    also that the condition $N≥4$ given in the problem is unnecessary.
3.   If the result of $B|A$ is zero, then A is divisible by B.
4.   Hours: $H-1|H$; Minutes: $60|H×60$
    The last solution should be tried for typical values of H. You will
    see that H is multiplied by 60 first, and then $60|H$ is obtained.
    More about order of execution in chapter 8.
5.   3!49
    Following the hint, there are three separators, each of which can be
    in any one of forty nine positions.
6.   4!30
7. $N-1|N$
    This works only for nonnegative values of N.
8.   1|$^-$1×N or 1-1|N

Chapter 5

```
1.              0  0  1  1∨0  1  0  1
       0   1    1  1
                1  0  1  0∧1  0  0  1
       1   0    0  0
                2  4  7  ‾2>6  ‾1  0  4
       0   1    1  0
                0  1  2  3=0  1  3  2
       1   1    0  0
                4  ‾5  ‾1  ‾6.8≥4  1  ‾1  2
       1   0    1  0
                8  7  6  5  4  3  2  1≤1  2  3  4  5  6  7  8
       0   0    0  0  1  1  1  1
                2  3  0<5  ‾1  4
       1   0    1
                3  1  2≠1  2  3
       1   1    1
                ~1  0
       0   1
                0  0  1  1⩒0  1  0  1
       1   0    0  0
                1  0  1  0⩑1  0  0  1
       0   1    1  1
```

2. The factors of an integer N are those integers which divide N. Hence set $0=1\ 2\ 3...N|N$.

3. $A≥0$ or $0≤A$ yields a logical vector with 1's in those positions corresponding to the accounts not overdrawn.

4. $A∨0=B$ works if either or both conditions hold while $A≠0=B$ works when only one of the conditions holds, but not both. Later, when the function $\sim$ (logical negation) is introduced, $A∨{\sim}B$ will also be a possible solution.

5. EXCLUSIVE NOR or NEXCLUSIVE OR.

6. Although logical negation $\sim$ won't be introduced until chapter 9, you should explore its action in the vector 0 1. If we give the name A to 0 0 1 1, then $A∧{\sim}A$ is always 0 and $A∨{\sim}A$ is always 1.

Chapter 6

```
1.              ~A∨~B
       0   1    0  1
                ~A∧B
       1   1    1  1
                ~B∨C
       1   0    1  0
                ~B∧~C
       1   0    1  0
                ~C≠D
       0   0    0  0
                ~D=B
       1   0    1  0
```

The results can be explained by assuming that logical negation $\sim$ acts on everything to the right of it. More about this in chapter 9.

2.
```
                B←2|A
                C←0=B
```
Also $B←A+1$ followed by $2|B$. If you understand the use of $\sim$, try $\sim2|A$.

3. $E \leftarrow 3 \ 7 \ 15 \ 2.7$
              $F \leftarrow E \star 2$
              $AREA \leftarrow 6 \times F$
              $AREA$
     54   294   1350   43.74
     This can be done in one step as $6 \times E \star 2$.

4. $X2 \leftarrow X \times X$
     $X3 \leftarrow X2 \times X$

5.   A) $Z \leftarrow S \times 0$ B) $W \leftarrow S \star 0$
                   $Z \leftarrow S - S$ $W \leftarrow S = S$
                   $Z \leftarrow S \neq S$ $W \leftarrow S \leq S$
                   $Z \leftarrow S \mid S$ $W \leftarrow S \div S$
                   $Z \leftarrow S > S$ $W \leftarrow S \circledast S$
                   $Z \leftarrow 0 \star S$ $W \leftarrow 0 \,!\, S$
                   $Z \leftarrow 0 \lfloor S$ $W \leftarrow S \,!\, S$
                   etc.

6. $B \leftarrow 2 \times A \leftarrow 3 \ 4 \ 5 \ 6 \ 7$

Chapter 7

1. $+/3 \ 7 \ ^-10 \ 15 \ 22$
     37
              $\div/3 \ 5 \ 2$
     1.2
              $\wedge/1 \ 1 \ 1$
     1
              $=/3 \ 2 \ 2$
     0
              $\lceil/1 \ ^-14.7 \ 22 \ 6$
     22
              $-/2 \ 4 \ 6 \ 8 \ 10$
     6
              $\star/3 \ 2 \ 1$
     9
              $\vee/0 \ 1 \ 0 \ 1$
     1
              $>/1 \ ^-2 \ ^-4$
     0
              $\times/2 \ 4 \ 6 \ 8 \ 10$
     3840
              $\wedge/1 \ 0 \ 1 \ 1$
     0
              $\vee/0 \ 0 \ 0$
     0
              $\lfloor/^-2 \ 4 \ 0 \ ^-8$
     $^-8$

2. $\wedge/$ returns a 1 if and only if all the components are 1, 0 otherwise.
     $\vee/$ returns a 0 if and only if all the components are 0, 1 otherwise.
     $=/$ (applied to a logical vector) returns a 0 if there are an odd
     number of 0's, 1 otherwise.

3. $+/3 \times AV$
     69
     which is the same as $3 \times +/AV$.

4. $\lceil/Q \leftarrow 1 \ 7 \ ^-2 \ ^-3$

5. $S\leftarrow.5\times+/L$ After the rules governing order of execu-
    $A2\leftarrow S-L$ tion are introduced in chapter 8, this
    $Q\leftarrow\times/A2$ can be done more compactly as
    $R\leftarrow S\times Q$ $S\leftarrow.5\times+/L$
    $AREA\leftarrow R*.5$ $AREA\leftarrow(S\times\times/S-L)*.5$

6. Since the X-coordinate of a point is customarily written first, it is
    not enough to take $\div/Q-P$ since this results in the difference in the
    X-coordinates divided by the difference in the Y-coordinates,
    which is the reciprocal of the slope, according to the definition
    given. Hence, $A\leftarrow\div/Q-P$ and $SLOPE\leftarrow1\div A$, or more compactly,
    $SLOPE\leftarrow1\div\div/Q-P$.

Chapter 8
1. $4*3\lceil3*4$
    $5.846006549E48$
            $(4*3)\lceil3*4$
    81
            $5*3\times5$
    $3.051757813E10$
            $1\div2+X\leftarrow{}^-5\ 6\ 0\ 4\ 8\ {}^-6$
    ${}^-0.3333333333\quad 0.125\quad 0.5\quad 0.1666666667\quad 0.1\quad {}^-0.25$
            $76\div+/2+3\times1\ 2\ 3\ 4$
    2
            $6\div2-4*3$
    ${}^-0.09677419355$

2. The first, second and fourth expressions are equivalent.
3. A) $(3\div4)+(5\div6)-7\div8$ or better, $+/3\ 5\ {}^-7\div4\ 6\ 8$
    B) $(-/9\ 8\div7\ 10)\div-/1\ 2\div3\ 5$
4. $(\times/X)*1\div+/X=X$
    6.386118449
5. $(\sim A)\vee\sim B$
    $1\quad 1\quad 1\quad 0$
            $A\vee C\wedge B$
    $1\quad 1\quad 0\quad 1$
            $(A\wedge\sim B)\wedge A\vee C$
    $0\quad 1\quad 0\quad 0$
            $(\sim B)\vee A\vee\sim C$
    $0\quad 1\quad 1\quad 1$
6. B will be compared with $B+A$ for equality, with A added to that result.
    The expression works only when A is 0. More generally, parentheses
    are needed around $A+B$.
7. Brute force solution:$(0\neq4000|Y)\wedge(0=4|Y)\wedge(0=400|Y)=0=100|Y$
    Better solution: $2|+/0=4\ 100\ 400\ 4000|Y$
    Still better solution: $-/0=4\ 100\ 400\ 4000|Y$
8. The minus sign in front of the middle term acts on everything to the
    right of it.
    Correct version: $(X*2)+({}^-2\times X\times Y)+Y*2$ or $(X*2)+(Y*2)-2\times X\times Y$.
9. $BETA\leftarrow10\times10\circledast I\div IO$
10. ${}^-8+X\times X\times2+{}^-3\times X*2$
11. $((+/X*2)\div+/X=X)*.5$
12. Jack is to propose if 1) he has the ring, 2) the weather is favorable,
    3) Jill is younger than Jack and 4) Jack isn't over the age limit
    for Jill's beaux.
13. Annual: $P\times(1+.01\times R)*T$
    Quarterly: $P\times(1+.01\times R\div4)*T\times4$

Chapter 9

1.
```
        L¯2.7|¯15
1
        ?10 10 10 10
2  8  5  6
```
Your random numbers may be different from those shown
```
        ⊕14.1 86 .108
2.646174797  4.454347296  ¯2.225624052
        ×¯5.6 0 42
¯1  0  1
        +8.7 ¯19.1 23
8.7  ¯19.1  23
        ⌈8.1|32.68
1
        *3 4.7 ¯1.5
20.08553692  109.9471725  0.2231301601
        ⌈¯1.8 0 ¯21 5.6
¯1  0  ¯21  6
        ?3 4 5
1  1  4
        ÷3.5 ¯67 ¯.287
0.2857142857  ¯0.01492537313  ¯3.484320557
        |3.1 0 ¯5.6 ¯8
3.1  0  5.6  8
        !3 5 7 4
6  120  5040  24
        L5.5 6.8 ¯9.1 ¯.12
5  6  ¯10  ¯1
        -¯1.2 ¯6.7 .52 19.5
1.2  6.7  ¯0.52  ¯19.5
        14×⌈5.8×¯31.046
¯2520
```

2. Floor: $X-1|X$
   Ceiling: $X+1|-X$ These expressions work for all real X.

3.
```
        *2+A1←(¯1+A*3)÷2
3269017.372
        ~(2≤A)∧∨/3=B
0
        C≠LC←((A*2)+(A+1)*2)*.5
0
```

4.
```
0=(LN÷10)|N
×(LN÷10)|N
```

5.
```
A←Y-1969
LY←L.25×A
B←1+7|3+A+LY or, on one line   B←1+7|3+A+L.25×A←Y-1969
```

6. A)   `10>|V or 0=L10⊕V`
   B)   `10≤|V or ~0=L10⊕V`

7.
```
        (10*¯1)×L.5+6.18×10*1
6.2
        (10*¯2)×L.5+4.75×10*2
4.75
(10*-D)×L.5+N×10*D
```

8. `-(10*-D)×L.5+|N×10*D`
   The solution for problem 7 works for both positive and negative numbers.

9.
```
        M←84.6129999993
        M
84.613
```

```
          1E5×M
     8461300
          ⌊1E5×M
     8461299
```

10. $(\lfloor X×10*-(\lfloor 1+10\circledast X)-N)=\lfloor Y×10*-(\lfloor 1+10\circledast Y)-N$
11. A) $\lfloor D÷B$
     B) $\lceil D÷B$
12. The results of these instructions are dependent on your implementation
     of $AP\widetilde{L}$. You cannot tell when the system evaluates an expression in
     parentheses. Hence, you should avoid writing commands like those
     shown in the problem.
13. $(\lfloor X+.5)-0=2|X-.5$
     $(\lceil X-.5)+\sim×2|X+.5$

Chapter 10

1.
```
              ∇Z←EQ X                        ∇Z←EQ1 X
     [1]      Z←0=×/X-2 3∇      or    [1]    Z←××/X-2 3∇
```
2.
```
              ∇R←H BB AB
     [1]      R←H÷AB∇
```
3.
```
              ∇T←HERO L
     [1]      S←.5×+/L
     [2]      T←(S××/S-L)*.5∇
```
4.
```
              ∇REFUND E
     [1]      +/.5×E⌊500 200∇
```
5.
```
              ∇RT←PR M
     [1]      RT←÷+/÷M∇
```
6.
```
              ∇R←SD X                        ∇R←SD1 X
     [1]      R←AVG X         or      [1]    R←(AVG(X-AVG X)*2)*.5∇
     [2]      R←R-X
     [3]      R←R*2
     [4]      R←(AVG R)*.5∇
```
7.
```
              ∇M←MR REL V
     [1]      M←MR÷(1-(V*2)÷9E16)*.5∇
```
8.
```
              ∇Z←X PLUS Y                    ∇Z←X MINUS Y
     [1]      Z←X+Y∇                  [1]    Z←X-Y∇
              ∇Z←X TIMES Y                   ∇Z←X DIVIDEDBY Y
     [1]      Z←X×Y∇                  [1]    Z←X÷Y∇
```

Chapter 11

1.
```
              ∇FICA←P TAX IN
     [1]      FICA←.01×P×7800⌊IN∇
```
2.
```
              ∇A SQDIF B
     [1]      T←(A-B)*2∇
```
3.
```
              ∇R←FERMAT N
     [1]      R←1+2*2*N∇
```
4.
```
              ∇CEILING X
     [1]      X+1|-X∇
```
5.
```
              ∇R←RANDOM
     [1]      R←?100 100 100 100∇
```
6.
```
              ∇COMP                          ∇COMP1
     [1]      (0=X|Y)∨0=Y|X∇    or    [1]    0=(X|Y)×Y|X∇
```
7.
```
              (3 HYP 4) HYP 3 HYP 1
     5.916079783
              4+3 HYP 4-3
     7.16227766
              (4+3) HYP 4-3
     7.071067812
```

8.   )LOAD 1 CLASS
        SAVED 15.02.39 07/29/69
              ∇ ARG1 D ARG2
        DEFN ERROR
              ∇ ARG1 D ARG2
                       ^
        D is a variable in 1 CLASS . (Execute)VARS D to check). The
        system will not let you have two objects in the same block of storage
        under the same name at the same time.
9.   F←10⊛A←AVG X

Chapter 12
1.   ∇STD[☐]
            ∇ STD N
        [1]   R←AVG N
        [2]   R←R-N
        [3]   R←AVG R*2
        [4]   ANS←R*0.5
            ∇
2. [5]   [4☐7]
   [4]   ANS←R*0.5
            ///1
   [4]   R←R*0.5
3. [5]   [0☐5]
   [0]   STD N
            5
   [0]   R←   STD N
4. [1]   [2]
   [2]

            ∨

5. [3]   [☐]
            ∇ R←STD N
   [1]   R←AVG N
   [3]   R←AVG R*2
   [4]   R←R*0.5
            ∇
6. [5]   [3]
   [3]   R←AVG (R-N)*2
7. [4]   [☐3]
   [3]   R←AVG(R-N)*2
   [4]   R←R*0.5
8. [4]   ∇
9.   ∇STD[1.5]R←R-N
10. [1.6]   [3☐10]
    [3]   R←R*0.5
            /5
    [3]   ANS ←R*0.5
    [4]   [.6]
11. [0.6]   +/N=N
    [0.7]   ∇
12.   )ERASE STD

Chapter 13
1. A)   )LOAD 1 CLASS
    SAVED   15.02.39 07/29/69
            C←52 78 90
    SYNTAX ERROR
            C← 52 78 90
            ∧
There is already a defined function by the name C in this workspace
(Execute)FNS C).
    B)   A←1+B←3
              T←F+7
    VALUE ERROR
              T←F+7
               ∧
              T←Z+7
              T
    12
F is a function name and has no value. When executed, Z receives a
value as a global variable.

2.   PERIM1   S←M PERIM2 R   S←PERIM3 R
            R   R   R
    14   3   3
            B   B   B
    2   2   2
            C   C   C
    5   5   5
            M   M   M
    7   7   7
            S   S   S
    1   20   10
This exercise is designed to give you practice in distinguishing
between local, dummy and global variables. To reset the values after
each execution, define a function like the following:
            ∇SETUP
    [1]   M←2+C←2+R←1+B←1+S←1∇
3.   ∇R←B PERIM2 C;P
    [1]   P←B+C
    [2]   R←2×P∇

Chapter 14
            ∇FN1 S
    [1]   S*10∇
            ∇FN2 V
    [1]   2⍟V≤X∇
            VAR1←÷1 2 3 4 5 6
            VAR2←⌈/VAR1
)SAVE WORKONE
    10.00.31 05/11/70
)CLEAR
    CLEAR WS
            ∇FN3 T
    [1]   ×T∇
            VAR3←*1 2 3 4 5
)SAVE WORKTWO
    10.01.26 05/11/70
)CLEAR
    CLEAR WS

```
       ∇A FN4 B
[1]    A-B*2∇
       VAR4←4 6 8 9
       )SAVE WORKTHREE
  10.02.22 05/11/70
       VAR5←-3 7 10 78
       )SAVE WORKFOUR
NOT SAVED, WS QUOTA USED UP
       )LIB
WORKONE
WORKTWO
WORKTHREE
       )DROP WORKONE
  10.07.04 05/11/70
       )LIB
WORKTWO
WORKTHREE
       )LOAD WORKTHREE
SAVED  10.02.22 05/11/70
       )FNS
FN4
       )VARS
VAR4
       ∇C FN5 D
[1]    (÷C≤?D)×4∇
       VAR6←1 0 7 ‾6 ‾8
       )SAVE WORKTWO
NOT SAVED, THIS WS IS WORKTHREE
       )SAVE WORKTHREE
  10.11.07 05/11/70
       )CLEAR
CLEAR WS
       )LOAD WORKTHREE
SAVED  10.11.07 05/11/70
       )FNS
FN4     FN5
       )VARS
VAR4    VAR6
       )ERASE FN4 VAR4
       )SAVE
  10.12.14 05/11/70 WORKTHREE
       )LIB
WORKTWO
WORKTHREE
       )FNS
FN5
       )VARS
VAR6
```

Note that when you load one of your own workspaces and then try to
save it under a different name, the system prevents you from so doing.
Also, when)SAVE is executed, the material will be saved under whatever
name the active workspace had prior to saving. The save doesn't take
place, however, if the active workspace was not given a name previously.
(CLEAR is not an allowable name for a workspace.)

Chapter 15

```
1.          )LIB 1
    CATALOG
    MINIMA
    WSFNS
    TYPEDRILL
    PLOTFORMAT
    NEWS
    CLASS
    APLCOURSE
    ADVANCEDEX
            )LOAD 1 WSFNS
    SAVED   23.45.54 07/07/69
            )FNS
    DELAY   DIGITS  ORIGIN  SETLINK WIDTH
            )VARS
    DESCRIBE
            DESCRIBE


        THE   FUNCTIONS   ORIGIN,   WIDTH,   AND   DIGITS   ARE   EACH
    SIMILAR TO THE COMMAND OF THE SAME NAME, EXCEPT THAT EACH IS
    A FUNCTION RATHER  THAN A COMMAN
```
(execution interrupted by pressing ATTN)
```
            )WSID
    1 WSFNS
            ∇L RECT W
    [1]     L×W∇
            )COPY 1 CLASS RECT
    SAVED    15.02.39 07/29/69
            ∇RECT[□]∇
        ∇ L RECT H
    [1]     2×L+H
    [2]     L HYP H
    [3]     L×H
        ∇
```
The original *RECT* is replaced by the version in 1 *CLASS*.
```
            )ERASE RECT
            ∇L RECT W
    [1]     L×W∇
            )PCOPY 1 CLASS RECT
    SAVED    15.02.39 07/29/69
```
This command will copy a global object in the same way as *COPY* only
if one doesn't exist with the same name in the active workspace.
```
            ∇RECT[□]∇
        ∇ L RECT W
    [1]     L×W
        ∇
            )SAVE JONES
       11.35.53 05/11/70
            )PORTS
    001 NFO
    OPR OPE
    012 RHO
    013 JHO
    019 NJD
    021 GKM
```

```
        )WSID SMITH
WAS JONES
        )SAVE
   11.36.56 05/11/70 SMITH
        )CLEAR
CLEAR WS
        )LOAD 1 NEWS
SAVED   15.26.37 04/02/70
        )SAVE 1 NEWS
IMPROPER LIBRARY REFERENCE
```
The ordinary user can't save into a common library because he wasn't
the one who put it in there originally.
```
        )CONTINUE HOLD
   11.38.19 05/11/70 CONTINUE
058   11.38.20 05/11/70 KGR
CONNECTED     0.08.25  TO DATE    51.27.40
CPU TIME      0.00.00  TO DATE     0.03.03
)5000:SJ
058) 11.38.45 05/11/70 KGRICE


   A  P  L \ 3 6 0

SAVED   11.38.19 05/11/70
        )LIB
JONES
SMITH
CONTINUE
        )FNS
APLNOW  CLEAR   CLEARSKED      CREATE  EDIT    FILE       FLE
FMTDT   INDEX   NJ      POS    POSITION        POSTSKED
PRINT   REWORK  RWK     SCHEDULE       SETDATE SKEDNOTE
START   TDATE   TRYTEXT TXF
        )VARS
DESCRIBE        I       LIBRARY MDX    MSGS    NEWSMAKING
PTX     RLIBRARY        SKD     SKNT   NS      SD
```
The command *CONTINUE HOLD* saves the active workspace in *CONTINUE* an
holds open the phone line for 60 seconds. The workspace is available to
the user when he signs on again.
2.   )SAVE CONTINUE
)LOAD GOOD
)COPY CONTINUE OK
)SAVE

<u>Chapter 16</u>
1.   ρA
     6
            ρρA
     1
            ρρρA
     1
            A⌈0.8×ι6
     0.8 8 2.4 4   6   10
            ι10
     1   2   3   4   5   6   7   8   9   10
            (ι5)+3
     4   5   6   7   8
```
```

```
      ¯7×ι1
¯7
      ιΓ/A
1  2  3  4  5  6  7  8  9  10
      +/ι15
120
      ÷ι5
1  0.5  0.3333333333  0.25  0.2
      ι28÷3+1
1  2  3  4  5  6  7
      ι10000
WS FULL
      ι10000
      ∧
```

The active workspace can hold just so much information at one time
See chapter 26 for a more complete discussion.

2.
```
      A←ι6
      ρA=6
6
      6=ρA
1
```
The first expression tells us how many elements of A have the value 6,
and the second tells us whether A has 6 components.

3.
```
      )LOAD 1 CLASS
SAVED   15.02.39 07/29/69
      ×/ρTAB0
1
      ×/ρTAB1
4
      ×/ρTAB2
12
      ×/ρTAB3
24
```
The instructions tell us how many elements are in each of the arrays.

4.
```
      A←0 8 ¯3 4 6 10
      ιρA
1  2  3  4  5  6
      ριρA
6
```
The first expression gives us a vector of indices for the elements in A,
while the second is equivalent to ρA. Compare ριρA with Γ/ιρA. How
do they differ? (Don't be too hasty in your answer.)

5. A)   ∇R←A1 N   B)   ∇R←B2 N
    [1]   R←+/(ιN)*.5∇   [1]   R←(+/ιN)*.5∇
    C)   ∇R←C3 N
    [1]   R←(×/ιN)*÷N∇

6.
```
      ¯1+2×ι8
1  3  5  7  9  11  13  15
      ¯12+5×ι5
¯7  ¯2  3  8  13
      .3+.3×ι6
0  0.3  0.6  0.9  1.2  1.5
      ¯350+100×ι6
¯250  ¯150  ¯50  50  150  250
      6-ι5
5  4  3  2  1
```

```
        2|ι6
1   0   1   0   1   0
```
7.   `ι3*ι3`
`RANK ERROR`
          `ι3*ι3`
          `∧`

The order of execution is such that ι3 will be generated first and
used as powers for 3, resulting in a vector for the right argument of
ι on the left. Since the index generator can be used only with nonnegative integers, the error message appears.

8.   `51≠ι50,  (ι50)=ι50,  (ι50)*0`
9.   `¯1+2×-/ι5`
      `+/ι5-1`
      `+/5=ι5+1`
      `+/0=6=ι5      +/~6=ι5`
10.   A)   `∇R←SERIES1 N`   B)   `∇R←X SERIES2 N;T`
      [1]   `R←-/÷ιN∇`   [1]   `R←+/(X*T)÷!T←¯1+ιN∇`
11.   `0=ρρA`

Chapter 17
1.   `ρM`
      `2   4`
              `(¯2) 1 2`
`SYNTAX ERROR`
              `(¯2) 1 2`
                 `∧`
              `¯2,1 2`
      `¯2  1   2`
              `ρρV`
      `2`
              `5 4ρV`

```
1   2   3   4
5   6   7   8
9   1   2   3
4   5   6   7
8   9   1   2
```
              `V,M`
`RANK ERROR`
              `V,M`
              `∧`
              `6ρ12`
```
12   12   12   12   12   12
```
              `10ρ100`
```
100   100   100   100   100   100   100   100   100   100
```
              `3 3ρ1,3ρ0`

```
1 0 0
0 1 0
0 0 1
```
              `5 4ρ0`

```
0 0 0 0
0 0 0 0
0 0 0 0
0 0 0 0
0 0 0 0
```

```
        5,4ρ0
  5  0  0  0  0
        ρρ0ρ9 10 11 12
  1
```
2.
```
        A←3 4 5
        B←ι8
        ρA,ρB
  4
        (ρA),ρB
  3  8
```
The first expression is equivalent to 1+ρA , while the second is the vector consisting of the lengths of A and B.

3.
```
        3 1ρ2                    3 1 1ρ2
                          2
  2              or
  2                       2
  2
                          2
```

4. `?100ρ10`
5. A)   `?(?8 8)ρ150`
   B)   `?(?8 8)ρ?299`
6. `R←12 4ρ(,A),,B`

   In the more general case, this is `R←((ρA)+1 0×ρB)ρ(,A),,B`
7. If E were a dyadic function, we would have to write 6 E 8 to execute it. Spaces or other delimiters (e.g., parentheses) are required around a function name.
8. `S,ι10` or `(ι0),S`
9. ```
   R←ι0
   R←R,Q
   ```
10. ```
            ∇W←INSERT V          In chapter 21 the function ↑ (take)
    [1]     W←((7-ρV)ρ0),V∇      will simplify this to ⁻7↑V
    ```

Chapter 18
1.
```
        'ABCDE'='BBXDO'
  0  1  0  1  0
        1 2<'MP'
DOMAIN ERROR
        1 2 <'MP'
          ∧
        ρρAL←3 3ρ'ABCDEFGHI'
  2
        ρV←'3172'
  4
        (ρV)ρV
3172
        3172=V
  0  0  0  0
        X,Y
MISSISSIPPIRIVER
        ρX,Y
 16
        +/X='S'
  4
        +/X≠'S'
  7
```

```
        X,' ',Y
MISSISSIPPI RIVER
        X='S'
0  0  1  1  0  1  1  0  0  0  0  0
        +/'P'=X
2

        +/(X,' ',Y)≠'S'
13

        v/X='R'

0
```

2. *D* is a character vector consisting of fifteen blanks.
3.
```
        ∇F A
[1]     'THE DIMENSION OF A IS:'
[2]     ρA
[3]     'THE RANK IS:'
[4]     ρρA
[5]     'THE NUMBER OF ELEMENTS IS:'
[6]     ×/ρA∇
```
In chapter 33 you will learn how to mix the numeric and literal output on a single line for greater compactness.

4.
```
        ∇M CAT R
[1]     (1 0+ρM)ρ(,M),R
[2]     '
THIS IS AN EXAMPLE OF
CATENATION IN APL'∇
```

5.
```
        )COPY 1 CLASS GEO3
SAVED    15.02.39 07/29/69
        ∇GEO3[0.5]
[0.5] ⍝THE LITERAL MESSAGE IN THIS FUNCTION
[0.6] ⍝IS KEYED TO THE ARGUMENTS USED
[0.7] ∇
        ∇GEO3[☐]∇
     ∇ L GEO3 H;X;FLAG
[1]     ⍝THE LITERAL MESSAGE IN THIS FUNCTION
[2]     ⍝IS KEYED TO THE ARGUMENTS USED
[3]     FLAG←((ρ,L)>1)v(ρ,H)>1
[4]     X←((4×~FLAG)ρ' IS:'),(6×FLAG)ρ'S ARE:'
[5]     'PERIMETER',X
[6]     2×L+H
[7]     'AREA',X
[8]     L×H
[9]     'DIAGONAL',X
[10]    L HYP H
     ∇

        3 4 GEO3 5 6
PERIMETERS ARE:
16   20
AREAS ARE:
15   24
DIAGONALS ARE:
SYNTAX ERROR
GEO3[10] L HYP H
              ∧
```

Comments introduced in this manner don't affect execution of the function unless branches (chapter 24) are used. Note also that in entering the comment the closing del was placed on the next line rather than at the end of the comment. Do you see why?

Chapter 19

1.
```
        (2<⍳5)/⍳5
3   4   5
        B/A
0   6.2   ¯2   25
        A[ρA],B[¯2+ρB]
25   0
        (3 2 7)[2 1 3]
2   3   7
        A[3 6]←2E5 4E¯4
        A
0   ¯5   200000   6.2   15   0.0004   25
        A[2 4 7]
¯5   6.2   25
        ρA[2 4 7]
3
        1 1 0 1\'TWO'
TW O
        A[8]
INDEX ERROR
        A[8]
        ∧
        A⍳⌈/A
3
        A[⍳ρA]
0   ¯5   200000   6.2   15   0.0004   25
        A[1]+A[2 3 4]×A[7]
¯125   5000000   155
        A[⌈/A⍳A]
25
        A[0ρ3]

        B\2 3 4 5
2   0   0   3   0   4   5
        C[1 16 12 27 9 19 27 1 12 7 15 18 9 20 8 13 9 3]
APL IS ALGORITHMIC
```
Note that A is respecified after fifth drill problem. This will affect the remaining problems.

2. A)   (D<.5)/D   D)   ((D<0)∧D>¯1)/D
    B)   (D>0)/D   E)   (D=2)/D
    C)   (4=|D)/D   F)   ((D<1)∧D≥¯2)/D

3.
```
        ∇Z←INSERT1 V
[1]     Z←((2×ρV)ρ1 0)\V
[2]     Z[2×⍳¯1+ρV]←'∘'∇        or
        ∇Z←INSERT2 V
[1]     Z←('∘',V)[1+((¯1+ρV,V)ρ1 0)\⍳ρV]∇
```
These functions as written work only for character vectors.

4.
```
        ∇Z←INCR V;T
[1]     Z←V[1+T]-V[T←⍳¯1+ρV]∇
```
When the drop function ↓ is introduced in chapter 21, line 1 can also be written as Z←V[1↓⍳ρV]-V[¯1↓⍳ρV]

5.
```
        ∇Z←F X
[1]     Z←3×X*2∇
        ∇Z←I AREA X
[1]     Z←+/I×F X[1]+I×⍳⌊|(-/X)÷I∇
```

6.
```
        ∇Z←W WITHIN R
[1]     Z←(R≥|W-+/W÷ρW)/W∇
```

7.   `(R=⌊R)/R`
8.   `∇R←A IN INT`
    `[1]    R←(+/INT[2]>|A-INT[1])×100÷ρA∇`
    `INT` is defined here as the vector `B,C`
9. `(⌈/V)>(+/V)-⌈/V` or `(⌈/V)>+/(V≠⌈/V)/V`
10. `Y[2×⍳⌊(ρY)÷2]` or `(2|1+⍳ρY)/Y` or `(~2|⍳ρY)/Y`
11.   `∇R←S INS X`
    `[1]    R←((S≥X)/X),S,(S<X)/X∇` or
            `∇R←S INS1 X`
    `[1]    R←X<S`
    `[2]    R←((R,0)∨0,~R)\X`
    `[3]    R[R⍳0]←S∇`
12. A)   `A←3`
            `⍳A[2]`
    `RANK ERROR`
            `⍳A[2]`
              `∧`
            `(⍳A)[2]`
    `2`
    The first expression is nonsense if `A` is a scalar or vector of length 1,
    while the second one is invalid if `A` isn't a positive integer ≥2.
    B)   `M←1 2`
            `N←3 4`
            `ρM,ρN`
    `3`
            `(ρM),ρN`
    `2   2`
    The first expression finds ρ of `1 2 2` (`M` with 2 catenated
    to the right end).
13. `V[ρV]`
14. The indices as given start with 0, which will result in an index error.
15. `(W=⌈/W)/⍳ρW` or `W⍳⌈/W`
16.   `∇Z←DELE V`
    `[1]    Z←((⍳ρV)=V⍳V)/V∇`
17. `+/Q[⍳8⌊ρQ]` or   `+/Q×8≥⍳ρQ`
18.   `∇R←X SELECT Y`
    `[1]    R←X[Y⍳⌈/Y]∇`
19. A)   `((¯1+ρV,V)ρ1 0)\V`
    B)   `(((2|ρV)+3×⌊.5×ρV)ρ1 0 1)\V`
    C)   same as B provided we don't want a zero on the right end
            when ρV is odd.
20.   `∇R←FACTORS N`   `∇R←FACTORS1 N`
    `[1]    R←(0=(⍳N)|N)/⍳N∇`   or   `[1]    R←(~×1|N÷⍳N)/⍳N∇`
21.   `∇Z←LIT N`
    `[1]    Z←+/(10*(ρN)-⍳ρN)×¯1+'0123456789'⍳N∇`
    This conversion of literal numbers to numerics can be done somewhat
    more compactly with the base function ⊥ to be introduced in chapter
    22, as well as by the inner product (chapter 31).
22.   `∇R←A COMFACT B`
    `[1]    R←(0=R|B)/R←(0=(⍳A)|A)/⍳A∇`
23.   `∇R←LONGEST X;J;M;N;P`
    `[1]    J←(X=' ')/⍳ρX`
    `[2]    M←⌈/N←¯1+(P←J,1+ρX)-0,J`
    `[3]    R←X[(P[N⍳M]+⍳M)-(1+ρ⍳M)]∇`

Chapter 20

```
        -/ι0
0
        */ι0
1
        ⊛/ι0
DOMAIN ERROR
        ⊛/ι0
        ^
        ⌈/ι0
⁻7.237005577E75
        ⌊/ι0
7.237005577E75
        |/ι0
0
        !/ι0
1
        ⍣/ι0
DOMAIN ERROR
        ⍣/ι0
        ^
        =/ι0
1
        ≠/ι0
0
        ≤/ι0
1
        >/ι0
0
        ≥/ι0
1
```

It should be clear that if we are to find an identity element *IMAX*
for ⌈, then it must be true that *N*⌈*IMAX* must result in *N* for all *N*.
Hence, *IMAX* must be the smallest number that can be represented in *APL*.
A similar argument holds for ⌊, where *IMIN* is the largest number
representable in *APL* .

Chapter 21

```
1.       3ϕA
   ⁻1   5  ⁻8   3   2   0
         2ϕA[ι4]
   0  ⁻1   3   2
         4↑A
   3   2   0  ⁻1
         2↑⁻3ϕA
   ⁻1   5
         ϕ0,ι3
   3   2   1   0
         2ϕϕι7
   5   4   3   2   1   7   6
         ⁻3↓A
   3   2   0
         A[⍋A]
   5  ⁻1   0   2  ⁻8   3
         A[⍒0 1 0 1 0 1]
   2  ⁻1  ⁻8   3   0   5
         (ι4)∈A
   0   1   1   0
```

```
            (3↑A)ε14
   1   1   0
            (16)=⍋A[⍋A]
   1   1   1   1   1   1
2.   ((|V)ε0,19)/V
3.   ∧/(S1εS2),S2εS1   or   ~0ε(S1εS2),S2εS1
4.   +/Sε'ABCDEFGHIJKL'
5.   ALF←'ABCDEFGHIJKLMNOPQRSTUVWXYZ '
     S[⍋ALFιS]
6.       ∇Z←BL S
     [1]    Z←(Cv1⌽C←S≠' ')/S∇
7.   (V,V1)[⍋V,V1]
8.   ∧/V[⍋V]=ιN   or   ∧/(VειN),(ιN)εV
9.   C[('X'=C)/ιρC]←'Y'
10.  (5<ι8)/X   and   ‾3↑X
11.      ∇R←MED X
     [1]    R←.5×+/X[(⍋X)[|⌈‾.5 .5×1+ρX]]∇
12.  A) This is a difficult problem.  The expression corresponds to a per-
        fect shuffle, in which a deck of cards is cut exactly in half and
        cards fed alternately first from the top half  then from the bottom
        half, to form a new deck.
     B) This expression is the algorithm used in APL for the deal function
        A?B
13.      ∇R←DECODE C
     [1]    R←ALF[PιALFιC]∇
14.      ∇COVIG M;C;D
     [1]    N←ALFιM
     [2]    M
     [3]    C←26|N+D←((ρN)ρKB)+(ρN)ρKA
     [4]    ALF[D]
     [5]    (ρM)ρ'‾'
     [6]    ALF[C]∇
```
VIG , incidentally, is an example of a well-known cryptographic scheme,
the Vigenére code, with COVIG being a more complicated variation.
Both this program and VERNAM (below) should be done in a workspace
with origin 0.
```
15.      ∇VERNAM M;V;N;C
     [1]    M
     [2]    V←?(ρM)ρ26
     [3]    C←26|V+ALFιM
     [4]    ALF[V]
     [5]    (ρM)ρ'‾'
     [6]    ALF[C]∇
```

Chapter 22
```
1.       (3ρ40)⊥8 7 2
     13082
            2⊥5 1 9 6
     68
            10⊥9 8 2 1 6
     98216
            1 ‾4.1 .8⊥11 2 3
     1.32
            7 8 9⊥7 8 9
     585
            3⊤5217
     0
```

```
                3  3T5217
     2   0
                3  3  3T5217
     0   2   0
                (5ρ3)T5217
     1   1   0   2   0
                (4ρ8)⊥¯14
    ¯8190
                1  4  6T345
     0   1   3
                2  4  5T78
     1   3   3
2.  A)          0  4  2⊥2  8  1
    B)          0  2000  16⊥3  568  13
3.  A)          8⊥2  1  7  7
    B)          2⊥1  0  1  1  0  1
    C)          (10ρ3)T8933
    D)          (10ρ5)T4791
4.  0  1TN
5.  XTX⊥Y
    X⊥XTY
```

Chapter 23

```
1.          ∇P←CONV D
    [1]     P←10⊥¯1+'0123456789'ι(D≠',')/D∇
2.  N=+/(10 10 10TN)*3
3.          ∇Z←C EVAL X
    [1]     Z←X⊥CV          (put 0's in for missing powers of X)
```

4. A) converts M into a vector of digits.

B) converts M into the corresponding scalar.

C) same as B.

```
5.  0=11|-/((⌊1+10⊛N)ρ10)TN
```

Chapter 24

1. A) If $5<W$ go to step 3, if $5>W$ go to 2, if $5=W$ go to the next step. W is assumed to be a scalar or vector of length 1.

B) Go to step 3 if $A=8$, otherwise drop through to the next step.

C) Go to END if $Y>1$, otherwise branch out of the program. At the same time R is reshaped as a 1 1 matrix containing a 1.

D) Go to step 7 if any element of B is a member of C, otherwise drop through to the next step.

E) If $A≤G$ go to 5, otherwise go to step 0.

F) Go to step 3.

G) Go to step 8 if $0≠J$, otherwise go to the next step. At the same time J is decreased by 1.

H) If the absolute value of X is greater than or equal to I, go to step 4, otherwise leave the program. I is also incremented by 1.

I) Go to $AGAIN$ if $N=10$, otherwise leave the program. R is also reshaped as a 2 4 matrix.

```
2.          ∇REM T
    [1]     I←1
    [2]     V←(T[I]≠V)/V
    [3]     →0×ιI≥ρT
    [4]     →2,I←I+1∇
```

This function, which involves branching, solves the problem by brute force. You'll appreciate the power of APL from the following:

```
            ∇REM1 T
    [1]     V←(~V∈T)/V∇
```

3.
```
        ∇Z←P DIGIT Q;M
[1]     Z←ι0
[2]     M←⌊P÷10
[3]     →(0≠M|P)/5
[4]     Z←Z,P
[5]     →(Q≥P←P+1)/2∇
```
4.
```
        ∇R←MED N
[1]     →(R=⌊R←.5×ρN←N[⍋N])/ST
[2]     →0,R←N[[R]
[3]     ST:R←.5×N[R]+N[R+1]∇
```
or
```
        ∇R←MED1 N
[1]     N←N[⍋N]
[2]     R←N[⌈.5×ρN]
[3]     →4×~2|ρN
[4]     R←.5×R+N[1+.5×ρN]∇
```
5.
```
        ∇R←N DUPL V
[1]     →0×ιρR←(N=V)/ιρV
[2]     'SCALAR NOT PRESENT'∇
```
6.
```
        ∇Z←ROOT S
[1]     →(0≠ρρS)/0
[2]     Z←S*.5∇
```
7.
```
        ∇R←SORT TEXT
[1]     ALF←'ABCDEFGHIJKLMNOPQRSTUVWXYZ'
[2]     R←''
[3]     →0×ι0=ρALF
[4]     R←R,(TEXT=1↑ALF)/TEXT
[5]     TEXT←(TEXT≠1↑ALF)/TEXT
[6]     ALF←1↓ALF
[7]     →3∇
```
or, without branching
```
        ∇R←SORT1 TEXT
[1]     TEXT←((ALFιTEXT)≤ρALF)/TEXT
[2]     R←ALF[R[⍋R←ALFιTEXT]]∇
```
Incidentally, a long vector of arbitrary characters can be entered in
the following way: define one line of TEXT as TEXT←'...' and each
succeeding line TEXT←TEXT,'...'. It is also possible to enter
large amounts of information into the system through a card reader
attached to an appropriate terminal.

8.
```
        ∇R←MODE N;V
[1]     V←R←ι0
[2]     AT:V←V,+/N[1]=N
[3]     R←R,N[1]
[4]     →(0≠ρN←(N[1]≠N)/N)/AT
[5]     R←R[(V=⌈/V)/ιρV]∇
```
9.
```
        ∇R←FIB N
[1]     R←1 1
[2]     END:→(N>ρR←R,+/¯2↑R)/END∇
```
10.
```
        ∇HISTOG A;I
[1]     I←⌈/A
[2]     I≤A
[3]     →2××I←I-1∇
```
To "clean up" the histogram, change line 2 to ' *'[1+I≤A]. This
function produces a vertical histogram. For a horizontal histogram try
the following:

```
        ∇HISTOG1 A
[1]     A[1]ρ'*'
[2]     →×ρA←1↓A∇
```
The composite function <u>outer product</u> (to be introduced in chapter
30) further simplifies the construction of histograms. Try
$A∘.≥ιⲅ/A$

11.
```
        ∇R INT P
[1]     'YR PRIN INT
'
[2]     I←1
[3]     IN←.01×⌊.5+100×P×R[1]
[4]     I,P,IN
[5]     P←P+IN
[6]     →((I←I+1)>R[2])/0
[7]     →3∇
```
Here $R[1]$ is the yearly interest rate in decimal form and $R[2]$ the
number of years to be evaluated. As in problem 10, the outer
product function will simplify considerably the job of generating
the table. Your table probably will not be formatted properly. More
about how to correct this in problem 11 at the end of chapter
30.

Chapter 25

1.
```
        V←'HELLO εωTHERE?'
        T←'?~ρεω'
        TΔREM←2 3 4
        REM T
REM[2] HELLO εωTHERE
REM[3]
REM[4] 2   2
REM[2] HELLO εωTHERE
REM[3]
REM[4] 2   3
REM[2] HELLO εωTHERE
REM[3]
REM[4] 2   4
REM[2] HELLO ωTHERE
REM[3]
REM[4] 2   5
REM[2] HELLO THERE
REM[3] 0
        TEXT←'DAB'
        TΔSORT←3 4 5 6
        SORT TEXT
SORT[3]
SORT[4] A
SORT[5] DB
SORT[6] BCDEFGHIJKLMNOPQRSTUVWXYZ
SORT[3]
SORT[4] AB
SORT[5] D
SORT[6] CDEFGHIJKLMNOPQRSTUVWXYZ
SORT[3]
SORT[4] AB
SORT[5] D
SORT[6] DEFGHIJKLMNOPQRSTUVWXYZ
SORT[3]
SORT[4] ABD
```

```
        SORT[5]
        SORT[6]  EFGHIJKLMNOPQRSTUVWXYZ
        SORT[3]
        SORT[4]  ABD
        SORT[5]
        SORT
        SORT[7]
```

Printing of the trace has been interrupted because of its length.   This is not a very efficient program (see *SORT1*), but in the case of a short literal vector like '*DAB*' the time would be reduced considerably by replacing *ALF* with *TEXT* on line 3.

```
        N←2 5 7 3 2 8 2 5 2
        TΔMODE←2 3 4 5
        MODE N
MODE[2] 4
MODE[3] 2
MODE[4] 2
MODE[2] 4    2
MODE[3] 2    5
MODE[4] 2
MODE[2] 4    2    1
MODE[3] 2    5    7
MODE[4] 2
MODE[2] 4    2    1    1
MODE[3] 2    5    7    3
MODE[4] 2
MODE[2] 4    2    1    1    1
MODE[3] 2    5    7    3    8
MODE[4]
MODE[5] 2
2
```

2.
```
            TΔGCD←ι4
            75 GCD 105
GCD[1]  75
GCD[2]  30
GCD[3]  75
GCD[4]  1
GCD[1]  30
GCD[2]  15
GCD[3]  30
GCD[4]  1
GCD[1]  15
GCD[2]  0
GCD[3]  15
GCD[4]  0
15
```

3.
```
            TΔΔACK←ι4
            2 ACK 1
ACK[1]
ACK[1]  3
ACK[1]
ACK[1]  3
ACK[1]  4
ACK[4]  2
ACK[3]  0    2
ACK[1]  4
ACK[4]  3
```

```
ACK[2]  0   3
ACK[3]  0   3
ACK[1]
ACK[1]
ACK[1]
ACK[1]  3
ACK[1]  4
ACK[4]  2
ACK[3]  0   2
ACK[1]  4
ACK[4]  3
ACK[2]  0   3
ACK[1]  4
ACK[4]  4
ACK[2]  0   4
ACK[1]  4
ACK[4]  5
ACK[2]  0   5
ACK[2]  0   5
      5
```

Chapter 26

1.
```
              1o1 2
1.743934249E¯16    ¯3.487868498E¯16
              180÷o1
57.29577951
              ¯2o1oo1÷2
0
              o1÷180
0.01745329252
              4o ι 3
1.414213562   2.236067977   3.16227766
              ¯1o1o1
1
              2oo1
¯1
              3o¯3oι5
1   2   3   4   5
              ¯1 ¯2o1 1o.5
0.5   1.070796327
```

2.   `11 1ρ1000,.05×ι10`

```
       0
       0.156434465
       0.3090169944
       0.4539904997
       0.5877852523
       0.7071067812
       0.8090169944
       0.8910065242
       0.9510565163
       0.9876883406
       1
```
This expression will generate the values called for by the problem,
but without identification as to the magnitude (in radians) of the
associated angles. With the transpose (chapter 29), such information
can be included: ⍉2 1 1ρ(oA),1ooA←(¯1+ι11)÷20 It can also be
done with the outer product (problem 2A, chapter 30).

3. Construct a function like *CHECK* below to obtain comparative com-
    puting times. The reason for the repetition of the calculations is
    that an accurate comparison isn't possible with just a single trial
    because of the shortness of the times involved.

```
          ∇CHECK
    [1]    CPUTIME
    [2]    I←1
    [3]    S←2!10
    [4]    →3×ι101≠I←I+1
    [5]    CPUTIME
    [6]    I←1
    [7]    S←(!10)÷(!2)×!8
    [8]    →7×ι101≠I←I+1
    [9]    CPUTIME∇
           CHECK
    0   0   0   1
    0   0   0   9
    0   0   0   17
```

    Don't forget to copy *CPUTIME* and *PREVIOUSTIME* from 1 *CLASS* .

4.   (202×ι5)=((20ι5)*2)-(10ι5)*2
    1   1   1   1   1

    For *X* a scalar, try the following: 0=-/(2 2 10ρ2 1 1×X)*1 2 2
    Can you explain why it doesn't work consistently for all *X*?

5.   ∇R←DATE
    [1]   R←'/0123456789'[1+(8ρ1 1 0)\1+(6ρ10)⊤ι25]∇

6.   ∇R←X TIME Y
    [1]   R←Y↑(X,3ρ60)⊤ι20∇

7. 1=+/(1 20X)*2
    This version works only for scalar *X*. For *X* a vector we can use
    the outer product (chapter 30) as follows:
    ∧/1=+/(1 2∘.∘X)*2

Chapter 27
1.   S+T

```
    21   21   21   21   21
    21   21   21   21   21
    21   21   21   21   21
    21   21   21   21   21
         2×S

    40   38   36   34   32
    30   28   26   24   22
    20   18   16   14   12
    10    8    6    4    2
         S⌊T

     1    2    3    4    5
     6    7    8    9   10
    10    9    8    7    6
     5    4    3    2    1
         3|T

     1   2   0   1   2
     0   1   2   0   1
     2   0   1   2   0
     1   2   0   1   2
```

```
          S≤T

    0  0  0  0  0
    0  0  0  0  0
    1  1  1  1  1
    1  1  1  1  1
          +/[2]T
   15   40   65   90
          +≠T
   34   38   42   46   50
          4+T

      5     6     7     8     9
     10    11    12    13    14
     15    16    17    18    19
     20    21    22    23    24
          ⌈/⌈/⌈/U
   24
          ⌈/,U
   24
          ×≠U

     13    28    45    64
     85   108   133   160
    189   220   253   288
          +/+/[1]T
  210
```
2.   (,M)[N?ρ,M]
3.   M←M+(ρM)ρ(1↓ρM)ρ0,N
4.   ∇GPA;GR;CR;M
   [1]   M←5 25ρ(25ρ4),(25ρ3),(25ρ2),(25ρ1),(25ρ0)
   [2]   GR←M×CR←(3×GR3)+(2×GR2)+GR1
   [3]   'THE GRADE POINT AVERAGES FOR EACH STUDENT ARE:'
   [4]   (+≠GR)÷+≠CR
   [5]   'THE CLASS AVERAGE IS:'
   [6]   (+/+≠GR)÷+/+≠CR∇
5.   ?4 4ρ100 or 4 4ρ?16ρ100
6.   ∇AR
   [1]   M←5 15ρV1,V2,V3,V4,V5
   [2]   'TOTALS BY CATEGORY ARE:'
   [3]   +/M
   [4]   'TOTALS BY CUSTOMER ARE:'
   [5]   +≠M
   [6]   'THE TOTAL OF ALL ACCOUNTS RECEIVABLE IS:'
   [7]   +/+/M
   [8]   'CUSTOMERS WITH OVERDUE INVOICES ARE:'
   [9]   (∨≠0≠3 15ρ30↓,M)/ι15∇

Chapter 28

1.   A[;2 5]

    2   5
    7   10
   12   15
          C[1;2 3;]

    5   6   7   8
    9   10   11   12

```
      ⁻1 1 2↓⊖C

  4   5
  8   9
      1 1 1 1 0 1\A

   1    2    3    4    0    5
   6    7    8    9    0   10
  11   12   13   14    0   15
      ⊖A

  11   12   13   14   15
   6    7    8    9   10
   1    2    3    4    5
      ⁻1 ⁻2 2 1 1⊖A

  11    7   13    9   10
   1   12    3   14   15
   6    2    8    4    5
      +⌿C[1 2;2;3]
11
      A[1 3;ι4]

   1    2    3    4
  11   12   13   14
      1 0 1 1\[2]C

   1    2    3    4
   0    0    0    0
   5    6    7    8
   9   10   11   12

  13   14   15    1
   0    0    0    0
   2    3    4    5
   6    7    8    9
      0 1/[1]C

  13   14   15    1
   2    3    4    5
   6    7    8    9
      3 1 2⌽A

   4    5    1    2    3
   7    8    9   10    6
  13   14   15   11   12
      ,⌽B
CBAFEDIHG
      B[1;2 3]
BC
      2 2 2↑⌽C

  4    3
  8    7

  1   15
  5    4
```

```
        1 0 1/B

ABC
GHI
        ⌽A

    5   4   3   2   1
   10   9   8   7   6
   15  14  13  12  11
       ¯1  ¯2 2⌽B

CAB
EFD
.IGH
        1 3 3 ⌽ 3 1 1 2 4⌽[1]A

    7   8  14  10   1
    4  15   6  12  13
    9   5  11   2   3
```

2. B[1;]←B[;3]
3. Assume each row is a name with no blanks on the left and filled out
   on the right with blanks.

```
        ∇DELE NAME;J
   [1]     J←0
   [2]     →6×ι(ρA)[1]≤J
   [3]     →2×ι~∧/A[(J←J+1);]=(1↓ρA)↑NAME
   [4]     A←(((J-1)ρ1),0,((ρA)[1]-J)ρ1)/A
   [5]     →0
   [6]     'NAME NOT FOUND'∇
```

   When the inner product is introduced in chapter 31, this function
   can be rewritten as

```
        ∇DELE1 NAME;T
   [1]     →4×ι∨/T←A∧.=(1↓ρA)↑NAME
   [2]     'NAME NOT FOUND'
   [3]     →0
   [4]     A←(~T)/A∇
```

4. The second is a 1 1 matrix, while the first is a scalar. Try
   ρ of each to check.
5. R←M[;M]
   Note that the indices themselves may have rank >1.
6.   ∇Z←MS N;Q
   [1]   Z←(N,N)ριN*2
   [2]   Q←(-⌈.5×N)+ιN
   [3]   Z←QθQ⌽Z∇
7.   ∇Z←V1 MAT V2
   [1]   Z←((ρV1),2)ρ0
   [2]   Z[;1]←V1
   [3]   Z[;2]←V2∇
              or
        ∇Z←V1 MAT1 V2
   [1]   Z←(V1,V2)[((ρV1),2)ρ(⌈.5×ι2×ρV1)+(2×ρV1)ρ0,ρV1]∇
```

   When the transpose function is introduced in the next chapter, this
   function can be reduced to a single line:  ⍉(2,ρV1)ρV1,V2
```

Chapter 29
1.   1 1⍉M
      1   6   1
                1 1 2⍉N

          1   2   3   4
         17   18   19   20
                ρ2 1 3⍉N
      3   2   4
                2 1 3⍉N

          1   2   3   4
         13   14   15   16

          5   6   7   8
         17   18   19   20

          9   10   11   12
         21   22   23   24
                ⍉⌽⊖M

          2   8   4
          1   7   3
         10   6   2
          9   5   1
                1 2 1⍉N

          1   5   9
         14   18   22
                ⌽2 1⍉M

          9   5   1
         10   6   2
          1   7   3
          2   8   4
                ⍉M

          1   5   9
          2   6   10
          3   7   1
          4   8   2
                ⍉⍉M

          1   2   3   4
          5   6   7   8
          9   10   1   2
2. 1 1⍉⌽B or 1 1⍉2 0 1⌽B
3.   ∇R←DIAG M
    [1]   R←10⊥1 1⍉M∇
4.   ∇R←X COLCAT3 V
    [1]   R←⍉(⍉X) ROWCAT V∇
5.   ∇Z←LIST N
    [1]   Z←⍉(3,N)ρZ,(!Z),÷Z←ιN∇
6. ∧/,S=⍉S
7. The result shows that A×B is a maximum when A=B, a conclusion
    well known to calculus students, who have worked since time immem-
    orial on problems like the following: Show that a square is that
    rectangle of greatest area for a given perimeter.

Chapter 30
1.   A∘.÷⌽A

   0.25   0.3333333333   0.5   1
   0.5   0.6666666667   1   2
   0.75   1   1.5   3
   1   1.333333333   2   4

     C∘.=B

1 0 0
0 0 0

0 1 0
0 0 0

0 0 0
1 0 0

     D∘.×A

  1   2   3   4

  2   4   6   8

  3   6   9   12

    A∘.⌈2⌽A

3 4 1 2
3 4 2 2
3 4 3 3
4 4 4 4

    1 3 9∘.>D

0
0
0

1
1
0

1
1
1

    1 0∘.∧1 0

1 0
0 0

    1 0 0 1 1∘.⍱0 1 0 1 1

0 0 0 0 0
1 0 1 0 0
1 0 1 0 0
0 0 0 0 0
0 0 0 0 0

    1 2 3∘.|⍳5

 0 0 0 0 0
 1 0 1 0 1
 1 2 0 1 2

```
        (ι5)∘.*0 1 2 3
```

```
    1                    1                 1                      1
    1                    2                 4                      8
    1                    3                 9                     27
    1                    4                16                     64
    1                    5                25                    125
```

2. A)   ⍉1 2∘.○○(0,ι5)÷6
    B)   ⍉(((1+ρ,B),10)ρ(ι10),,B∘.⍟ι10
    C)   'AEIOU'∘.=S
    D)   (ι10)∘.*1 2 .5
3. 4 2 2   or   2 2 4
4.   ∇R←DIST L
    [1]   R←⌊.5+((((L[;1]∘.-L[;1])*2)+(L[;2]∘.-L[;2])*2)*.5∇
              or
              ∇R←DIST1 L
    [1]   R←⌊.5+(+/1 3 2 3⍉(L∘.-L)*2)*.5∇
5. +/'ABCDEFG'∘.='CABBAGE'
6. SUM←B|C+D
    CARRY←B≤C+D
            ∇ADDTAB B;T
    [1]   T←INT∘.+INT←⁻1+ιB
    [2]   (B|T)+10×B≤T∇
7.   ∇Z←C1 MULT C2
    [1]   Z←+/[1](1-ιρC1)⍉C1∘.×C2,0×1↓C1∇
8. A)   X←⁻5+ι9
          F←(⌽X)∘.=|X
          GRAPH
```

```
  ∘           +            ∘
     ∘        +         ∘
        ∘     +      ∘
           ∘  +  ∘
  +  +  +  +  ∘  +  +  +  +
              +
              +
              +
              +
```

```
    B)    F←(⌽X)∘.=⁻5+X*2
          GRAPH
```

```
  ∘           +          ∘
              +
              +
              +
              +
  +  +  +  +  +  +  +  +  +
     ∘        +        ∘
              +
              +
        ∘   +   ∘
```
```

8. C) $F \leftarrow (\phi X) \circ . \leq X + 1$
            $GRAPH$

```
            +         o   o
            +       o   o   o
            +   o   o   o   o
                o   o   o   o   o
    +   +   +   o   o   o   o   o   o
        o   o   o   o   o   o   o   o
    o   o   o   o   o   o   o   o
  o   o   o   o   o   o   o   o
  o   o   o   o   o   o   o   o
```

D) $F \leftarrow ((\phi X) \circ . \leq X + 1) \wedge (\phi X) \circ . \geq 3 - |X$
        $GRAPH$

```
            +         o   o
            +       o   o   o
            +   o   o   o   o
            +       o   o   o
    +   +   +   +   +   +   +   o   o
            +               o
            +
            +
            +
```

E) $F \leftarrow (\phi X) \circ . \leq 3 | X$
        $GRAPH$

```
                +
                +
  o         o   +       o
  o     o   o   +   o   o       o
  o   o   o   o   o   o   o   o   o
  o   o   o   o   o   o   o   o   o
  o   o   o   o   o   o   o   o   o
  o   o   o   o   o   o   o   o   o
  o   o   o   o   o   o   o   o   o
```

9.
$$Y \leftarrow \phi X \leftarrow \,^-13 + \iota 25$$
$$R \leftarrow (0 = (\,^-3 \times Y) \circ . + (2 \times X) - 2) \vee 0 = (2 \times Y) \circ . + X - 8$$
$$R$$

```
0 0 0 0 0 0 0 0 0 0 0 0 0 0 0 0 0 0 0 0 0 0 0 0 0
0 0 0 0 0 0 0 0 0 0 0 0 0 0 0 0 0 0 0 0 0 0 0 0 0
1 0 0 0 0 0 0 0 0 0 0 0 0 0 0 0 0 0 0 0 0 0 0 0 0
0 0 1 0 0 0 0 0 0 0 0 0 0 0 0 0 0 0 0 0 0 0 0 0 0
0 0 0 0 1 0 0 0 0 0 0 0 0 0 0 0 0 0 0 0 0 0 0 0 0
0 0 0 0 0 0 1 0 0 0 0 0 0 0 0 0 0 0 0 0 0 0 0 0 0
0 0 0 0 0 0 0 0 1 0 0 0 0 0 0 0 0 0 0 0 0 1 0 0
0 0 0 0 0 0 0 0 0 1 0 0 0 0 0 0 0 0 0 0 0 0 0 0
0 0 0 0 0 0 0 0 0 0 0 1 0 0 0 0 0 0 1 0 0 0 0 0
0 0 0 0 0 0 0 0 0 0 0 0 1 0 0 0 0 0 0 0 0 0 0 0
0 0 0 0 0 0 0 0 0 0 0 0 0 1 0 0 0 0 0 0 0 0 0 0
0 0 0 0 0 0 0 0 0 0 0 0 0 0 0 0 1 0 0 0 0 0 0 0
0 0 0 0 0 0 0 0 0 0 0 0 1 0 0 0 0 0 0 1 0 0 0 0
0 0 0 0 0 0 0 0 0 0 0 0 0 0 0 0 0 0 0 0 0 1 0 0
0 0 0 0 0 0 0 0 0 0 1 0 0 0 0 0 0 0 0 0 0 0 0 1
0 0 0 0 0 0 0 0 0 0 0 0 0 0 0 0 0 0 0 0 0 0 0 0
0 0 0 0 0 0 0 1 0 0 0 0 0 0 0 0 0 0 0 0 0 0 0 0
0 0 0 0 0 0 0 0 0 0 0 0 0 0 0 0 0 0 0 0 0 0 0 0
0 0 0 0 1 0 0 0 0 0 0 0 0 0 0 0 0 0 0 0 0 0 0 0
0 0 0 0 0 0 0 0 0 0 0 0 0 0 0 0 0 0 0 0 0 0 0 0
0 1 0 0 0 0 0 0 0 0 0 0 0 0 0 0 0 0 0 0 0 0 0 0
0 0 0 0 0 0 0 0 0 0 0 0 0 0 0 0 0 0 0 0 0 0 0 0
0 0 0 0 0 0 0 0 0 0 0 0 0 0 0 0 0 0 0 0 0 0 0 0
0 0 0 0 0 0 0 0 0 0 0 0 0 0 0 0 0 0 0 0 0 0 0 0
0 0 0 0 0 0 0 0 0 0 0 0 0 0 0 0 0 0 0 0 0 0 0 0
```

The 1's correspond to integer number pairs satisfying the two
simultaneous linear equations 3Y=2X-2 and 2Y=8-X (conventional
notation). The point of intersection (4,2) is the common solution of both equations.

10. Since this problem is intended to be only illustrative, not all
the examples will be shown.

10. A) $X \leftarrow \iota 20$
             $Y \leftarrow X * 2$
             $Z \leftarrow 2 \times X * 2$
             40 60 *PLOT Y AND Z VS X*

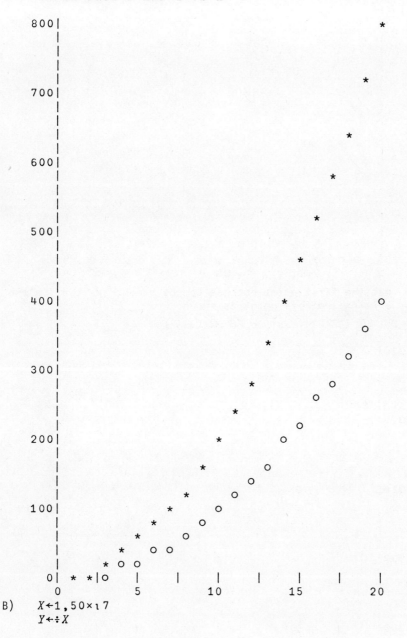

     B) $X \leftarrow 1, 50 \times \iota 7$
             $Y \leftarrow \div X$

10. B)   20 30 *PLOT Y VS X*

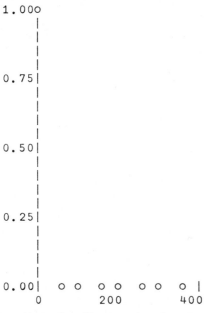

```
1.000○
     |
     |
     |
     |
0.75|
     |
     |
     |
0.50|
     |
     |
     |
0.25|
     |
     |
     |
0.00|  ○ ○   ○ ○   ○ ○   ○  |
    0       200       400
```

Notice that the first point botches up the graph. We can fix the
plot by eliminating this point as shown:

        20 30 *PLOT Y[1+ι7] VS X[1+ι7]*

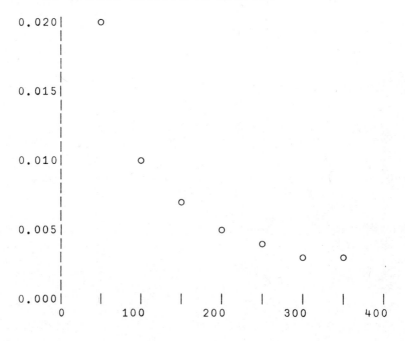

```
0.020|     ○
     |
     |
     |
0.015|
     |
     |
     |
0.010|        ○
     |
     |           ○
     |
0.005|              ○
     |                 ○
     |                    ○   ○
     |
0.000|   |    |    |    |    |    |    |    |
    0      100      200      300      400
```

10. D)   *Y AND Z*

```
0.000000000E0         1.000000000E0
1.736481777E⁻1        9.848077530E⁻1
3.420201433E⁻1        9.396926208E⁻1
5.000000000E⁻1        8.660254038E⁻1
6.427876097E⁻1        7.660444431E⁻1
7.660444431E⁻1        6.427876097E⁻1
8.660254038E⁻1        5.000000000E⁻1
9.396926208E⁻1        3.420201433E⁻1
9.848077530E⁻1        1.736481777E⁻1
1.000000000E0         1.743934249E⁻16
9.848077530E⁻1       ⁻1.736481777E⁻1
9.396926208E⁻1       ⁻3.420201433E⁻1
8.660254038E⁻1       ⁻5.000000000E⁻1
7.660444431E⁻1       ⁻6.427876097E⁻1
6.427876097E⁻1       ⁻7.660444431E⁻1
5.000000000E⁻1       ⁻8.660254038E⁻1
3.420201433E⁻1       ⁻9.396926208E⁻1
1.736481777E⁻1       ⁻9.848077530E⁻1
1.743934249E⁻16      ⁻1.000000000E0
⁻1.736481777E⁻1      ⁻9.848077530E⁻1
⁻3.420201433E⁻1      ⁻9.396926208E⁻1
⁻5.000000000E⁻1      ⁻8.660254038E⁻1
⁻6.427876097E⁻1      ⁻7.660444431E⁻1
⁻7.660444431E⁻1      ⁻6.427876097E⁻1
⁻8.660254038E⁻1      ⁻5.000000000E⁻1
⁻9.396926208E⁻1      ⁻3.420201433E⁻1
⁻9.848077530E⁻1      ⁻1.736481777E⁻1
⁻1.000000000E0       ⁻1.743934249E⁻16
⁻9.848077530E⁻1       1.736481777E⁻1
⁻9.396926208E⁻1       3.420201433E⁻1
⁻8.660254038E⁻1       5.000000000E⁻1
⁻7.660444431E⁻1       6.427876097E⁻1
⁻6.427876097E⁻1       7.660444431E⁻1
⁻5.000000000E⁻1       8.660254038E⁻1
⁻3.420201433E⁻1       9.396926208E⁻1
⁻1.736481777E⁻1       9.848077530E⁻1
```

        Y VS X

```
0.000000000E0         0.000000000E0
1.745329252E⁻1        1.736481777E⁻1
3.490658504E⁻1        3.420201433E⁻1
5.235987756E⁻1        5.000000000E⁻1
6.981317008E⁻1        6.427876097E⁻1
8.726646260E⁻1        7.660444431E⁻1
1.047197551E0         8.660254038E⁻1
1.221730476E0         9.396926208E⁻1
1.396263402E0         9.848077530E⁻1
1.570796327E0         1.000000000E0
1.745329252E0         9.848077530E⁻1
1.919862177E0         9.396926208E⁻1
```

(not all of display shown)

11.   10 5 *DFT* (÷ι10) *AND* (÷ι10)*.5

```
1.00000    1.00000
0.50000    0.70711
0.33333    0.57735
0.25000    0.50000
0.20000    0.44721
0.16667    0.40825
0.14286    0.37796
0.12500    0.35355
0.11111    0.33333
0.10000    0.31623
```

Chapter 31

1.   *A+.=A*
      3
            B×.-C

```
‾18    0    4    0
  0   ‾6   ‾8    0
  0   24   70   18
 24   12    0   36
```
            B∨.<C

```
1 1 1 1
1 1 1 1
0 0 0 0
1 1 1 1
```
            A∧.>C
```
0  0  0  0
```
            A∨.≠B
      LENGTH ERROR
            A∨.≠B
            ∧
            3+.×B
```
66   48   60
```
            B×.=A
```
0  0  0  0
```
            C|.-B

```
  0   0   2
  1   0   1
  0   2   0
```
            (⍉*C*)⌈.+*A*
```
11   10    9   11
```

2. A) $A\wedge.=B$ results in a 1 if A and B are identical, 0 otherwise.
            $M\wedge.=B$ produces a logical vector with a 1 for each row of M
            which is identical to B
            $A+.\neq B$ gives the number of pairs of corresponding dissimilar
            elements in A and B.
            $(M=0)\wedge.\geq U$ produces a logical matrix which reproduces the
            initial 1's in each row of $M=0$ and fills the rest of the row
            with 0's, i.e.

            M

0	0	0	3	2	0	0	0
0	0	1	7	9	2	8	0
6	4	0	0	0	1	6	0

            $M=0$

1	1	1	0	0	1	1	1
1	1	0	0	0	0	0	1
0	0	1	1	1	0	0	1

            $(M=0)\wedge.\geq(\iota 8)\circ.\leq\iota 8$

1	1	1	0	0	0	0	0
1	1	0	0	0	0	0	0
0	0	0	0	0	0	0	0

            It may be considered a simulation of the "and-scan" $\wedge\backslash M=0$
            (not yet implemented).
            $A\times.\star B$ is equivalent to the times reduction of A raised to
            the B power. One possible use could be in getting a number
            from its prime decomposition. Here is an example of this
            latter use:
            $2\ \ 3\ \ 5\ \ 7\times.\star 2\ \ 1\ \ 0\ \ 1$
84

    B) $R[I;J]$ is 1 if and only if the Ith column and the Jth row
       of N have at least one 1 in the same location. It is used to
       represent two-stage connections, as in pecking orders or cir-
       cuitry. (See the defined function RUN in this chapter.)
    C) For $R\leftarrow C+.=D,R[I;J]$is the number of matching pairs of
       elements of $C[I;]$ and $D[;J]$
       For $R\leftarrow C\lceil.\lfloor D,\ R[I;J]$is the largest of the smaller of $C[I;]$
       and $D[;J]$ taken pairwise.
3. A) $R\leftarrow 0\neq.=4\ \ 100\ \ 400\ \ 4000\circ.|Y$
    B) $\nabla REFUND1\ E$
    [1] $.5\times 200\ \ 500+.\lfloor 1\ \ 1\circ.\times EV$
    C) $\nabla Z\leftarrow LIT1\ N$
    [1] $Z\leftarrow(^{-}1+'0123456789'\iota N)+.\times 10\star\phi^{-}1+\iota\rho NV$
    D) $\nabla R\leftarrow N\ DUPL1\ V$
    [1] $R\leftarrow'SCALAR\ NOT\ PRESENT'$
    [2] $\rightarrow 0\times\iota 0=N\vee.=V$
    [3] $R\leftarrow(N=V)/\iota\rho VV$
4. $\nabla R\leftarrow X\ POLY\ C$
    [1] $R\leftarrow C+.\times X\circ.\star^{-}1+\iota\rho,CV$

5. Without the inner product a straightforward sort function is
```
        ∇A←ALFSORT M;I
[1]     M←(ALF←' ABCDEFGHIJKLMNOPQRSTUVWXYZ')ιM
[2]     I←16
[3]     M←M[⍋M[;I];]
[4]     →3×ι0≠I←I-1
[5]     A←ALF[M]∇
```
Much more elegant, however, is
```
        ∇A←ALFSORT1 M
[1]     A←M[⍋ (ALFιM)+.×⌽27*¯1+ι16;]∇
```
Because the largest number which APL can handle is approximately
7E75, there is an inherent limitation in ALFSORT1. By experi-
menting with various matrices of similar names, see how many places
out the sorting extends to. When the function ⊥ is extended to
matrices (not yet implemented at this time), the algorithm in
ALFSORT1 can be further simplified, as for example
M[⍋,27⊥⍉ALFιM;]

6.
```
        ∇Z←EXP A
[1]     Z←.14 .10 .06+.×(75⌊A),(50⌊0⌈A-75),0⌈A-125∇
            or
        ∇Z←EXP1 A
[1]     Z←.01×4 4 6+.×(75 25,⌊/ι0)∘.⌊A∇
```
which will handle both vector and scalar arguments.

7.
```
        ∇R←BASE M
[1]     R←M+.×⌽10*¯1+ι¯1↑⍴M∇
```
A more general solution for some radix vector B operating over
the columns is
```
        ∇R←B BASE1 M
[1]     R←(×/0 ¯1↓(0,⍴B)↓(1 2×⍴B)⍴(×/2,2⍴⍴B)⍴(1↓B=B),B)+.×M∇
```

8.
```
        ∇R←N COS1 V
[1]     R←(V∘.*N)-.÷!N←¯2+2×ιN∇
```
This function will take an array of any rank as its right argument.

Chapter 32

1.
```
        ∇R←F X
[1]     R←*X∇
        1E¯6 SLOPE ι10
2.718283187  7.389059793  20.08554696   54.59817733
    148.4132333  403.4289952  1096.633707  2980.959477
    8103.087978  22026.47681
        *ι10
2.718281828  7.389056099  20.08553692   54.59815003
    148.4131591  403.4287935  1096.633158  2980.957987
    8103.083928  22026.46579
```
In calculus courses it is shown that *X is its own derivative.

2. In general execute INV (N,N)⍴1,N⍴0. A specific example
    might be
```
        INV 3 3⍴1 0 0 0

        1               0               0
        0               1               0
        0               0               1
```
from which it should be evident that the identity matrix is its
own inverse.

3.
```
        (INV 3 3⍴2 1 3 4 3 ¯1 2 1 ¯4)+.×10 13 3
3.5  2.220446049E¯16  1
```

```
4.          ∇LIN W;G
   [1]      →(0=G←(W[1]×W[5])-W[4]×W[2])/L1
   [2]      'X IS:'
   [3]      ((W[5]×W[3])-W[2]×W[6])÷G
   [4]      'Y IS:'
   [5]      ((W[1]×W[6])-W[4]×W[3])÷G
   [6]      →0
   [7]      L1:'NO UNIQUE SOLUTION'∇
            ∇ABC SOLVE DEF
   [1]      ⍝ABC IS A 3-ELEMENT VECTOR A,B,C
   [2]      ⍝DEF IS A 3-ELEMENT VECTOR D,E,F
   [3]      →OK×⍳0≠-/×/(ABC,DEF)[2 2⍴1 5 2 4]
   [4]      'NO UNIQUE SOLUTION'
   [5]      →0
   [6]      OK:(INV(ABC,DEF)[2 2⍴1 2 4 5])+.×ABC[3],DEF[3]∇
5.          ∇R←F X
   [1]      R←X×300+⁻2×X∇

            1E⁻6 SLOPE 0 100 200
299.999998   ⁻100.000002   ⁻500.0000001
            1E⁻6 SLOPE 0 20 40 60 80
299.999998   219.9999972   139.9999974   59.99999757
            ⁻20.00000222
            1E⁻6 SLOPE 60 65 70 75
59.99999757   39.99999717   19.99999768   ⁻2.728484105E⁻6
```
The sides of the rectangle are each about 75 feet long.
```
6.          ∇R←F X
   [1]      R←÷X∇
            .001 AREA 1 2
0.6928972431
            ⍟2
0.6931471806
```
Readers with a background in the calculus will recall that the
natural logarithm of N is equivalent to the area under the
curve $Y←÷X$ from $X=1$ to $X=N$.

Chapter 33
```
1.          ∇MULT1 N;X
   [1]      X←?N,N
   [2]      1↑X;'×';1↓X
   [3]      →(⎕=STOP,×/X)/0,CORRECT
   [4]      'TRY AGAIN'
   [5]      →3
   [6]      CORRECT:'CORRECT'
   [7]      →1∇
2.          ∇MULT2 N;X
   [1]      X←?N,N×I←1
   [2]      1↑X;'×';1↓X
   [3]      →(⎕=STOP,×/X)/0,CORRECT
   [4]      →ANS×⍳4=I←I+1
   [5]      'TRY AGAIN'
   [6]      →3
   [7]      ANS:'ANSWER IS ';×/X
   [8]      →1
   [9]      CORRECT:'CORRECT'
   [10]     →1∇
```

```
3.              ∇MULT3 N;X
     [1]        X←?N,N×I←1
     [2]        1↑X;'×';1↓X
     [3]        →(□=HELP,STOP,×/X)/AID,0,CORRECT
     [4]        →ANS×ι4=I←I+1
     [5]        'TRY AGAIN'
     [6]        →3
     [7]        ANS:'ANSWER IS ';×/X
     [8]        →1
     [9]        CORRECT:'CORRECT'
     [10]       →1
     [11]       AID:'COUNT THE STARS FOR THE ANSWER:'
     [12]       Xρ'*'
     [13]       →5∇
4.              ∇MULT4 N;X
     [1]        X←?N,N×I←1+0×AKT←I19
     [2]        1↑X;'×';1↓X
     [3]        →(□=HELP,STOP,×/X)/AID,0,CORRECT
     [4]        →ANS×ι4=I←I+1
     [5]        'TRY AGAIN'
     [6]        →3
     [7]        ANS:'ANSWER IS ';×/X
     [8]        →1
     [9]        CORRECT:⌊((I19)-AKT)÷60;' SECONDS'
     [10]       →1
     [11]       AID:'COUNT THE STARS FOR THE ANSWER:'
     [12]       Xρ'*'
     [13]       →5∇
5.              ∇SPELL[6]'THE CORRECT SPELLING IS ',SPL[N+1;]∇
6.              ∇ENTER;A
     [1]        R←''
     [2]        →DONE×ι0=ρA←,□
     [3]        R←R,20↑A
     [4]        →2
     [5]        DONE:R←(1+,0 20┬¯1+ρR)ρR∇
```

Chapter 34

```
1.              )LOAD 1 CLASS
        SAVED   15.02.39 07/29/69
                Y←ι10
                )ORIGIN 0
        WAS 1
                TAB3[0;2;1]
        132
                Yι4 5 6
        3   4   5
                )DIGITS 5
        WAS 10
```

```
        ÷TAB3

   0.009009      0.0089286     0.0088496
   0.0082645     0.0081967     0.0081301
   0.0076336     0.0075758     0.0075188
   0.0070922     0.0070423     0.006993

   0.0047393     0.004717      0.0046948
   0.0045249     0.0045045     0.0044843
   0.004329      0.0043103     0.0042918
   0.0041494     0.0041322     0.0041152
        )WIDTH 60
WAS 120
        )FNS J
MEAN      PI      RECT     REP     REVERSE ROWCAT  RUN      S
SD        SETVARIABLES      SIGN    SORT    SPELL   SQRT     STAT
STATISTICS         SUB      SUMSCAN TIME    TIMEFACT         TRA
TRACETIME
        )LOAD 1 WSFNS
SAVED  23.45.54 07/07/69
        X←DIGITS 6
        ÷ι7
1  0.5  0.333333  0.25  0.2  0.166667  0.142857
        X
10
        DIGITS X
6
        ÷ι7
1  0.5  0.3333333333  0.25  0.2  0.1666666667  0.1428571429
```

2. Because both indexing and the index generator are affected in the
   same way by the change of origin.

3.
```
        )ORIGIN 0
WAS 1
        ι0

        ι1
0
        ρι0
0
        ρι1
1
```

5.
```
        A←9.222222222222222
        B←9.22222222222227
        C←ι10
        A=B
1
        A∈B
1
        A-B
⁻4.884981308E⁻15
        C[3.000000000000008]
3
```

6.   ∇SUB[1.1]
    [1.1] T←ORIGIN 0
    [1.2] P←P,?P
    [1.3] T←ORIGIN T
    [1.4] [2]
    [2]
              ∨

    [3]   ∇

Bibliography

Berry, P.C., APL\360 PRIMER, IBM Corporation, 1969, Publication No. H20-0689

Berry, P.C., APL\1130 PRIMER, IBM Corporation, 1968, Publication No. C20-1697

Breed, L.M., and R.H. Lathwell, "The Implementation of APL\360," ACM SYMPO-
SIUM ON EXPERIMENTAL SYSTEMS FOR APPLIED MATHEMATICS, New York and
London: Academic Press, 1968, pp. 390-399

Falkoff, A.D., and K.E. Iverson, APL\360 USER'S MANUAL, IBM Corporation,
1968, Publication No. H20-0683

Falkoff, A.D., and K.E. Iverson, "The APL\360 Terminal System," ACM SYMPOSIUM
ON EXPERIMENTAL SYSTEMS FOR APPLIED MATHEMATICS, New York and London:
Academic Press, 1968, pp. 22-37

Falkoff, A.D., K.E. Iverson and E.H. Sussenguth, "A Formal Description of
System\360," IBM SYSTEMS JOURNAL, Volume 3, Number 3 (1964) pp. 193-262

Iverson, K.E., A PROGRAMMING LANGUAGE, New York: John Wiley, 1962

Iverson, K.E., ELEMENTARY FUNCTIONS: AN ALGORITHMIC TREATMENT, Chicago:
Science Research Associates, 1966

Iverson, K.E., THE USE OF APL IN TEACHING, IBM Corporation, 1969, Publication No. 320-0996, (also available as Volume 13, Queen's Univ. Papers
in Pure and Applied Math., Kingston, Canada, 1968)

Pakin, S., APL\360 REFERENCE MANUAL, Chicago: Science Research Associates,
1970

Rose, A.J., Videotaped APL Course, IBM Corporation, 1968

Smillie, K.W., STATPACK2: AN APL STATISTICAL PACKAGE, Publication No. 9,
Department of Computing Science, University of Alberta, Edmonton,
Canada, 1969

Supplement
Extensions to the APL language

This supplement contains a number of additions and extensions to the *APL*
language which were not generally available at publication time, but which
are included in the *APL* program product announced by IBM in June, 1970.
In addition, some examples will be shown of tabs, formatting and large file
capability, features of *APL PLUS*, an *APL* time sharing service available
through Scientific Time Sharing Corporation (U.S.) and I. P. Sharp
Associates Ltd. (Canada). The service is based on *APL\360* and includes
certain proprietary extensions to be discussed.

Matrix division

This is a primitive function which can be used to solve sets of linear
equations (dyadic), invert matrices (monadic), and find least squares solutions. For example, suppose we are given (conventional notation)

$$\begin{cases} 2X + 4Y - 3Z = -4 \\ 6X + 17Y - 8Z = -15 \\ 4X - 2Y + 3Z = 20 \end{cases}$$

Then, letting A be the matrix of coefficients and B the vector of constants,

```
      A
  2    4    ‾3                    (note that the extra line has been
  6   17    ‾8                    eliminated from the display of arrays
  4   ‾2     3                    of rank >1)
       B
‾4   ‾15   20
```

the solution can be obtained by taking B matrix divide A. The domino ⌹ for
matrix division is formed by overstriking the quad with the divide symbol.

```
      X←B⌹A
      X
3   ‾1   2
      A+.×X
‾4   ‾15   20
```

Used monadically, ⌹A results in the inverse of A. A must be square and invertible or a domain error results. Compare this with the defined function *INV* in chapter 32.

```
      Y←⌹A
      A+.×Y
 1.000000000E0     ‾8.326672685E‾17   5.551115123E‾17
 1.998401444E‾15   1.000000000E0      0.000000000E0
‾4.440892099E‾16   8.326672685E‾17    1.000000000E0
```

Catenation

Two variables whose shapes are conformable can now be joined along an existing coordinate. If no coordinate is specified, the catenation is over the last coordinate. Notice that scalar arguments are extended for purposes of catenation.

```
      Q
□□□□□□□
□□□□□□□
□□□□□□□
□□□□□□□
      R
OOOOOOO
OOOOOOO
      S
*******
      T
△ △ △ △
      Q,[1]R
□□□□□□□
□□□□□□□
□□□□□□□
□□□□□□□
OOOOOOO
OOOOOOO
      Q,[1]S
□□□□□□□
□□□□□□□
□□□□□□□
□□□□□□□
*******
      Q,T
□□□□□□□△
□□□□□□□△
□□□□□□□△
□□□□□□□△
      W←'*'
      Q,W
□□□□□□□*
□□□□□□□*
□□□□□□□*
□□□□□□□*
```

```
      Q,[2]W
□□□□□□□*
□□□□□□□*
□□□□□□□*
□□□□□□□*
      Q,[1]W
□□□□□□□
□□□□□□□
□□□□□□□
□□□□□□□
*******
```

Lamination

Lamination joins two variables along a new coordinate. Here are some examples of the syntax and use of this function:

```
      Q,[.5]W
□□□□□□□
□□□□□□□
□□□□□□□
□□□□□□□

*******
*******
*******
*******
      Q,[1.4]W
□□□□□□□
*******

□□□□□□□
*******

□□□□□□□
*******

□□□□□□□
*******
      R,[2.3]W
O*
O*
O*
O*
O*
O*
O*


O*
O*
O*
O*
O*
O*
O*
```

The syntax is of the form $C \leftarrow A, [I]B$, where for $0 < I < 1$, $C[1;;] \leftarrow A$ and $C[2;;] \leftarrow B$; for $1 < I < 2$, $C[;1;] \leftarrow A$ and $C[;2;] \leftarrow B$; for $2 < I < 3$, $C[;;1] \leftarrow A$ and $C[;;2] \leftarrow B$, etc., rank permitting. As in catenation, scalars are extended.

Decode and encode

These functions extend to arrays as follows:

```
      H
0   1   2   3   4   5
      J←3 2 1⊤H
      J
  0   0   1   1   2   2
  0   1   0   1   0   1
  0   0   0   0   0   0
      I
0   1   2   3   4   5   6   7
      K←2 2 2⊤I
      K
  0   0   0   0   1   1   1   1
  0   0   1   1   0   0   1   1
  0   1   0   1   0   1   0   1
      L←3 2 1⊥J
      L
0   1   2   3   4   5
      M←2 2 2⊥K
      M
0   1   2   3   4   5   6   7
      2⊥K
0   1   2   3   4   5   6   7
```

From these examples it should be clear how the shape of the result is related to the shape of the arguments.

Adjustable fuzz

Normally when a comparison is done in APL the final ten bits of the arguments are disregarded. To change this fuzz (see page 265), copy the function $SETFUZZ$ from 1 $WSFNS$ and execute $SETFUZZ\ N$ where $0 \le N \le 31$. The number of bits disregarded is then changed to N, with the previous fuzz returned as a result.

```
      1=1.0000000000001
1
      )COPY 1 WSFNS SETFUZZ
SAVED   15.29.04  05/15/70
      SETFUZZ 0
10
      1=1.0000000000001
0
```

(The following are proprietary extensions of *APL PLUS*. For further information, refer to the publications listed in the Bibliography at the end of this supplement.)

Tabs

Since the TAB and CLR/SET keys on the Selectric keyboard are not part of the *APL\360* system, *APL PLUS* has a tab feature which incorporates tab stops to speed up terminal input-output, especially in printing displays with lots of "white space".

To use tabs, first set the tab stops at regular intervals (for instance, every fifth position), using the CLR/SET key on the left side of the keyboard. The tabs may be set by typing

```
      )TABS 5
WAS 0
```

When printing, *APL PLUS* will then use tabs instead of multiple spaces wherever possible.

On input, *APL PLUS* treats a tab exactly like the equivalent number of spaces. An interesting application of input tabs is in using ⎕ to build the rows of a matrix. If the tabs are set to the column dimension of the resultant matrix, then tabbing to the next typed word will assure that the resultant character matrix will have text on each line, left justified.

Here is an example, with the tabs set at 10, 20, 30 etc. The symbol ∘ denotes where the tab key was struck.

```
      )TABS 10
WAS 5
      ∇R←INPUT
[1]    R←⎕
[2]    R←((.1×ρR),10)ρR∇
      T←INPUT
JONES∘    KELLEY∘   ADAMS∘
      ρT
3   10
      T
JONES
KELLEY
ADAMS
```

Corresponding to the)*TABS* command, a *TABS* function is available in the w.s. 1 *WSFNS*. The syntax is $R←TABS\ N$. N is the new tab setting, and R is the old setting. The normal mode of the system is *TABS* 0. Caution: tab settings, if used, must be equally spaced. Non-uniform tab stops can cause erratic terminal behavior.

Working with data files

The *APL PLUS* File Subsystem lets you work with much more data than can be held in a workspace, and do it far more conveniently than by using the *COPY* commands. All the file operations are in the workspace 1 *FILES*.

```
      )LOAD 1 FILES
SAVED    20.32.24 07/27/70
      DESCRIBE
```

WORKSPACE 1 FILES

THIS WORKSPACE CONTAINS FUNCTIONS FOR USING APL PLUS DATA
FILES,   AS   DESCRIBED   IN   APL_PLUS_FILE_SUBSYSTEM,
SCIENTIFIC TIME SHARING CORPORATION, 1970,   AND AVAILABLE
FROM SCIENTIFIC TIME SHARING CORPORATION AND I. P. SHARP
ASSOCIATES LTD.   THE FOLLOWING FUNCTIONS ARE PROVIDED:

FAPPEND	PLACES A NEW COMPONENT ON A FILE
FCREATE	CREATES AND OPENS A NEW FILE
FDROP	DELETES COMPONENTS FROM A FILE
FERASE	ERASES A FILE
FHOLD	REQUESTS TEMPORARY EXCLUSIVE USE OF FILE(S)
FLIB	NAMES OF FILES IN LIBRARY
FLIM	GIVES FILE COMPONENT NUMBERING
FNAMES	NAMES OF FILES CURRENTLY TIED
FNUMS	NUMBERS OF FILES CURRENTLY TIED
FRDAC	GIVES FILE ACCESS AND LOCK INFORMATION
FRDCI	GIVES COMPONENT INFORMATION
FREAD	READS A COMPONENT FROM A FILE
FRENAME	CHANGES LIBRARY NUMBER AND NAME OF A FILE
FREPLACE	REPLACES A COMPONENT IN A FILE
FSTAC	DEFINES ACCESSES AND LOCKS FOR USERS
FSTIE	OPENS FILE FOR SHARED USE
FTIE	OPENS FILE FOR EXCLUSIVE USE
FUNTIE	UNTIES FILE(S)
FE	PRIMITIVE FILE FUNCTION UPON WHICH ALL OF THE ABOVE ARE BASED. REQUIRED FOR USE OF ANY OF THE ABOVE.

A file consists of a number of components, each of which is an APL value
of any type - character or numeric; scalar, vector, matrix, or of any
number of dimensions.

Users may have more than one file, each with its own name. For example,
suppose that you have two files as shown below (it will be demonstrated
later how they might have been built). The file named PERSONS has four
components, each a vector of characters, and the file SALES also has four
components, each a vector of numbers.

file-name	PERSONS	SALES
1	'SMITH'	5 6 3 1 4
component 2	'JONES'	2 6 10
number 3	'KELLEY'	4 6 2 9 1 5
4	'BECKER'	20 6 4

File names belonging to an account number (or common library) may be obtained by the function FLIB, the syntax of which is

result ←FLIB account number

The result is a character matrix, each row of which is the name of a file:

```
FLIB  1234
1234  PERSONS
1234  SALES
```

The following program prints each of the components of the file named *PERSONS*, along with the sum of the numbers in the corresponding component of *SALES*:

```
      ∇ PROG1;X;I
[1]    'PERSONS' FTIE 1
[2]    'SALES' FTIE 2
[3]    'NAME       SUM'
[4]    I←1
[5]   LOOP:X←FREAD 2,I
[6]    (10↑FREAD 1,I);+/X
[7]    I←I+1
[8]    →LOOP×ιI≤4
[9]    FUNTIE 1 2
      ∇
```

The *FTIE* operation establishes a connection between the file name and an integer value (of your choice), called a <u>file-number</u>. In *PROG1*, *PERSONS* is given the file-number 1, and *SALES* is given the file-number 2. The ability to reference files by number permits 'stepping' through several files in order, or accessing different files on the basis of a calculation. The syntax is

'file-name' *FTIE* file-number

Here, the left argument is a vector of characters forming the name of a file. The right argument (the file-number) is a scalar integer value.

FREAD brings a replica of a file component into the active workspace. This replica may be placed in a variable, as in line 5 of *PROG1*. It may be used in an expression, as in line 6. In many ways, reading a component from a file is similar to using any *APL* function that returns a value. The syntax of the *FREAD* operation is

result ←*FREAD* file-number, component-number

Note that the right argument is a two-element vector.

FUNTIE has the syntax

FUNTIE file-number(s)

It is used to break the connection between a file and its file-number. Several files may be untied with one application of *FUNTIE*, as in line 9 of *PROG1*. After being untied, both the file-name and the file-number may be retied to some other file-number and file-name.

Two operations are provided to help you find what files you have tied. *FNAMES*, with syntax

result ←*FNAMES*

returns a matrix of characters, each row of which is the name of a file currently tied. *FNUMS* returns a vector of file-numbers corresponding to the names given by *FNAMES*. Its syntax is

result ←*FNUMS*

The simplest way to untie all tied files is the expression *FUNTIE FNUMS*, since the vector returned by *FNUMS* is exactly what *FUNTIE* needs in order to untie all files.

New files are brought into existence with the *FCREATE* operation and new components are placed on the file with the *FAPPEND* operation. The following program might have been used to build the two files *PERSONS* and *SALES*:

```
      ∇ PROG2
[1]    'PERSONS' FCREATE 5
[2]    'SALES' FCREATE 20
[3]    PMAT← 4 6 ρ'SMITH JONES KELLEYBECKER'
[4]    I←1
[5]   LOOP:NAME←PMAT[I;]
[6]    'ENTER VALUES FOR ',NAME
[7]    □FAPPEND 20
[8]    ((NAME≠' ')/NAME) FAPPEND 5
[9]    I←I+1
[10]   →LOOP×ιI≤1↑ρPMAT
[11]   FUNTIE 20 5
      ∇
```

The syntax of the *FCREATE* operation is

'file-name' *FCREATE* file-number

An empty file, with the desired name, is made available, and then tied as in the *FTIE* operation.

FAPPEND puts at the end of a file a new component consisting of a replica of an *APL* value from the active workspace. Its syntax is

value *FAPPEND* file-number

Examples of appending to files *SALES* and *PERSONS* are found in *PROG2* on lines 7 and 8.

There are no restrictions regarding what may be appended to a file. The components of a file need not be similar in type or dimension.

When a file is no longer needed, it can be erased as follows:

'file-name' *FERASE* file-number

This removes the file and frees both the space it occupied and the name for new files to be created.

PROG3 is an example of changing the arrangement of some filed information. The components of *PERSONS* and *SALES* are to be merged into a new file, *RECORDS*. Each odd-numbered component of *RECORDS* will come from *PERSONS* and the following even-numbered component will come from *SALES*. The two original files are erased after the operation is finished.

```
    ∇ PROG3
[1]    'PERSONS' FTIE 2
[2]    'SALES' FTIE 1
[3]    'RECORDS' FCREATE 3
[4]    I←1
[5]  LOOP:(FREAD(1+2|I),⌈I÷2) FAPPEND 3
[6]    →LOOP×ι8≥I←I+1
[7]    FUNTIE 3
[8]    'PERSONS' FERASE 2
[9]    'SALES' FERASE 1
    ∇
```

In this example, the file-numbers 1 and 2 did not appear with *FUNTIE* because the erasure of *PERSONS* and *SALES* also untied them.

Shared files

A shared file is stored information to which a group of users may have
simultaneous access. Through the use of shared files, *APL PLUS* can be
used for reservation systems, management control systems, many-person games,
simulation studies, and message switching.

The airline reservation system presented here is typical of many inventory
applications in which several people must access and modify a data base,
in real time. The reservation system consists of a 'control center',
which makes available an inventory of airplane seats, and any number of
'agents', whose task it is to sell the available seats.

To initialize the system, the control center creates two files using the
program *SETUP*. The first of these files, named *SUPPLY*, holds the currently available number of seats for each of a number of flights. The
second file, named *TRANSACT*, will hold a record of each transaction made
by the agents.

The control center operator makes more seats available (by simulating
departures and arrivals) through the use of the *REPLENISH* program. The
operator enters the flight numbers and the number of additional seats to
be made available on those flights.

Agents place orders against the inventory through the use of the program
SALES. An entry here should be a two-element vector consisting of which
flight number and how many seats are requested. For the purposes of the
example, a reward structure is built into the sales program: orders
which can be filled yield the agent one dollar each; orders which cannot
be filled cost the agent 50 cents per seat; and invalid entries reduce
his earnings by one-half.

Entries of the first two types above are recorded on the transactions
file. The program *OBSERVE*, which is run by the control center, prints
the transactions of the agents in real time, identified by time, city,
and nature of transaction. When there are more than ten transactions
waiting to be printed, the observe program blocks further transactions by
the agents until printing has caught up again.

Here is a diagram of the file organization followed by the above-referenced
programs and associated variables:

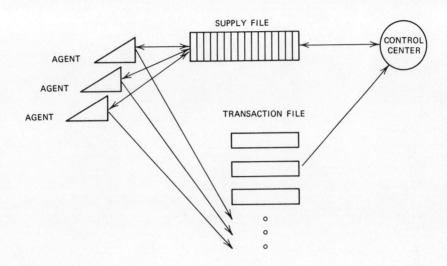

Agent program:

```
     ∇ SALES;STOP;B;P;A;INV
[1]     STOP←*1
[2]    ↙→ORD×ι∧/ 1 2 ∈FNUMS
[3]     (OWNER,' SUPPLY') FSTIE 1
[4]     (OWNER,' TRANSACT') FSTIE 2
[5]   ORD:,'⍞EARNINGS: ⍞.F9.2,X3,⍞ENTER ORDER⍞' ∆FMT EARN
[6]     →DONE×ιSTOP=1↑P←,⎕
[7]     →ORD×ι0=ρP
[8]     →ER×ι2≠ρP
[9]     →ER×ι~(A←1↑P)∈ι10
[10]    →ER×ιB≠|⌈B←1↓P
[11]    FHOLD 1
[12]    INV←FREAD 1 1
[13]    →NOT×ιINV[A]<B
[14]    INV[A]←INV[A]-B
[15]    INV FREPLACE 1 1
⌈16]    FHOLDι0
[17]    'ORDER FILLED'
[18]    (1,P,EARN←EARN+B) FAPPEND 2
[19]    →ORD
[20] NOT:FHOLDι0
⌈21]    'ORDER CANNOT BE FILLED'
[22]    'ONLY ';INV[A];' ON HAND'
[23]    (0,P,EARN←0⌈EARN-0.5×B) FAPPEND 2
[24]    →ORD
[25] ER:'INPUT ERROR--ORDER NOT VALID'
[26]    EARN←EARN÷2
[27]    →ORD
[28] DONE:'YOUR EARNINGS ARE ',,'F10.2' ∆FMT EARN
[29]    FUNTIE FNUMS
     ∇
```

Control center programs:

```
      ∇ SETUP;A;X                          ∇ RR←REPLENISH;INV;X;Y
[1]     OWNER←,'I10' ΔFMTI29         [1]     RR←ι0
[2]     'WHO IS TO SHARE?'          [2]     'WHICH ONES?'
[3]     A←(A≠I29)/A←□,0             [3]     X←,□
[4]     'SUPPLY' FCREATE 1          [4]     →ER×ι~∧/X∈ι10
[5]     'TRANSACT' FCREATE 2        [5]     'HOW MUCH EACH?'
[6]     X←((ρA),3)ρ0               [6]     →ER×ιYv.≠⌈|Y←,□
[7]     X[;1]←A                     [7]     →ER×ι(ρX)≠ρY
[8]     X[;2]←85                    [8]     FHOLD 1
[9]     X FSTAC 1                   [9]     INV←FREAD 1 1
[10]    X[;2]←8                     [10]    INV[X]←INV[X]+Y
[11]    X FSTAC 2                   [11]    INV FREPLACE 1 1
[12]    FUNTIE 1 2                  [12]    (2,INV) FAPPEND 2
[13]    'SUPPLY' FSTIE 1            [13]    FHOLDι0
[14]    'TRANSACT' FSTIE 2          [14]    →0
[15]    NEXT←1                      [15] ER:'INVALID ENTRY, TRY AGAIN.
[16]    (10ρ0) FAPPEND 1            [16]    →1
      ∇                              ∇
```

```
      ∇ RR←OBSERVE;Z;MTRX
[1]     RR←ι0
[2]     →S0×ι∧/ 1 2 ∈FNUMS
[3]     'SUPPLY' FSTIE 1
[4]     'TRANSACT' FSTIE 2
[5]   S0:SW←0
[6]     MTRX← 3 16 ρ'⍇    NO⍇,2I4,F9.2⍇   YES⍇.2I4,F9.2⍇ MORE⍇,
        2I4,20I4'
[7]   S1:→OK×ιNEXT≠1↓FLIM 2
[8]     'CAUGHT UP'
[9]     FHOLDιSW←0
[10]  S5:DELAY 2
⌈11⌉    →OK×ιNEXT≠1↓FLIM 2
[12]    →S5
[13]  OK:Z←(FRDCI 2,NEXT),FREAD 2,NEXT
[14]    (8↑9↓TIME Z[3]),CITIES[ANUMιZ[2];],,MTRX[1+Z[4];]
        ΔFMT(ι1)∘.×4↓Z
[15]    NEXT←NEXT+1
[16]    →S1×ι(SW=1)vNEXT≥⁻10+1↓FLIM 2
[17]    'HOLDING'
[18]    SW←1
[19]    FHOLD 1 2
[20]    →S1
      ∇
```

Pertinent global variables:

```
      EARN                              '5A1,I6'  ΔFMT  (CITIES;ANUM)
0                              N.Y.   1411
      NEXT                     L.A.   1412
1                              P.A.   1413
      OWNER                    TOR    1414
   78974                       PHIL   1415
      SW                       WASH   1416
0                              HQS    78974
                               MTL    1417
                               OTT    1418
                               ANY
```

Report formatting

In the workspace 1 *PLOTFORMAT* on the *APL PLUS* system is a special function, called *ΔFMT*, which is useful for preparing neat output of data. *ΔFMT* is a dyadic function which returns an explicit result. The left argument is a character vector of format codes, and the right argument is a list of the values to be printed. For example, using the matrix *SPL* in 1 *CLASS*, suppose we wanted to produce the following display:

```
ZERO    IS   0      0.0000       0.0000       0.0000
ONE     IS   1      1.0000       1.0000       1.0000
TWO     IS   2      1.4142       1.2599       1.1892
THREE   IS   3      1.7321       1.4422       1.3161
FOUR    IS   4      2.0000       1.5874       1.4142
FIVE    IS   5      2.2361       1.7100       1.4953
SIX     IS   6      2.4495       1.8171       1.5651
SEVEN   IS   7      2.6458       1.9129       1.6266
EIGHT   IS   8      2.8284       2.0000       1.6818
NINE    IS   9      3.0000       2.0801       1.7321
```

The statement which will do this is

```
'5A1,X2,⎕IS⎕,I3,3F10.4'  ΔFMT  (SPL;⁻1+ι10;(⁻1+ι10)∘.*÷2 3 4)
```

The format code *A* is used to print character information. *5A1* asks for five repetitions of a character field one position wide. Then the *X2* code means space over two positions. The phrase *⎕IS⎕* causes printing of the characters *IS* in the next positions. *I3* takes three spaces to print the values 0, 1, 2, 3, ..., 9 as integer fields. And last, the square roots, cube roots, and fourth roots are printed out each in ten spaces, with four positions allowed for the decimal part (*3F10.4*).

ΔFMT will handle scalars, vectors, and matrices in the right argument. It always treats vectors of length n as though they were n×1 matrices (i.e., vectors will be printed vertically). To print the elements of a vector across on a single line, *ΔFMT* may be used in either of the following ways:

```
      X←2.4 4.982 304 1000.23123
      'F10.2' ΔFMT X
      2.40
      4.98
    304.00
   1000.23

      'F10.2' ΔFMT (1,ρX)ρX
      2.40       4.98      304.00    1000.23
```

In the above statement *X* is made into a matrix with one row, and in the
following example the resulting matrix of characters is raveled:

```
      ,'F10.2' ΔFMT X
      2.40       4.98      304.00    1000.23
```

Compared to formatting routines such as *DFT*, *ΔFMT* uses typically only
5-10% of the CPU time required for the former. *ΔFMT* also contains
qualifier and decoration codes to position and decorate fixed point and
integer results within the space allotted to them by the format phrase.

Input and output of large amounts of data

Large amounts of data can be inputted rapidly by the *APL PLUS* Computer
Center card reader and magnetic tape units. Typically, the data is prepared on standard 80-column punched cards, which are submitted to the
Computer Center with instructions for what file to place the data in.
Although there are many ways to have the data organized in the file, a
good starter is to have each component of the file be an 80-element
character vector, corresponding exactly to a punched card. Then, using
the File Subsystem, the information can be converted to any desired form.

The high speed printer at the Computer Center can be used to print results
which would take a lot of time on a typewriter terminal. To use the
printer, the results to be printed are placed in a file, and the program
PRINTREC in workspace 1 *FILEPRINT* is executed. *PRINTREC* is a con-
versational program, and it will request your name and mailing address.

The file to be printed must consist of characters only, and *ΔFMT* can be
used to advantage here. The *PRINTREC* program includes facilities for
titling, page numbering, margins, 'skipping', etc.

Miscellaneous *APL PLUS* features

If you form an incorrect character, or if a transmission error occurs
while you are entering information from your terminal, *APL PLUS* will
print *CHAR ERROR* and then return to you the readable portion of the
line, for you to retype the rest of it. Standard *APL*, under either of
these circumstances, would return either *CHARACTER ERROR* or *RESEND*
and would require that you type the entire line over again.

The *COPY* command in *APL PLUS* now accepts the names of more than one
variable, function, or group. For example, the command

```
      )COPY 1 CLASS SPL SUB TAB3 SPELL
```

will copy all four objects from the workspace 1 *CLASS* considerably more rapidly than by separate *COPY* commands. This extension applies to the *PCOPY* command as well.

Wide-platen terminals can now print more than 130 positions in a line. The *)WIDTH* command accepts a specification of up to 254. Any width greater than 130 must be specified in a clear workspace, and once a width greater than 130 is given, it cannot be changed. To apply a large width to an existing workspace, use the sequence *)CLEAR*, *)WIDTH* 154 (or whatever), and *)COPY*. The increased width applies only to printed output.

After any incorrect sign-on command, your terminal will overprint the error message with a short line of nonsense symbols, like this:

)HELLO
𝕯𝕰𝕯𝕽𝕰𝕱𝕴𝕰𝕿𝕽𝕰𝕱𝕰𝕽𝕰𝕯𝕹𝕴𝕰

so that the next input may be typed without leaving a legible record of your account number or password. The system command *)BLOT* also produces a nonsense pattern, and may be used to conceal confidential information, for example, a lock in a system command. Type *)BLOT* and then enter your next line over the result.

Bibliography

Breed, L. M., <u>FILEPRINT</u>, Washington: Scientific Time Sharing Corporation, 1970

Breed, L. M., <u>REPORT FORMATTING IN APL PLUS</u>, Washington: Scientific Time Sharing Corporation, 1970

Breed, L. M., and Rose, A. J., <u>APL PLUS FILE SUBSYSTEM</u>, Washington: Scientific Time Sharing Corporation, 1970

Index